St. John

ATLANTIC OCEAN

CARIBBEAN SEA

HERMITAGE

PALESTINA

FORT

MAGAZINE

EMMAUS

Picture Point

BORDEAUX

BORDEAUX MOUNTAINS

LAMESHUR

ANNABERG RUIN

FREDERIKDAL

Mamey Peak
1144'

Bordeaux Mountain
1277'

REEF BAY ESTATE HOUSE

REEF BAY SUGAR MILL

Camelberg Peak
1193'

WATERFALLS,
CARIB INSCRIPTIONS

SEVEN RIDGE

CANEEL BAY

CANEEL BAY

BETHANY

CRUZ BAY

CANEEL BAY PLANTATION
CANEEL BAY

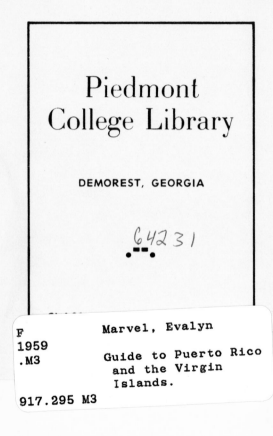

Guide to Puerto Rico and
The Virgin Islands

Guide to Puerto Rico and The Virgin Islands

by

EVALYN MARVEL

REVISED EDITION

CROWN PUBLISHERS, INC. · NEW YORK

PICTURE CREDITS

Puerto Rico News Service: pp. 12, 13, 19, 23, 26, 27, 31, 36, 43, 48, 53 (2), 54, 56, 58, 73, 76, 79, 80, 83, 85, 89, 90, 93, 96, 99, 100, 103, 104, 109, 111, 118, 120 (2), 124, 134, 137, 138, 141, 143, 145, 150, 152, 154
University of Puerto Rico: pp. 69, 73, 75
Richard Meek: p. 85
Jack Volkman: pp. 114 (2), 147
Roberto Cole: pp. 128, 130, 134
Pan American World Airways: p. 164
Department of Tourism, Virgin Islands: pp. 170, 198, 222 (2), 225, 226, 233, 238, 239, 244, 245, 246, 250
Ben Robles: p. 189
Don Toschi: pp. 175, 179, 180, 185, 187, 189, 192, 200, 203, 213
Lillian C. Griffith: pp. 180, 184
Sam Falk: pp. 205, 206, 208, 210
Fritz Henle: p. 214
Louis Dormand: pp. 218, 230, 237, 243
Robert Martin: pp. 220, 221
Eastern Airlines: p. 229
Sprat Hall: p. 249

First Printing, December, 1960
Revised Edition, 1963

© 1960 by Evalyn Marvel
© 1963 by Crown Publishers, Inc.

Library of Congress Catalogue Card Number: 60-15394

Printed in the United States of America

Dedication

From the beginning it was my intention to dedicate this book to the new and kind friends who helped me in my search and research, giving me time, effort, information, and enthusiasm. I have found, not without pride, that the list is too long to enumerate. But *they* will know—for they are no longer new, but good, friends—that this is my inadequate gesture of appreciation and that they are responsible for my love of this portion of the Caribbean. One can write a travel book on sights seen and basic information garnered. However, I hope this book has a little more of the personal touch—and a knowledge and understanding of the people who, in the final analysis, give these islands their peculiar charm.

Contents

SECTION II—*The Virgin Islands*

Introduction

This book is written for all who like to travel, but particularly for those who sometimes are discouraged by the delays and restrictions of crossing a frontier. It is addressed to everyone who dreams of an ideal vacation—a change of scene, a change of atmosphere, and a change of pace. It is written, too, for those with a love of adventure—preferably adventure easily and comfortably achieved.

The American West Indies—which consist of Puerto Rico and the Virgin Islands—have all the enchantment of foreign lands without the accompanying difficulties. No passport is necessary; no money has to be exchanged, and therefore there is no puzzling and fatiguing translating of local currency into ours—"If nine of those equal one dollar, twenty-four of them would be—" A dollar is still a dollar and a 25-cent tip is exactly that.

To secure a passport, a vaccination certificate is required, and for some countries, typhus, malaria, or yellow fever inoculations are also advisable. But in this Caribbean oasis the standards of health are as good as our own—in some respects, better. This may be due partially to the relaxing year-round balminess; the sun is a trifle hotter in summer, but the gentle trade winds make it quite bearable and assure a refreshing night's sleep.

There are, moreover, no language barriers in these isles, and so there are no comic misunderstandings like ordering soup for steak, and no suspicion that one is being cheated on every hand because of his ignorance of the native tongue. Puerto Ricans, although inheritors of a Spanish culture, are generally bilingual. Don't forget that they are Americans too. They hold independent Commonwealth status, but they are nevertheless proud of their dual nationality. The Virgin Islands are an American protectorate; the only tongue there is English, spoken with a strange lilt and, often, a curious twist of phrase that gives it piquancy.

Not the least of the assets of this Caribbean next-door-to-paradise is the ease of reaching it. Jet planes from New York make the trip shorter than a train ride to Boston, but even the old-fashioned carrier does it in five and a half hours. Three lines—Eastern, Pan-American, and Trans Caribbean—have a large choice of daily flights and the best bargain on the aviation market, a $115.50-round-trip Thrift Flight to San Juan, with equally reasonable Tourist and First Class offerings. There are also jet flights originating from Miami, and for those who like a restful sea voyage, numerous freighters offer first-class accommodations for twelve passengers. Alcoa Steamship has a regular weekly run from New York to Puerto Rico, St. Thomas, and St. Croix. Various other lines service ports as far north as Boston, and also New Orleans and Houston in the south and Seattle on the West Coast. Among the companies with more or less continuous service are Antilles, Bull, Isbrandtsen, and Waterman.

The fabulous, luxurious hotels of San Juan have received their proper share of glory, either by word of mouth or in the travel pages of periodicals. Those in the Virgin Islands, although perhaps less grandiose, are also exceedingly fine. In Puerto Rico, outside of San Juan, several magnificent hotels have been built and some delightful inns are now in operation. Many hotels, particularly those in San Juan itself, are self-contained palaces in which guests can—and all too often do—live isolated from the interesting life which surrounds them. Such hostelries offer a delightful setting and a certain amount of entertainment. Guests can swim, they can gamble, they have a choice of bars and dining rooms, or they can go to the supper club to watch the show, which is changed almost every week. But as one frustrated visitor was heard to wail, "What *else* do you do?" It seems appalling that this poor tourist in a strange land not only lacked initiative, but had no knowledge of the sights, amusements, and recreation available outside the hotel portals. Curiously few of these have been mentioned in guidebooks or otherwise given proper attention.

Many an interested vacationer cannot afford, or is unwilling to pay, the prices of the luxury palaces. And often this type of hotel does not appeal to him anyhow. Other prospective tourists are frightened off (or at least hesitant) because they mistakenly believe these are the only places to stay. In actuality, both Puerto Rico and the Virgin Islands have hotels of every category, a variety to please the taste of everyone.

Travelers go to other lands to see and live in other environments. They certainly should not travel in the expectation of finding the identical atmosphere they know at home. Here in the tropics, under the American flag, are two different countries, each with a history, culture, and way of life distinctly its own. They put a voyage of discovery within easy reach of everyone, and it is this writer's hope that her book will help many tourists discover and enjoy the delights that are almost at their doorstep.

SECTION I

Puerto Rico

CHAPTER 1

Island in the Trade Wind

(Clothes—Hotels—Entertainment—Means of Transportation)

THE trade winds that come in from the northeast and blow across to the Caribbean are responsible for the equable climate of Puerto Rico. The farther east on the island you are, the more the climate is tempered. So it is that San Juan, on the northeast coast, on the Atlantic Ocean, is cooler than the southern or Caribbean side of the island. The winds are slightly stronger here, ruffling the hair, but they are warm, soft breezes and even the most allergic will find them pleasant.

The woman preparing for a stay in San Juan should tuck in her suitcase a light scarf, chiffon preferably, to tie around her head to hold the waves in place. Or in San Juan she can buy one of those attractive jeweled or beaded caps—actually, coarse hair nets—made of colored plastic or raffia string, which are both practical and becoming.

Summer clothes are worn here the year around, since the difference in season is more a question of whether the word is spelled with a small or a capital "S." The Season runs officially from December to May, but its most noticeable distinctions are that hotel rates are higher and there is more lavish use of evening clothes. Even then, evening dress is not obligatory; a cocktail gown is quite adequate. For men, a dark suit will do, although a dinner jacket is a better accompaniment to a woman's evening gown.

Seasonal changes in temperature are slight, the variation between winter and summer (and noon and night) being

9

about ten degrees. The average temperature on a winter day is 75 degrees. For the Season, or cooler, period, it is wise to take along a light wrap like a stole or sweater, although it may be needed more as a protection against air-conditioning than outdoor temperature.

In town, the ordinary daytime attire is a light-weight sleeveless dress. For motoring trips, a cotton skirt and blouse are the most practical; sports shirt and slacks for the men.

Most travelers assume that in such a balmy atmosphere, shorts should make up a major portion of their wardrobe, but a word of warning is necessary on this subject. The Puerto Rican's background is Latin and conservative. Wearing shorts outside the precincts of the hotels or, to be more specific, the beach areas is not only disapproved of, but actually against the law. There have been one or two embarrassing episodes in downtown San Juan resulting from tourists' ignorance of this ordinance and of what the Puerto Rican, in any case, considers a disregard of the proprieties.

Of course shorts are acceptable for sailing or fishing just as they are on a beach. And slacks are suitable attire for those hardy souls who like mountain climbing, or spelunking (there are enough caves to thrill the most ardent), or horseback riding. Otherwise, however, there is no use for them.

Of late the seasonal ebb and flow of visitors has been less marked, for more and more vacationers are discovering that Puerto Rico is as welcome an escape from sticky heat as from snow and cold. I have known the thermometer to touch 90 degrees on a rare August day in San Juan, but thanks to the trade winds, the heat was tolerable and at night I slept peacefully. That same day, it was a humid 96 degrees in New York and 102 in Miami.

The Puerto Rican, in fact, prefers the summer, which here, as elsewhere, produces a greater profusion of flowers. Oddly, it is also the only season when he goes swimming, despite the wonderfully warm water all through the year. Why this is so, no one has satisfactorily explained. Some say the water is cleaner and purer then, but no such difference is apparent to us outsiders. Natives mention the period when the fish are spawning, but that does not account for eight or nine months of the year. The custom obviously dates back a long time, to reasons lost in obscurity. Today more than a few young people are tempted to disregard it. A partial explanation might be the autumn equinox, when hurricanes are in the making and the sea is likely to be rougher. But on the Atlantic side of the island it is foolhardy to go swimming in any but sheltered bays at any time, since the ocean bed quickly drops to great depth and there is, moreover, a heavy undertow in the open sea.

Although hurricanes are born in the Caribbean area at the end of August or in early September, fortunately most of them drift out and dissipate in the Atlantic. Puerto Rico has suffered but two in twenty years, a more reassuring record than is held by Florida or even the New England states. Incidentally, Puerto Ricans disregard such official hurricane designations as 'Edith,' "Edna," and so on, naming the hurricanes which did not spare them San Filipe and Santa Clara after the saints' days on which they struck.

Outside of such unlikely visitations, Puerto Rico and the Virgin Islands—thanks to their easterly geographic location— enjoy a practically foolproof climate. Blessed with rain, Puerto Rico is lush, too, but the rain is rarely—very rarely—more than a ten-minute downpour, and they can honestly brag of only "eight days of rain a year." By that, they mean days of *real* rain.

The big hotels of San Juan are justly famed. They are beautiful, often architecturally unique, and provide the acme of luxury. Outside of San Juan the Dorado Beach, twenty miles away, El Ponce Intercontinental on the south coast and El Conquistador on the east coast also offer luxury surroundings.

These fabulous hostelries are like the realization of a dream to both the owners and the guests, but it seems to me that not enough is known of the very comfortable alternative accommodations. During the Season prices average $20.00 to $30.00 single, $25.00 to $35.00 double, at the Caribe Hilton, La Rada, Condado Beach, La Concha, El San Juan, Americana, and El Convento.

El Miramar Charterhouse and Hotel Pierre charge somewhat lower rates. While not on the beachfront, they arrange beach facilities for guests.

Nowadays, out-of-season slashes in charges are slight, although outside the San Juan area there are bigger cuts.

11

Aerial view of San Juan's "gold coast." The Caribe Hilton is in the left background. To the right, on the mainland, are other large hotels—Condado Beach, La Concha, El San Juan, and Americana.

Almost adjoining some of these palatial hotels, however, are such moderately-priced ones as the Normandie, Escambron, Atlantic Beach, and Coral Beach. A special attraction of all of them is that they are situated on the sea front.

A block or two back from the beach are smaller hotels such as El Portal and the Olimpo Court at greatly reduced cost. San Juan also has a number of attractive guest houses—Hil's, Duffy's, Don Pedro, La Playa and some thirty others—costing around $7.00 and even as low as $5.00 without bath.

Several one-room kitchenette apartments are also available on a weekly basis of $9.00 a day, and some of these are practically next door to the grand hotels. Moreover, some of the ocean-front hotels—the Escambron and El San Juan, for example—permit transients to use their swimming facilities for a dollar or two a day. The three best beaches for ocean swimming are at the Caribe Hilton (limited strictly to guests), the Normandie-Escambron, and the El San Juan. There are also several public beaches in the San Juan area. (Consult Chapter 16.) The visitor who rents a car will find numerous bathing spots within easy reach of the city.

Out on the island there are many good hotels, some very

modern, with conveniences for fishing, boating, and bathing, at a fraction of the cost of the hotels in the capital. These others will be discussed later on. A travel agency can be very helpful in this respect, and the Puerto Rico Department of Tourism (offices are at 666 Fifth Avenue, New York, or Dupont Plaza Center, Miami, Florida) will be glad to provide an up-to-date, complete listing of hotel rates.

Nevertheless, the water-front palaces of San Juan have certain outstanding features, and they merit a visit. The utterly charming décor of the Caribe Hilton, its gardens with their flamingos, should not be missed, nor the recently-opened El Convento, across from the cathedral. The Condado Beach—the oldest hotel, built by a Vanderbilt in 1919—has been much renovated, but it retains an elegance which makes it still the most popular with Puerto Ricans and longtime residents. La Concha and El Miramar Charterhouse have roof bars, with fascinating views of modern San Juan; when the Sheraton is finished, it will have a roof restaurant. All the large hotels have government-controlled gambling rooms and supper clubs with variety shows. If so inclined, the tourist can see a new show almost every night. There are numerous new night spots which are listed in the chapter on modern San Juan.

One of the first things to secure upon arrival is a copy of

Guests at La Rada, one of San Juan's fabulous luxury hotels, can enjoy water-skiing on the lagoon.

Que Pasa, a monthly giveaway to be found on every hotel desk. Printed in English, it gives detailed information on current activities, from sports and theatres to fiestas and art shows, as well as a listing of restaurants in and out of town, and a map of old San Juan—in short, it is a good amusement guide and practical assistant.

In addition to all the above, the Tourism Information Booth located at the International Airport in Puerto Rico will answer any of your questions. Simply dial 791-1014. Or if you should have questions during the planning stage of your trip, write to Puerto Rico's Department of Tourism at 666 Fifth Avenue, New York City.

Once there was a railroad around the island, but the only tracks to be found today are the narrow-gauge ones for hauling cane on the sugar plantations. Cars are now the sole means of conveyance, but Puerto Rico boasts more and better roads than any of its Caribbean neighbors.

Obviously the pleasantest and most convenient scheme is to rent a drive-yourself. The prices are comparable to those in the States, and, in fact, such familiar companies as Hertz and Avis are in business here too. Both the familiar American makes and the smaller European cars are available, the latter being more popular. On the main highways a large car presents no problem, but on some circuitous mountain roads the Volkswagen, M-G, or Fiat has a decided advantage.

There are, of course, alternative means of getting about. Transportation within San Juan is extremely efficient and all-encompassing. The buses (fares are ten cents) are clean and comfortable, and the drivers are courteous and helpful. Taxis, too, are plentiful; they are metered and are not expensive. Less tipping is expected here than Stateside, often none for short hauls, although tourists do customarily tip.

Outside the city there is that wonderful innovation, the *publico*, a sort of interurban jitney service that falls into two categories: the independent owner-drivers to be found in the central plaza of any town, recommended only for short hauls, and those belonging to a *linea* or line. The latter have roomy cars of recent vintage, which carry five passengers; they are convenient because they pick you up at your door and deposit you at your exact destination. Several reputable lines have offices on Recinto Sur, above but more or less facing the main post office, and just below, on the water front, is *Choferes Unidos de la Marina*. These companies are listed under "Transportation" in *Que Pasa*, or the Department of Tourism will give you, upon request, the schedules of the principal ones.

I personally adore *publicos*. It may take half an hour or so to get out of a town, for you go from one neighborhood to another picking up the assorted passengers, but this is a pleasant means of getting acquainted with the city. Once on the road, the car makes good speed, yet the drivers have a well-earned reputation for careful driving. The car radio is turned on to soft Latin-American music, equivalent to our Muzak, and you settle back in contentment.

All of these cars bear the word "Publico" on their license plates, a fact worth remembering if you are driving, for they do sometimes stop peremptorily for a passenger. For safety's sake it is a good idea to remain a full car-length distance in back of them.

There is still a third means of transportation, particularly if your time is limited. Caribair provides commutation service to Ponce and Mayagüez, the second and third largest cities, and from them you can pick up a local *publico* to any outlying town. The cost of these flights is $11.00 round trip, as against the standard *publico* rate of $2.50 and $3.00 each way. If possible, it is desirable to go at least one way by car in order to see the countryside.

Interurban bus trips are *not* recommended, for the buses are filled as much with livestock and produce as with passengers. With two minor exceptions, there are no excursion buses to provide service for tourists. Anyway, to my mind, it is far pleasanter to discover places at your leisure than to be herded in and out of crowded caravans.

Whether you drive yourself or take a *publico*, you should secure a map and orient yourself. The newest and by far the most complete map is the one put out by Mobil Oil. This provides in detail not only the island and San Juan, but all of the larger cities as well. With it, you can find your way almost anywhere.

Bon voyage!

CHAPTER 2

First Acquaintance with San Juan

(Initial Impressions—Governmental Status—Operation
Bootstrap—the People and Racial Equality)

WHATEVER the means of transportation and wherever the
final destination, San Juan is almost certainly the first Caribbean port of call and there are few tourists who don't make it
a stopover. As the vast majority of visitors come by air, the San
Juan Airport, with its flowers, ponds, and airport hotel, has
been designed to tempt even the most transient-minded.

The mere act of stepping off the plane, however, seems to
produce an extraordinary sense of well-being. The effect can't
be called invigorating, because the soft air is too relaxing. Perhaps buoyancy is a better term. But whatever it is, others have
told me that they had the same immediate reaction. Doubtless
several ingredients make up the sensation, and while you wait
for your luggage and vaguely try to analyze this euphoria, a
pretty girl steps up and says, "May I offer you a Welcome
Cocktail?" This is a frozen daiquiri, mild but not completely
sherbet-like as it is in some places, and the world seems even
rosier, thanks to Rums of Puerto Rico.

The pretty girl at the airport who helps to set your mood, or
the awesome sight of El Morro and the old city walls as your
ship enters the harbor—each in a way typifies Puerto Rico. And
whether you drive into town on the four-lane highway from
the airport, or taxi to your destination through the narrow
streets of old San Juan, both are representative of this land
where modernity is happily blended with an old civilization.

Whichever your approach, you are sure to be impressed—
perhaps surprised too—by the extreme cleanliness of the city,·

16

for a good deal has been written and said about the slums and the great poverty of Puerto Rico. These still exist, but even in the worst days the Puerto Rican made a fetish of personal cleanliness. Were you to poke your head into one of the miserable hovels which yet remain, you would be astounded by the gleam of the rough wood floor and the single plank walls. Today there is also modern hygiene—proper sewage disposal, purified water, and excellent medical facilities—which has wiped out the scourge of disease besetting the people a mere decade ago.

This is a healthy country, and the visitor can see it in the smiling faces. Like the girl at the airport, everyone seems to welcome you. It is not unusual, even in the city, for a stranger to say good-day in passing, and if you should stop on the street, momentarily bewildered, someone is sure to step up and offer to guide you.

You sense a letdown in tempo here. On the whole, Puerto Ricans do things with an efficiency dear to us in the States, but without the hectic hurry we are accustomed to. Watch the way your porter moves. He doesn't dash off for the taxi, nor does he drag his feet, but you are on your way with no more delay than elsewhere.

The Puerto Rican blends an American overlay with an ancient heritage. He is, first of all, a citizen of Puerto Rico, but he is also an American. Precisely worded, Puerto Rico is a self-governing commonwealth "freely associated with the United States." Because of the Puerto Rican's dual citizenship, we from the States are identified as "continentals," a tactful designation we should remember to employ.

That today there is some political grumbling on a local level in the island is a healthy sign. The largest and only governing party up to the present is the Populares (Partido Popular Democratica), instigators of the Commonwealth. There is also a vociferous Statehood party, which prefers that Puerto Rico follow the line of Alaska and Hawaii. The Independence group comes in a poor third, for most Puerto Ricans want to retain an American passport.

Until around 1940 Puerto Rico received little attention from Washington. It was a land almost entirely ill-housed, ill-clothed,

17

ill-fed. The mass of the people were illiterate. As Governor Muñoz Marín later stated, "The trouble with us in those days was that we were too prone to blame others for our troubles." Fortunately, within the small educated group there were dedicated, incorruptible leaders who fought for a better way of life. Realizing that in the final analysis the betterment of the people was dependent upon their own determination, they demanded independence of the homeland as a means of arousing them out of their lethargy.

It was on this basis that Operation Bootstrap evolved, and the Puerto Rico one sees today is a somewhat breath-taking exposition of its phenomenal achievements. The good health, the schools, the new houses and factories, the roads and the clean streets are all attributable to the hidden energy and determination of a once hopeless, starving, and sick people. Glimpsing some of the improvements on the way to the hotel gives you a feeling of suppressed excitement, an impression of actually partaking in a renaissance, which may partially explain that sensation of well-being experienced on arrival.

San Juan, a city of half a million, is run by a woman. Like Governor Muñoz, she held office prior to the advent of the Commonwealth and has been elected four times. Doña Felisa Rincón de Gautier is as colorful, anachronistic a figure as was ever seen in political office. Handsome, with an Old World femininity (her abundant gray hair done up intricately, a fresh flower or ribbon thrust into it, and an active little fan inevitably in her hand), she looks like a Spanish duenna. Childless but maternal, she is a godmother to literally hundreds of poor children. This shrewd, indomitable, and tireless woman runs her office by methods that are both original and successful. She is known to go about the streets calling many of the citizenry by name, and in the poorer quarter will stop and scold them as if she were a member of the family. "I have two garbage collections a day, and yet you allow that litter to accumulate! Clean it up right away!" Appreciative of all she has done for them, they hasten to obey. Although the Puerto Rican was always personally clean, until recently he had no sense of public neatness. This, too, he has now acquired.

They affectionately refer to the mayoress as Doña Fela, an

Ocean Park, a recent housing development in the San Juan area.

intimate but respectful derivative of her name, because she is accessible to everyone. On Wednesday mornings she holds open house at city hall, the Alcaldía, where the humblest can bring their problems. It may be that husband José has unjustly lost his job, or son Ramón is in trouble, or the question of whether daughter Carmen should marry the man. She listens to each intently, giving advice, and takes action when it is justifiable. To Doña Felisa more than any other one person, goes the credit for the San Juan of today.

Officially the country is Puerto Rico, Porto Rico being an ancient corruption of the Spanish language. It has been claimed that the United States is responsible for the modern usage of Porto Rico, but this is not so. It can be seen on early seventeenth-century maps, although it is impossible to discover where or how the original blunder occurred. Nevertheless, even today, to say "Porto Rico" is a sign of ignorance of the land.

19

Originally the island was called Boriquen or, as it is more frequently spelled nowadays, Borinquen, which was the Indian name for it. Tainos, a tribe of Arawaks who came from the delta of the Orinoco in South America, lived here. They were gentle, peaceable Indians who, before the advent of the white man, were already troubled by attacks from the Carib tribes of the Lesser Antilles. They did not, however, survive the conquistadors, but before they were exterminated, their blood had found its way into Spanish veins. The conquistadors imported African slaves and were not entirely averse to marrying them, so today these three racial strains are apparent in Puerto Rico. Later, Frenchmen escaped here from the uprising in Haiti, as some had previously fled Louisiana after the Purchase, and at one period Chinese laborers were also brought here, on a temporary basis, to build the first roads. But the three primary strains—Spanish, Indian, and Negro—generally mixed together, represent the average Puerto Rican today.

This is not to say that a pure Spanish caste no longer exists. It does, and in some instances is guilty of snobbish class distinctions. But officially and, with the rarest exceptions, unofficially, there is no racial discrimination.

This is a partial answer to the recurring question of newly-arrived tourists: "Why are the Puerto Ricans here so different from those in the States?" Disarmed from the moment of landing by the direct, friendly approach of the people, many tourists cannot help recalling the closed, sullen faces of the Puerto Ricans on the streets of New York or various other large cities, and thinking of the newspaper headlines pointing out starkly horrible juvenile crimes. These realities are puzzling contradictions.

Of course the people of the island and those who have emigrated to the States are one and the same, except that the latter have been affected by a policy of almost consistent discrimination. Trusting in our oft-repeated utterances of equality, they came to the States confident that they were going to the Land of Opportunity. What they found was quite the opposite. Poor though they were in Puerto Rico, in many instances they lived under conditions far better than the miserable existence awaiting them on the continent, where they are usually ill-housed and have little chance of improvement. Their opportunities for work are circumscribed, and they are soon aware of the hostility surrounding them.

This is the adult reaction. The immature youth is conditioned by the atmosphere in which he grows up in the States. It is the juvenile delinquent, not the adult, who makes the headlines. It is the youth whose mind is warped and twisted by resentment—a sad commentary on our vaunted way of life.

Contrary to general belief, the government never encouraged migration, and as conditions on the island have improved, the rate of emigration has dropped. There is even a trickle of returnees coming back to the homeland.

One single word explains the situation—discrimination. In Puerto Rico a man can hold his head high with self-respect, in the knowledge that he is equal not only before the law but beside his fellow citizen. Surely it is a by-product that in San Juan it is perfectly safe on the streets at night, even for a woman alone.

If you have brought any prejudice to Puerto Rico with you, discard it as you would an outworn garment, for wherever you go—to a theatre, a restaurant, or the most exclusive hotel—you will find ample evidence of racial equality. It may be a new experience, but it is also a very pleasant one.

CHAPTER 3

Establishing the First Settlement

(Discovery and Early History of Puerto Rico—Ponce de León
—Wars and the Building of Fortifications.)

THE singularly fierce and warlike Caribs, having wrested the
Lesser Antilles from the Arawaks, were intent on taking the
island of Borinquen from the Tainos, another Arawak tribe.
The Tainos were an agricultural people; the Caribs were sea-
farers who, unlike other Indians, used sails on their canoes.
When, therefore, seventeen huge ships with sails bigger than
any the Tainos had ever seen, appeared one November day in
1493 at the entrance to the west coast Bay of Aguadilla, they
fled in terror, and all Christopher Columbus found was a
deserted village.

It was his second voyage to the New World, and he had no
intention of stopping long here, as he was still looking for a
passage to the Orient. He took on some water, which he needed
badly, for he had been driven off several outlying islands by
the Caribs before he could replenish his supply. Then he im-
planted the flag of Spain and a cross in the ground, and moved
on to Hispaniola, where he had left a settlement on his previous
voyage the year before. On his arrival he found that the entire
garrison of Navidad (Ciudad Trujillo today) had been wiped
out. Leaving the soldiers who had accompanied him on this
trip to re-establish a fort, he returned to Spain still unaware
that a continent blocked his progress to the Far East.

On his fourth and last voyage to the New World, Columbus
again stopped in the same west coast bay of the large island
he had claimed for Spain. He had named the island San Juan
Bautista. The harbor on the northeast coast near which, not

long after, the first settlement was established became known simply as Puerto Rico, or rich port, but because of some confusion in making out the official documents, the names were interchanged. The island became Puerto Rico and the new colony took the name of San Juan.

On this last voyage (1504), the Indians did not flee when Columbus arrived, nor did they fight. They were not co-operative, however, and Columbus had great difficulty in securing food from them. He had a calendar on which eclipses were indicated, and he noted that one was expected shortly. "Tomorrow," he told them, "I will black out the sun." When his promise was fulfilled, he received the necessary provisions without further trouble, for the Tainos naturally felt sure he had supernatural powers and were convinced that he was immortal as well.

Possibly this explains why, four years later when an army captain led a group from Hispaniola to settle the island, he was so quickly able to establish friendly relations with the Tainos. The captain's name was Juan Ponce de León, famous in our childhood history books as the seeker of the Fountain of Youth. He had accompanied Columbus on that second voyage in 1493 and remained behind with the new garrison on Hispaniola. By edict of King Ferdinand, he became the first governor of Puerto Rico.

Sailboats in the harbor at San Juan.

Ponce, like Columbus, landed on the western shores, but he enlisted the aid of a tribal chieftain and was guided around the coast until he reached the superb deep harbor of present-day San Juan. It was ideal in many respects, the port being sheltered by a small island. Moving inland a few miles where conditions were better suited to agriculture, the Spaniards began the building of their first colony of Caparra. The entrance to the harbor, nevertheless, was vital to their safety, and so after thirteen years the settlement removed to the island in the bay, and the construction of fortifications was soon begun.

Old San Juan is such a compact town just because it is an island. It is marvelously easy for sightseeing and, particularly because of its walls and forts, equally easy to understand in historical perspective. Work on permanent fortifications was started in 1533, when the base of La Fortaleza and a lookout tower at El Morro were commenced, but it was over two hundred years before the city was completely fortified.

In the beginning, the slow progress was caused by a lag in supplies from the homeland. For instance, the lookout of El Morro was replaced by more substantial ramparts, but they took a discouraging thirty years in the building. The colonists were short of both labor and materials. Later, when San Juan's strategic position in relation to the other Spanish colonies in the Western Hemisphere became apparent, El Morro was elevated to a citadel. The other forts were also reinforced and the perimeter of defense extended.

Puerto Rico soon proved a disappointment to the gold-thirsty Spaniards. Her gold mines were negligible compared to those in Mexico and South America, and soon were all but exhausted. Losing interest, the motherland ignored the pleas for gunpowder and building materials. As the other colonies prospered, however, San Juan's strategic and protected harbor gained in value both as a shelter for the heavily-laden ships returning to Spain and as a port of repairs. At the height of Spain's glory, Cartagena and San Juan were the main bastions of the Spanish Empire.

La Fortaleza, which faced partially inland, was at first considered the primary fort, since it was from this side that most of the Indian assaults came. The good relations with the Tainos had been of brief duration, for the Spaniards, following their customary practice, pressed the Indians into servitude. Those who remained free fled to the security of the mountainous interior.

Moreover, doubt of the immortality—and therefore the invincibility—of the white man had been growing, and the Tainos finally decided to put it to the test. A group of them agreed to guide a young conquistador to some mines. They carried him in their arms to ford a stream, and halfway over, one of them pretended to stumble. The Spanish colonist fell into the water, and the Indians held his body down until it moved no more. To be doubly sure, they waited three days on the riverbank to see if he would awaken. When it was abundantly clear that the young colonist was both dead and mortal, the word was rapidly spread. With the end of the myth, the once peaceable Tainos declared war to the death on the white man.

In the middle of the sixteenth century, within thirty years of the establishment of the permanent settlement, French corsairs and English pirates were adding to the harassment of the colony. Caribs also continued their attacks on the island, but El Morro, facing seaward, had by this time been strengthened and now replaced La Fortaleza as the major fort.

Sir Francis Drake, who was given letters of marque by Queen Elizabeth, spent a number of years as a privateer in the West Indies and off the coasts of South and Central America before his defeat of the Spanish Armada. Knighted, a respectable and respected admiral, he then returned to the Caribbean. He knew all the channels and bays of the region and, in particular, the harbor of San Juan. Consequently, in 1595, when word was received that he planned to attack the port, there was panic. Sir Francis, the scourge of the Spaniards, was thought to be unbeatable.

One Alexander O'Reilly, known as Don Alejandro, a deserter from the Royal Navy then living in San Juan, scoffed at the colonists' terror. A Spanish convoy from Cuba, laden with gold and silver destined for Spain, had put into San Juan for repairs after a storm. The precious cargo was stowed in La Fortaleza, and the ships themselves were sunk in the harbor entrance; then the garrison sat back, waiting tensely for the attack. But soon they were stung by Don Alejandro's continu-

*La Fortaleza (now the Governor's Mansion), with the
old city wall beneath.*

ing jibes. Their pride insulted, they switched to the offensive,
met Drake with a bombardment, and inflicted a resounding
defeat. It was the most ignominious that Drake had ever
suffered, and it is said that some days later at sea he died of
disappointment. That may have been a contributing factor, but
the real cause was dysentery.

By this time two additional forts had been constructed—
Escambron, the ruins of which can still be seen on the far side
of the beach of the Escambron Hotel, and Murillo, between
it and El Morro. They were not sufficient, however, to with-
stand the siege of the Earl of Cumberland, who captured the
city three years after Drake's attack.

During the English occupation an unsuspecting caravel—a
small ship of that era—arrived laden with pearls. Cumberland
confiscated the valuable cargo and decided to take it to England without delay. He requisitioned slaves of the residents and
helped himself to the organ, bells, and sacred vessels of the
cathedral. He left a force in the city, but shortly after his
departure yellow fever broke out, and the remaining troops also
hurriedly re-embarked, after having held the city only five
months.

Following their departure, it was decided to convert El

Morro from a fort to a citadel. This change had been contemplated for some time, and the commander had petitioned the King several years previously to "send negroes and stone-breakers, for white people die in two days." Over and over he repeated "send negroes," for the slave trade was flourishing. At last his request was granted. El Morro was expanded and another new fort, San Gerónimo, was put up on the eastern end of the small island. The Earl of Cumberland, instead of attacking in the orthodox way, had shrewdly landed in the Condado section of the mainland, approaching the island settlement where its defenses were weakest. San Gerónimo and San Antonio, another fort farther inland, rectified this condition.

San Antonio is now demolished, but San Gerónimo is today under restoration on the edge of the Caribe Hilton gardens. Incidentally, at the right of the entrance to the Caribe Hilton grounds, almost camouflaged by the plantings, is a sentinel outpost of the fort attached to a fragment of the connecting wall.

Except for continuing raids by the Indians and the occasional visitation of a pirate ship, San Juan was unmolested until 1625. Meanwhile another fort had been built—San Gabriel,

El Morro.

commonly called "El Cañuelo" or the Channel Fort, on the Isla de Cabras opposite La Fortaleza.

The Dutch West India Company, entering with a fleet, immediately captured it and laid siege to the city. For four days they kept on firing, causing great destruction and even partially occupying the city, but finally Spanish forces from the mainland reached the settlement, crossing from Santurce via the San Antonio bridge, and the Dutch, seeing themselves almost surrounded, fled. During that same year the French also attempted a landing, but were repulsed.

Again the defenses were strengthened. San Cristobal, just off the Plaza Colón, was started and a tunnel dug to connect it with El Morro. Another tunnel led to the arsenal supplying both forts, and a third led to the small bastion protecting the city gate of Santiago, also called Puerta de Tierra or Land Gate, which opened onto the Plaza Colón. In Muñoz Rivera Park there is another powder house which was for the use of Forts Escambron and San Gerónimo. It is not now identified as such, but instead houses the tiny natural history museum and zoo, a short walk from the Supreme Court building. The lovely vine-covered wall with apertures, partially encircling it, was transplanted from the ruins of Fort San Antonio, all that remained intact.

To make San Juan impregnable, work went ahead on the city walls filling the gaps between forts. When this was completed, San Juan was at last entirely fortified. She had long been sufficiently protected against visitations of pirates, and the Indians were all but exterminated. Toward the end of the eighteenth century, Spain and England being once more at war, the British fleet attempted another landing. For two weeks they besieged the city, but then withdrew. The fortifications were unassailable.

With the fear of attack lifted, the grimness of colonial existence gave way to the amenities of social life. San Juan was a city of rich merchants and plantation owners who had close attachments to the mother country. The fine furnishings of their homes were almost entirely imported from Spain. The slave trade was at its height and there was no dearth of servants. It was a life of luxury and leisure, a feudal existence—and a satisfactory one for those in control.

CHAPTER 4

Old San Juan

(Fiestas—the Main Square—Plaza Colón—Calle del Cristo, the Chapel, and Casa del Libro)

ON JUNE 24, the entire population of San Juan goes swimming. They congregate on the beach the night before, and at the stroke of midnight (some rush the hour) the whole family— father, mother, sons, daughters, and grandparents—are in the water. The older generation, not usually seen at the beach, is often fully garbed, and fat, elderly women, giggling like children, splash each other in the shallow water. Many of them simply sit down so the sea can reach to their shoulders.

Along the shore bonfires crackle merrily. There is a good deal of shouting and singing and swapping of picnic suppers. For most, it is an all-night affair, this Fiesta of San Juan Bautista, patron saint of the city. And what more appropriate way could there be to honor St. John the Baptist?

As with most fiestas, the celebration continues for several days. Steel bands play, there are games in the parks and dancing in the streets. Although the arbitrary Puerto Rican ruling regarding the correct season to bathe is lost in obscurity, at least the starting date is comprehensible. Only the ill and utterly infirm would fail to observe the Fiesta of San Juan, particularly as it is believed to be a harbinger of good luck. Except for Christmas, or the Feast of the Three Kings, this is the greatest holiday of all.

Christmas has traditionally been a strictly religious celebration, and Twelfth Night or the Fiesta of the Three Kings is the time for exchanging presents. Children here, instead of writing letters to Santa Claus and trying to keep awake to see

29

him squeeze down the chimney, collect grass to be stowed away in a box under the bed in order to feed the camels when the Three Wise Men, or Kings, arrive. But the Kings also have the disappointing habit of coming so late that one can't keep one's eyes open.

The American influence has now added Christmas to the holidays, greatly delighting the young ones but causing a heavy strain on parental pocketbooks. Frequently a stalk of sugarcane is used for decoration, gilded or sprayed with silver and sometimes hung with light ornaments. In some families a tree has replaced it, but firs are not indigenous to the island. Besides, many prefer the beauty of the cane, with its long, graceful leaves. The children have an affinity for the cane stalk; it makes an ideal hobbyhorse to race with the neighborhood youngsters, and the flowering tassel tosses like a mane.

The singing of Christmas carols, or *aguinaldos*, on the other hand, was brought from Spain rather than borrowed from us. The word *aguinaldo* means gift, and the Spanish carols are somewhat different from ours. They signify the giving of presents, when even the most humble and poor offer their cherished possessions to the newborn Christ Child, or "niño Jésus." For centuries groups have roamed the countryside and streets of towns singing these exquisite songs to the soft accompaniment of a guitar and, sometimes, gourds.

Whether costumes are a Puerto Rican innovation, I do not know, but the singers generally masquerade. One young man usually encases himself in a cotton horse—in lieu of a camel, which undoubtedly needs two experts to manipulate. Sometimes the singers wear gilt-paper crowns; frequently they don masks, but most often they stain their faces dark, for which reason they are called *negritos*. One of the Wise Men, if you remember, was supposed to be black.

The energetic Mayoress of San Juan has a great fondness and respect for these age-old traditions. On the Fiesta of San Juan she, too, goes wading in the water. Not very far out, it is true, but still she never fails to put in an appearance. On Christmas Eve, by her express orders, a beautiful nativity is set up outside the City Hall. And she personally started a fund (it is now augmented by contributions) for the purchase of toys for poor children. She distributes the toys herself, and ad-

*San Juan's beloved
Doña Felisa.*

monishes the parents who come to collect them that they be faithful to the legend and tell the children the toys are gifts from the Three Kings.

The Alcaldía (city hall) somehow always has a festive air. Under the arcade on any ordinary day there is an inevitable line-up of flower vendors. Curiously, there are comparatively few flower sellers either in San Juan or other parts of the island. The Puerto Rican is so accustomed to being surrounded by blooms outdoors that he considers it a ridiculous extravagance to spend money for them to grace the interior. These flower vendors add charm to what might at first glance seem an austere building. Go inside, though—the attendant at the entrance is only too pleased by your interest—and look at the patio. It is small, with a simulated well in the center and wooden balconies suspended from the second floor, as if it were a private home. This is exactly what it was until the city purchased it around the end of the eighteenth century. It was quite an old residence then, having been built in 1602, but lent itself easily to the plan for making a replica of the City Hall in Madrid. Upstairs are a small museum and library, open to the public and interesting as examples of early Spanish architecture.

Diagonally across the square, which was once the public market, is the Intendencia, or Treasury building, which I love

31

for its neo-classic façade. Although it dates from the exact middle of the seventeenth century (1650), it was both refurbished and enlarged in the nineteenth. It, too, was once the home of a rich merchant.

However, it is less confusing for sight-seers to start from the Plaza Colón, where all bus routes terminate. As the entire city is an islet a mile and a half long and a mile across at the widest point, and the original San Juan took up but a third of it, it is both convenient and more rewarding to do the trip on foot. To drive around yourself, in any case, is a nuisance, especially finding parking places on the narrow jammed streets.

The buses stop in front of, or close to, all the large hotels, and it is a short, pleasant drive along the Avenida Muñoz Rivera or, by return, the Avenida Ponce de León. One word of warning—it is preferable to come in at four o'clock or after, when the sun has lost its intensity, and to stick to the shady side of the street. When I first came to Puerto Rico, being a fast walker, I took to the less crowded side and very quickly discovered why it was empty. I also learned to walk more slowly, as the Puerto Ricans do. It is hot at midday.

In the early days the Plaza Colón marked the boundary of the city, with huge guarded gates opening to the fields beyond. On the far side of the plaza, in back of the bus terminal and between the two main arteries leading in and out of the city, stands the Institute of Culture, a baroque gray building with white trim. It was an exclusive social club in the nineteenth century, until people began "moving out of town." A cool-looking and quite imposing building, it nevertheless gives but slight hint of its truly magnificent interior, with high carved ceilings, classic pillars, and marble staircase. It houses a permanent exhibit of Puerto Rico's modern artists of excellent caliber, temporarily shelters early relics from buildings under repair, such as a wood-carved Madonna and head of San Francisco awaiting return to Porta Coeli at San Germán, and quite likely a current art show.

When I first heard of the Institute of Culture, a government agency, I secretly laughed. It sounded naïve, as if culture were a mere matter of inoculation, like an injection of vaccine. When I went there, however, I completely reversed my opinion. Since before Operation Bootstrap the vast majority of Puerto Ricans were illiterate—and even now a plurality of them have only a rudimentary education—the Institute may seem like merely an extension of the schools. In some respects this is correct. When a student shows aptitude, he is given further opportunity for training in his particular field. For example, the Institute has both a Graphic Arts and Plastic Arts Workshop, taught by men and women of demonstrable ability, and it is around their work that the permanent exhibition revolves. The Institute assays and offers scholarships for those interested in other artistic media, such as music and dance.

It also fulfills another need. The Puerto Rican has a natural appreciation of beauty, but much which he has admired and with which he has lived has had, until recently, only a vague aesthetic value. Occasionally he was aware that the village church was very old, and having a sentimental attachment to it, he was distressed to see it collapsing in disrepair. Many fine monuments of early date have been marred by the well-intentioned but inexpert ministrations of local carpenters and plasterers.

Today, historic buildings throughout the island are classified, and all repairs are supervised by the Institute of Culture. The Institute is also dating and co-relating them according to epoch, instead of leaving these monuments to the vagaries, imaginings, and exaggerations of the local populace. In my own travels I was sometimes faced with three or four contradictory dates, occasionally spread over almost a century. It was for this reason that I called on the head of the Institute, Señor Ricardo Alegría, an erudite, hard-working, and very conscientious young man, with an M.A. from the University of Michigan. He specializes in archaeology. He was immediately able to dispel some myths, and to produce accurate dates and back them up with evidence. He was also able to direct me to further examples of a given period.

Across the *avenida* from the Institute stands the Tapia Theatre, a lovely old playhouse of the same generation of buildings, with its ticket office on the sidewalk under the colonnade. Spruced up inside as well as out, it has retained its double balconies of boxes, the center one on the second level bearing the Seal of State to indicate the Governor's box. Of soft rose

33

with white trim, the theatre is not only delightful to look at but, more important than sheer physical beauty, has excellent accoustics.

Many still refer to the Tapia as the Spanish Theatre, since until recently it has had an almost unbroken record of Spanish productions. Those came to an end, however, to be followed by the now defunct Drama Festival, an annual event starting the second Tuesday in January and continuing for eight years. In that period, recent Broadway plays were performed by top stars (Joan Bennett, Fay Bainter, Boris Karloff, to mention a few).

As late as the thirties, though, the Tapia was mentioned with an indulgent laugh for the broken-down stock companies which were its tenants. In the nineteenth century it no doubt had a fine reputation, but actors, like other artists, earned a poor livelihood. On certain nights the theatre held galas, a polite term for benefit performances. On such nights the star of the troupe took over the functions of the box office. She sat in the foyer selling tickets, with a basket beside her, and the Spanish gentlemen—exceedingly generous in certain circumstances—dropped pesos in liberal handfuls into the container. They were proud of their theatre and felt a sentimental devotion to the actors.

Directly opposite the Tapia, on the far side of the plaza, is the start of the Calle Fortaleza. Follow it through the commercial district for six blocks and then turn to the left. This is the lower end of Calle Cristo, one of the earliest paved streets in the Western Hemisphere, some say *the* earliest. Surely it must be the oldest in continuous use; its worn blocks are the original glazed bricks brought over from Spain. These bluish cobblestones were carried as ballast in ships from the homeland, as were some of the fine bricks used in early constructions, and also the gorgeous tiles found decorating patios and interiors of homes.

In this section of the city, where the first colony settled, you are surrounded by beautiful old houses of the eighteenth and nineteenth centuries and even a few of earlier date. Many still need repair, but under the guiding hand of the Institute of Culture rapid progress is being made. The magnificent El Convento Hotel, which long ago housed Carmelite nuns, is a splendid example.

Many homes have been converted to use as apartments and restaurants; some house attractive shops, and several are designated for early opening as de luxe pensions. Look at them carefully, even the shabby ones, and note the beautiful wrought-iron balconies or, through the open tenement door, the fine old tiles lining the risers of the stairs. Notice the heavy wooden supports and, occasionally, the balconies of wood. This is *ausubo*, an excessively hard native wood, which has withstood both the climate and the assaults of termites and lesser insects. Much of it looks almost suspiciously recent, but its appearance is not due to any specific treatment, but to its own unusually fine properties. It is largely thanks to these excellent beams and planks that the houses have survived so many years of neglect.

One of the renovated eighteenth-century residences on the Calle Cristo is the Casa del Libro at #255, opened as a museum in 1958. It was started by the late Elmer Adler, a retired curator of Princeton University, for whom it was a labor of love. He got a government subsidy for it, raised funds by public subscription, and received gifts of valuable manuscripts. The present director is David Jackson McWilliams.

As the name suggests, this Casa is a museum devoted to examples of fine printing and historical documents. The museum occupies the ground floor only. The upper story, air-conditioned, is for the storage and preservation of those books and manuscripts not on display. Once or twice a year the exhibit is changed. When I visited it the collection was called "Columbus and the Book." It was there I saw the original *calendarium* foretelling the eclipse, which Columbus used to such good avail with the Indians. The most valuable documents on view, however, were two royal cedulas signed by Ferdinand and Isabella, valued at $10,000 each. One dated May 20, 1493 requisitioned provisions for Columbus' second voyage, the one on which he made his first landing in Puerto Rico. On that same date he was granted his coat-of-arms and designated "Captain-General of the Fleet."

A fine example of early typography was also on display, a book of Seneca's printed in 1492, with the prophetic lines:

> Time will come in distant ages
> When the ocean will reveal its mysteries
> An immense land will appear...

The Casa del Libro is recommended not only because of its collection of rare manuscripts and books but as an illustration of intelligent restoration. So excellently have the original details been reproduced that Delft tiles were imported to replace the damaged or missing ones. Although this residence was built long after Spain's domination of the Low Countries, the Spaniards must have retained an appreciation of the superiority of the Dutch tiles. The larger tiles backing the wall fountain in the patio, my favorites, are surely the originals; their soft, faded colors exude an antique beauty.

It is only a few steps from the Casa del Libro to the foot of the street, almost blocked by the little Capilla Cristo, or Christ Chapel. Long deserted, it has mercifully suffered no thoughtless rebuilding, although it has undergone some restoration. It is most effective when seen from a distance, for it blends in as if it were a continuation of the onetime sea wall and creates the illusion of another city gate.

Small as a wayside shrine (not even the width of the narrow Calle Cristo), it is without doors, open to but protected by glass from the public. Over its miniscule belfry is a weather vane surmounted by a cock. An unknown pope of medieval times, it seems, once ordered weather vanes like these, the cock

San Juan's old city wall, with the top of Capilla Cristo (Christ Chapel) just visible at the foot of Calle Cristo.

being an emblem of St. Peter, to be placed on all churches of that era. Probably this one was ordered put on the chapel to recall old churches in Spain.

One can look below the city wall beside the chapel at what is reclaimed land, as the foot of Calle Cristo used to end at the sea. In the eighteenth century, it was the starting point for horse races, the course running uphill the full length of the street past the Cathedral and finishing in front of the church of San José. These races were very festive events, with colored ribbons strung across the street from balcony to balcony, on each of which hung a large ring. The young bloods contested in the spearing of these rings as they raced along on their mounts.

The city wall was low at this spot, and it seems surprising that many accidents did not occur. Once a caballero with an especially lively steed had trouble controlling him. Suddenly both horse and rider plunged over the wall into the sea. A certain general by the name of Tomás Mateo Prats, a spectator on a nearby balcony, seeing the disaster, called out, "Save him! Save him, Blessed Christ of Health!" Miraculously the caballero *was* rescued, and seeing him brought back in safety, the general crossed himself and vowed to build a commemorative chapel in thanks for the divine intervention.

The chapel was dedicated in 1753, fulfilling the general's vow within the year. The pastime of racing horses through the streets persisted for almost another hundred years despite the danger. They were finally prohibited by a reproving ordinance of 1849, which pointed out that "horse races in towns are not permitted in any civilized country in the world."

The chapel altar is of rococo hammered silver. Over it was hung a painting of the Crucifixion which, the echo of the general's supplication still fresh, became known as "The Blessed Christ of Health." In view of the holy intercession which the chapel commemorated, it was logical to endow the painting with mystic powers. Word of illness cured and wounds healed soon spread, and for a while the chapel was a shrine for pilgrims. On Calle Cristo in those days they also held a celebration in honor of "The Blessed Christ of Health." With the passage of time, belief in its curative properties dimmed, and by the next generation the little chapel was deserted.

CHAPTER 5

More About Old San Juan

(Some Further History—La Fortaleza, the Cathedral, and
San José—Ponce de León and Casa Blanca—El Morro)

CALLE CRISTO was the only street which bisected the island and
it was, therefore, the big thoroughfare of old San Juan. In the
eighteenth century when the vogue for horse races was at its
peak, San Juan extended several streets back from it. The
Plaza de Armas, then the Plaza Baldorioty, where the City
Hall stands, was the market place, and between it and the
Plaza Colón quite a few fine mansions had been erected. The
original colony, however, was built close to the fortifications at
the base of the island and Calle Cristo was the undisputed main
street.

In 1529, a mere eight years after the colony had transferred
from Caparra, there were 120 dwellings and the settlement had
acquired a look of permanence. Several of the houses were of
stone and the Dominican monastery, as well as San José church,
had been erected. The cathedral, however, was still a wood and
thatch structure. Work by Indians impressed into service was
continuing in desultory fashion on La Fortaleza and the lookout of El Morro.

These proved sufficient bulwarks against the depredations of
Caribs and pirates and, at the end of the century, the more
formidable assault of the English. With the importation of
Negro slaves, who withstood the heat better than the Indians,
work was accelerated and additional fortifications constructed,
but the attack of the Dutch in 1625 was devastating. After
capturing El Cañuelo, the newly-finished fortress on Isla de
Cabras, they turned their guns on the city. The narrow channel

separating the two islands made San Juan an easy target, and it quickly turned into an inferno. The holocaust consumed many homes, damaged the new stone Cathedral and Bishop's Palace, and partially destroyed Casa Blanca and La Fortaleza.

Many of the colonists were already dispirited. Not only was San Juan in a constant state of siege, but at all too regular intervals storms added to the destruction. Moreover, the far greater wealth which their compatriots had found in Mexico and South America provided an enticing excuse for migrating there. At the time of the Dutch attack, the colony had diminished to less than two hundred inhabitants. But in the middle of the seventeenth century, when San Juan had gained prestige as a bastion of the Spanish Main, it began to expand and the town could boast of 350 homes. Some of these were wooden shacks, but the greater number were built of limestone and brick for durability. They are the basis of San Juan today.

Returning from Capilla Cristo to Calle Fortaleza, and turning left toward the governor's mansion, the sight-seer pauses from sheer delight at the unmarred perfection of this street of colonial homes. Calle Fortaleza, and the short Caleta de San Juan beyond—tree-shaded, with the mellowed soft colors of the houses blending into the green, their balconies almost touching—exude the restful charm of a bygone era. These early-nineteenth-century houses are products of the age of prosperity, at least for the plantation owners, when war no longer threatened Puerto Rico and there was an unlimited market for sugar.

At the end of the street stands La Fortaleza, still called The Fortress, although it has been the governor's residence for over three hundred years. The governor and military commander, however, were synonymous for a long time. In its original state, La Fortaleza consisted simply of a stone tower and quarters sufficient for a lone guard. Although it was quickly acknowledged to be inadequate as a defense post and El Morro superseded it in importance, its enormous underground storage space —both for ammunition and the protection of valuable cargo on its way to Spain—was invaluable. There was, in time, a labyrinth of subterranean passages connecting it with the various forts of the city.

Despite its solid stone construction, La Fortaleza had been

badly damaged by the Dutch; in the rebuilding it was made suitable for residential use. The Chapel of Santa Catarina, on the spot where the San Juan Gate now stands, was torn down and rebuilt within the confines of the fort, for construction of the city walls was also in progress at the time. For this reason La Fortaleza was occasionally called the Palace of Saint Catherine.

These repairs and additions were made in 1639, following which the governor transferred his headquarters from Casa Blanca. During the ensuing centuries there were further embellishments and additions although, oddly, La Fortaleza was not officially decreed as the governor's residence until late in 1822. In 1846, the incumbent governor undertook to change its aspect to that of a palace, enlarging the entrance and remodeling the austere facade into the gracious, classic lines it has today. Theodore Roosevelt, visiting La Fortaleza during his presidency, described it as "half-castle, half-fortress," which I consider far from an apt description. No major changes have been made since the earlier Roosevelt's visit, but I find it a charming, livable—in some aspects, almost cozy—home.

The large entrance doors lead into a huge patio, used on official occasions as a ballroom, but ordinarily it is the driveway to garages, or old carriage houses. The upper level consists of white latticed shutters, which open onto the square inner terrace. This first floor is broken up into reception and dining rooms, a coffee bar, and to the rear, the ancient, unaltered kitchen. (This kitchen is simply retained as a museum piece.) On the floors are embossed wool rugs of fine soft colors, with the Seal of State and other emblems brightening the corners of the otherwise monotone carpets. These very excellent native products come from Arecibo; they are sold to United States decorators, but are not as yet, unfortunately, available for retail purchase. The furniture, although not outstanding, shows a tasteful appreciation such as one expects in any amateur collector of antiques.

The gardens, cut up into small patios filled with flowers, have an intimate warmth. Even the huge main terrace is inviting, despite the ancient cannon which reminds you of the true meaning of La Fortaleza. Built flush with the city walls, this terrace commands a view of the harbor entrance, of Isla de Cabras and Cataño on the opposite shore, with the shaded blue mist of mountains in the background. To the right of it, on the northwest corner, is the original tower, its flat-surfaced roof forming a small terrace on the edge of the patios.

La Fortaleza can be visited, but only with a guide. The guard at the entrance will make the arrangements for you. If the governor is in residence, only the gardens can be seen; at other times the second floor is also open to the public.

San Juan Gate, once known as the Water Gate, is two streets beyond. This is not only the oldest, but the sole gate remaining, of the four which once led into the city. Here the ships docked, and the voyager at once devoutedly headed up the street to the Cathedral to offer a prayer of gratitude for his safe arrival.

Today, in front of the gate there is a broad cement walk which leads around the base of La Fortaleza, turning into the bay where ships now dock, but it requires no great imagination to visualize the rough wood pilings where the caravels and galleons once tied up. Here in this corner of the isle is the essence of old San Juan.

Walk over one short street before retracing your steps to Calle Cristo. Halfway up the block, to the left on the ascent, is the Callejon Las Monjas, named for the Carmelite nuns whose seventeenth-century convent used to back onto this alley and whose later, nineteenth-century edifice is now renovated to house the guests of El Convento Hotel. The only significance of the Callejon Las Monjas today is as the last remaining street of steps, commonplace in the period before modern traffic. A street of humble working people, it quite fascinated me because of the ease with which one could look into their private quarters. The unshuttered, wide-open doors and windows were almost an invitation. Some say it is not so much that the people want you to look in as that they like to look out and see what is going on. Whatever the reason, I noticed that this open-house arrangement is not confined to any one class; it is quite commonplace in all quarters of the city.

The houses on the street of steps are modest ones, consisting of tiny one- or—at the most—two-room apartments, but I was struck by two things: the impeccable neatness and cleanliness, and the astonishing sight of a modern electric refrigerator in almost every living room. I was informed that the refrigerator is put in a place of honor because it is their most valuable possession, a thing to be shown off; however, it occurs to me that it represents one of the bad habits the Puerto Rican has picked up from us—installment plan buying, which keeps the poor man constantly in debt. Many of these otherwise sparsely furnished rooms also boasted a TV set!

The Plazuela de las Monjas, on which the Carmelite convent once faced and where the semi-modern Cathedral stands, seemed to me—until the plastic surgery on El Convento—devoid of charm, but in the ancient city it was the central square and bore a different, if not always pleasant, aspect.

That was the era of the Inquision, which was as zealously carried on in the New World as in old Spain. One of Ponce de León's earliest acts upon settling in Caparra was to build a church; within five years of the colonization, it was designated the first bishopric in the Western Hemisphere. Naturally the diocese was transplanted with the colony to the islet of San Juan, and even though the first cathedral was simply a palm-thatched hut, its first bishop bore the resounding and terrifying title of General Inquisitor of the Indies. First in the thatched hut and later in the stone replacement, for almost three hundred years the backsliders and delinquents were tried, tortured, made to do penance, or marched to their execution. When the Dutch took transient possession of the city, they found "sambenitos" hanging in the new vestry—coarse sacks with large crosses and pictures of the devil painted on them in red, which the penitent and condemned alike were forced to wear.

By this period the Cathedral presented an appearance of greater solidity. The thatch structure had been almost immediately wiped out by hurricane. It was rebuilt of wood, but this was constantly damaged by storm and as frequently repaired, and stone walls eventually replaced the frail timber. The coats-of-arms of the king and the bishop were suitably carved on the façade, and fine silver altarpieces, imported from Spain, adorned the interior. The Earl of Cumberland, during the British occupancy of San Juan, was sufficiently impressed to write: "The Cathedral is as fine as any in England, very perfect and lovely. It has a lovely organ..." As already mentioned, the latter pleased him so much that he included it, as well as the church bells and sacred vessels, in the loot which he took home.

The Cathedral has been restored and rebuilt so many times

San Juan Cathedral.

since, that little remains of the earlier epochs. It was rebuilt after the Dutch siege, again damaged by hurricane, again restored. At the end of the seventeenth century the roof was blown off, and of necessity it was again temporarily covered with thatch. In the early nineteenth century it was shaken by an earthquake, after which it was reconstructed, enlarged, and given the appearance it bears today. Of the original permanent structure the Gothic ceiling over the altar, the circular staircase to the pulpit, and the tower are all that remain.

The modern sculptured marble tomb of Ponce de León gives one no sense of history. On the other hand, the ornate gold-leaf middle-nineteenth-century chapel of the Virgin, all the way forward on the left side of the nave, has great charm. The extraordinarily sweet sadness of her face as she grasps the play-fully raised arm of the Infant, unconventionally sprawled across her lap, has a rare human maternal appeal.

The Cathedral is befittingly grandiose, and no doubt for this reason the remains of Ponce de León were transferred there from San José—a church of his time and of which his grandson became presbyter—on the four-hundredth anniversary of Ponce's arrival in Puerto Rico.

Less grandiose but far more interesting is the church of San José. It can, in certain respects, claim to be the oldest church in Puerto Rico, since its foundations were begun, along with the adjoining Dominican monastery, in 1523. Unlike the Cathedral, it withstood both hurricanes and wars, with the exception of damage to its façade by an American shell in 1898. Even this façade dates from 1635. Both the church and the Dominican convent (in Spanish the word "convent" is used interchangeably for both male and female orders; this one belonged to the priesthood and was, in our language, a monastery) were somewhat renovated during the nineteenth century.

San José needs a thorough restoration, which the Institute of Culture has just begun. At present it is a hodgepodge of good and bad taste, splendid remains of early colonial art and horrible examples of later epochs. The first reaction of tourists acquainted with the old churches of Europe is certain to be one of disappointment. The exterior walls are weathered and peeling, and those in the interior are not only equally flaky but reveal an artist's inexcusable conception of cement blocks. In addition, the columns carry painted fluting (a commonplace in countries where marble and granite are lacking), intricate decorative curlicues over doors, and—perhaps greatest desecration of all—a painted stained-glass window next to a quite ordinary one, not to mention the lifelike, utterly silly little altar boys strategically placed for offertories.

But I implore you not to judge too hastily and turn your back. Study first the pure lines of the traditional Spanish façade, with its small wooden balcony over the portals, from which, during times of siege, the priest used to address his frightened flock in the square. Inside, look up at the essentially simple Roman vaulting. Peeking through the flaky painted blocks is the earlier lovely cerulean blue which once covered these arches.

In the nave on either side of the altar rail are two large canvases (eighteenth century) by Campeche, Puerto Rico's greatest painter. They are so in need of expert cleaning as to be almost indistinguishable at present. A small, revered oil of the Madonna suckling the Christ Child, known as the Madonna of Belen, is in the small chapel farthest forward on the right. Many legendary tales have been told of its supernatural properties, but nothing is really known of it beyond the experts' pronouncement that it is Flemish in origin and dates from the period when Spain occupied the Low Countries.

On the opposite side of the nave, in the center chapel, is the greatest relic of the church. This is the Crucifix of the Ponces, an almost life-sized figure of painted wood, harrowingly realistic with its waxlike flesh.

Ponce de León, after requesting and being granted ornaments, chalices, and bells for the original cathedral in Caparra, separately sent gold and ordered an Andalusian crucifix for his personal chapel. This was consigned to a later vessel, which reached San Juan at the peak of a storm. The ship was wrecked on the rocks of the Isla de Cabras, and presumably everything and everybody aboard were lost. According to fairly well authenticated records, one lone box was found floating off El Morro. It contained the Ponce crucifix. Ponce's granddaughter donated it to San José when her brother, after the death of his wife, entered the priesthood and became presbyter.

At that period the church was not San José but Santo Tomás, named for St. Thomas of Aquinas, the revered intellectual of the Dominican Order, which built the church. Later it became Santo Domingo, or St. Dominick, in honor of the founder of the Order. In the 1830's, however, when there was civil war in Spain over the succession to the throne, the Regent Queen Maria-Christina sanctioned the suppression of monasteries and convents for the purpose of gaining funds to fight the Carlists. This also fortuitously spelled the official abolition of the Inquisition, which, as a matter of fact, had been much less stringent for the past century. Five hundred thousand pesos had been levied on Puerto Rico, and her governor was instructed to take over religious properties, if necessary, to raise the sum. The Dominicans thereupon found themselves dispossessed, and when conditions were again normal a decade or so later, it was the Jesuits who took over administration of the church, which they rebaptized San José.

The monastery itself, given over to secular purposes, retained the appellation of Dominican. Once it was part of a vast property, the largest single tract of land in San Juan, with gardens and orchards reaching to the entrance of El Morro. Now all you can see are the two buildings fused together, the monastery's wooden-barred windows outlined in brown in attractive contrast to its yellow walls. In this mild climate buildings do not become as quickly weathered as, say, in Europe and often do not look their age. If the fresh paint seems to dispel the illusion of antiquity, it must be emphasized that the monastery, despite refurbishing, remains essentially the same as in the days when the colonists fled to its cloisters for refuge against the attacks of Caribs and Europeans. In this monastery also was the school for the colonists' children, the first native-born Puerto Ricans. Only once prior to the confiscation of the property was it abandoned, and that was during the five months of English occupancy of the city, when the Earl of Cumberland requisitioned it as his headquarters.

When the Jesuits took over San José in the middle 1800's, it was already in disrepair, and while necessary work was being done, certain changes were also made. The original carved altar was given to the church in Loíza Aldea, which somehow seems regrettable, even though the present more pretentious altar has obvious beauty. At that period, too, the remains of Ponce de León, which his grandson had transported from Cuba, where he had died, and which had rested here undisturbed since 1559, were presumably only temporarily removed. But they now lie beneath a new monument in the Cathedral.

However, San José still contains many reminders of the Ponce family—the family crucifix, the grandson who was presbyter, the burial places of other members of the family. The Ponce coat-of-arms is placed high on the wall to the left of the altar. In the square by the side of the church is a statue of the founding father of Puerto Rico, supposedly made of captured English cannon.

Incidentally, if the front entrance to San José should be closed, try the doors opposite the statue. It is puzzling to me that the churches on the island are not, as elsewhere, always open. Apparently they are locked to prevent vandalism when no one is in attendance, but I have never found any thoroughgoing explanation. Be that as it may, the chances of entering, particularly at the noon hour, are poor.

46

The large building diagonally across the square on the corner of Calles Cristo and San Sebastian is the bishop's palace. Unfortunately it is not open to the general public, for it is a lovely building, less changed than many of the city's edifices. Tradition has it that when the house was purchased for the episcopal palace in 1728, it was a private residence already of considerable age and falling into decay. A sizable sum was spent on putting it into shape, restoring it much as it is today.

The palace seems to guard the entrance to Casa Blanca, today the residence of the commander of the U.S. Army Forces Antilles and open to the public, by appointment, on Wednesdays at 10 A.M. (Call 722-0000, ext. 3106, for arrangements.) This is an old landmark, sometimes described as having been the home of Juan Ponce de León. The land, in fact, was given to him by the Crown because he was displaced from office. Ponce, appointed governor by the king, had served only two years when Columbus' son, governor of Hispaniola, installed his own nominee, declaring that Puerto Rico was under his jurisdiction and the appointment of its governor was his prerogative—a decision the king eventually accepted.

In 1513 Ponce had left on an expedition—he, too, in search of a passage to the Orient—and discovered Florida, which he conceived to be an island. From the Indians he had heard vague but repeated tales of waters with recuperative powers, and in Florida he found wonderful springs that seemed to answer the description. On his second exploratory trip he was mortally wounded by the Florida Indians, and the survivors of the expedition fled with him to nearby Cuba, where Ponce died. This was in 1521, the very same year that the colony moved from Caparra to the islet of San Juan. A small frame house had been erected for him, but he never occupied it.

As the land had been given in perpetuity to the Ponce family, his eldest daughter and her husband, Garcia-Troche, took possession. Ponce had fathered only daughters, so his son-in-law petitioned, and was granted, the right to take the family name. The frame house was destroyed by storm like so many others, and Garcia-Troche commenced the present stone structure. Originally, like La Fortaleza, it consisted principally of a tower plus limited living quarters.

From time to time Casa Blanca was enlarged and embel-

Sentry box on wall of La Fortaleza, next to the San Juan gate.

lished, eventually emerging as a charming mansion. In 1773 the Casa Ponce, as it was generally called, was sold by the family to the Spanish government, which designated it the residence of the military commander (by then a separate official from the governor). So, with a U.S. Army general in residence, it now continues to fulfill its traditional function.

Across from and slightly to the right of San José is the National Park Service (U.S.A.), from whose eminence one can see not only the gates of El Morro, known officially as Fort Brooke since it serves as a base for the U.S. Army, but a bit beyond to the golf course. El Morro perhaps has a unique distinction in having the only moat in the world to serve such a purpose. It looks very pretty—filled in, covered with grass, and dotted with palm trees—and the bunkers, no doubt, present rather unusual hazards. The course is open to any golf enthusiast upon request.

Dignified old El Morro has some humorous history, too. A delightfully comic touch was provided in World War I at the moment of our declaration of war, when a German ship in the harbor lifted anchor and hurried out to sea on the instant the news was received. A conscientious soldier on duty, also apprised of the situation, took the only action he deemed possible. On his own, he fired one of the fort's ancient and long disused cannons at the fleeing ship. The shot was not so successful as its aftermath. Whether the marksmanship was good or not is uncertain, but the old cannon itself hurtled into the air and then toppled into the sea with a thunderous noise and a memorable arch of flame. The German captain, believing he was at the mercy of a new and terrifying weapon, ran up the white flag of surrender and returned to port, where he and the crew were interned for the duration.

For anyone interested in the sober historical significance of El Morro, excellent free tours are offered four times daily—at 9:30 and 11:00 A.M., 2:00 and 3:30 P.M. The National Park Service has a tour of Casa Blanca too, but this only on Monday mornings and arrangements must be made in advance.

After taking such a tour, I no longer wondered why the watchtower is so frequently used as an emblem of San Juan. The particular sentry box represented, by the way, is a lonely outpost on the water's edge of San Cristobal (now open to the public on all days from 8:30 A.M. to 4 P.M.)—the recipient of nostalgic affection. It is known as the Devil's Sentry Box. The legend goes that the relieving sentry appeared early one morning to find only the gun, armor, and outer clothing of the soldier who had preceded him; the man himself had disappeared in the vaporous morning air. Legends, to prove their authenticity, always have repeat performances, and this one is supposed to have had several repetitions, all of which occurred, one following close on another, around the eighteenth century. A mundane, and therefore unpopular, version is that there was but one lost sentry, who was discovered some years later cheerfully alive and well on a farm near Caguas. My personal version—after stepping in and taking measurements of several old sentry boxes—is that the soldier suffered from claustrophobia. True, people of that era were shorter in stature, but I felt that only a couple of inches separated me from the roof, and it was impossible to take as few as two steps in the standard lookouts. In any case, although the sentry box symbol supposedly represents this particular one, it was the standard design of all the Spanish forts.

CHAPTER 6

Modern San Juan

(Geography and Architecture—Artistic Attractions—Night
Clubs and Other Amusements—Restaurants—Shopping)

In their last attempt to capture San Juan, the English went
ashore on the mainland farther down the coast at Boca de
Cangrejos, for the Spaniards, using huge rocks, had blocked the
narrow channel separating the island from Santurce. These
rocks, by the way, can still be observed—a dribble of them off
Fort San Gerónimo. In the intervening century and a half, the
Spaniards had also turned the defense post which guarded the
San Antonio bridge into a full-fledged fort, connected with San
Gerónimo.

Santurce, at the period, was an agricultural region in which
some residents of San Juan had country estates. These people
hurried back to the protection of the city walls, and the old
drawbridge was pulled up. Fort San Antonio proved a much
stronger defense than the British had anticipated, and they
were defeated.

Nothing remains of the fort today (except that lovely piece
of wall transferred to Muñoz Rivera Park), and where the old
drawbridge once stood, three cement bridges interlace and
consolidate metropolitan San Juan. Santurce makes up such a
vast part of San Juan that it is frequently used as a postal
address by itself, as if it were a separate city. The real reason
for this is that the present San Juan encompasses numerous
townships with a repetition of street names, and a resident of
necessity must indicate that *his* street is the one in Rio Piedras,
Hato Rey—or Santurce.

Actually, Santurce is the core of modern San Juan. The

Condado section of beach front contains many of the new hotels and apartment houses. Miramar, with some other hotels, is also an excellent residential district, and farther along, the Avenida Ponce de León, main artery and longest street, cuts through today's business center. You will note, if you study your map, that Santurce just escapes being an island itself, its boundaries being outlined by channels and lagoons except for the narrow strip of land connecting it with Isla Verde. Isla Verde, where the airport, the El San Juan, the new Americana Hotel, and several popular restaurants are situated, seems quite as much a part of San Juan as Santurce does, but officially, at this writing, it remains a suburb.

By usage, "Old San Juan" indicates the island and the original settlement, but even this is an inexact distinction, as the colony never filled the islet. That section between the Plaza Colón and the bridges might be termed semimodern, since its architecture (dating from the twenties and thirties) forms a charming transition from the old town to ultra-modern Santurce. Driving downtown on the one-way Avenida Muñoz Rivera, with the sea on the right, you pass the handsome School of Medicine, the classic-domed Capitol and the Casa de España, a social club, with a blue and white tiled roof and Spanish ceramics adorning its white walls.

Private cars, instead of turning into the Plaza Colón, can continue along the coastline past the fortifications of San Cristobal up to the entrance of El Morro. There are some fine old buildings on the land side, unfortunately lacking any conveniences and still inhabited by poverty-stricken citizens. These buildings are to be renovated, but the process of slum clearance is of necessity slow, as adequate quarters must first be found for the evacuated. Blessedly almost hidden from gaze on the embankment below the sea wall is probably San Juan's worst remaining slum, which bears the outrageous misnomer of "La Perla." Not so many years ago it was twice as large, but what remains of it urgently needs attention.

As you return on the Avenida Ponce de León, you will see a beautiful white building highlighted with mosaics, with bas-reliefs flanking the door. This is the Ateneo Puertorriqueño, an independent adjunct of the Institute of Culture, supported by private funds. It holds a concert on the average of once a month, offers European films, sponsors lectures, art contests, and exhibits. It also contains a small permanent collection of old paintings, the works of José Campeche being outstanding among them.

Campeche was the son of a freed slave and artisan employed by the church as a wood-carver and restorer of early paintings. The family lived at 43 Calle Cruz, on the corner of Calle San Sebastian, just two streets away from San José. The lower story of the building contains a *comado,* or grocery. Campeche was a native son who turned down invitations to go to Europe, but so highly was his work regarded even during his lifetime that the Spanish king purchased two oils, which are now hanging in the Prado in Madrid.

The Ateneo is next door to the Carnegie Library, which is adjoined by the Casa de España, the Capitol, and the School of Medicine—all three of which extend from the incoming boulevard to the outgoing one. These, in turn, are succeeded by several departmental buildings. With the exception of the Capitol, they are all recent Spanish-style architecture, some brightly colored, some ornamented with tiles, gay and yet not too ornate.

Suddenly the colorful display is broken by the restful green of the park, where dirt paths under mammoth trees with interlocking trunks and thick, lacy foliage lead toward the new Supreme Court Building at the far end, the first of many interesting examples of completely modern design. This rectangular structure is built on stilts over an artificial pond, with an inconspicuous flat dome covering the circular courtroom. It has none of the antiseptic, purely functional air that makes so much modern architecture essentially drab. At night, particularly, seen rising mistily above its spotlighted fountains, with globules of light spotting the pond beneath, it has an almost dreamlike quality.

The extraordinary originality of the new architecture—from hotels to churches to private homes—has a cachet that is decidedly Puerto Rican. Their tremendous fondness for color sometimes runs riot in the poorer quarters, finding expression in such amazing juxtapositions as, say, a pink porch attached to a green house, or a lemon and red trim on blue. Any combination is entirely possible, and although it may be noncon-

Detail of San Juan's new Supreme Court Building.

Handsome, delicate grillwork on a private home in San Juan.

formist, it has preserved many a shack from complete degradation. In public buildings and the finer homes the use of color is naturally more restrained, but there is a laudable amount of it to please the eye, and in the low-priced housing developments there are pleasant splashes of color to break the monotony of uniformity.

The constant use of grillwork also seems to me outstandingly Puerto Rican. Thanks to the climate, intricate wrought-iron grills often replace glass windows and doors, as well as shelter terraces and close off gardens. Since there is almost no ferrous metal in Puerto Rico, the extensive use of wrought-iron trimmings is surprising (a holdover, doubtless, from the days when it was ballast on Spanish ships), but occasionally cement lattices are used to achieve a similar effect.

Both the Caribe Hilton and La Concha hotels are excellent specimens of the present trend in Puerto Rican architecture. They bear not the slightest resemblance to each other, with a single exception—both have open-air lobbies. The question of cold does not have to be considered, and protection from wind and an occasional storm is managed through directional angles and overhangs. On the sea or windward side, of course, there is glass.

For a pleasant ride and a glimpse of some of the new private homes, drive out the Calle Loíza to Isla Verde as far as Boca de Cangrejos. This latter, by the way, has a most inviting, unspoiled beach and not far offshore a coral reef called the "submarine gardens," a wonderful place to go snorkeling. Plans are afoot to erect a hotel there. Just before you reach this spot, on the edge of the Ocean Park development is another good public beach, with an attractive snack bar complete with terrace and tables across the road.

Union Church (interdenominational) at Punta Las Marias.

Turn off Calle Loíza at Calle Taja (or, if you take the Loíza bus, request to be dropped at the corner) and walk the three or four streets to the sea. A yellow post marked "Parada," by the way, is the standard indication of a bus stop.

In the wooded area of Punta Las Marias, seemingly part of Isla Verde but in reality on the edge of Santurce, you might like to stop and visit the interdenominational Union Church. It is built of brick and cement, with the grounded metal beams supporting its rounded walls joined in a peaked arch above the pews. What appears from the exterior to be a vast chimney is transformed on the inside into an altar of simple dignity. Although my personal preference is for churches of less austerity and greater warmth, this one is unquestionably an interesting experiment in design.

In the private homes you will observe a great range of individuality. Look up and down the side streets and you will not find two alike, but rarely will they be freakish. Throughout the island, wherever there are new real estate developments, one finds delightful examples of native modern architecture, but they are especially evident in the rapidly expanding city of San Juan.

Incidentally, notice the distinctive Puerto Rican touch on the front lawns: egg shells covering the sharp tips of cactus plants. Some say they are to protect you from scratches, others that they keep insects away, and some that they are merely decorative—probably the most logical explanation.

In the originality of Puerto Rican architecture there is a definite hint, which is not without foundation, of a general artistic renascence. At least two of the large hotels usually house current shows of Puerto Rican artists. They can be found just off the entrance to the lobby of La Concha, and on the mezzanine of the Condado. There are also several downtown galleries, as well as the exhibitions of the Institute of Culture and the Ateneo Puertorriqueño. Puerto Rico is producing some first-rate painters, and the exhibits are usually well worth visiting. Among the established names are Julio Rosado del Valle (whose murals flank the staircase of the Caribe Hilton), Augusto Marin, Rafael Tufiño, Lorenzo Homar, Guillermo Sureda Arbelo, and Epifanio Irizarry. Two quite apposite paintings of Irizarry's

*Garden cactus deco-
rated with eggshells—a
distinctive Puerto
Rican touch.*

still haunt me—one of masked carnival figures, the other a
head of Christ.

The decision of the great Pablo Casals to settle in San Juan
has given impetus to activity in the musical field. Casals' mother
was Puerto Rican, but, strangely, he had never seen her native
land until at the age of eighty, in 1956, he came for a visit—
and decided to stay. Now the Festival Casals is held annually.
A very old man, but still vigorous and indisputably one of the
world's finest living musicians, he himself plays in the chamber
music programs and alternates with Alexander Schneider as
conductor of the Puerto Rico Symphony Orchestra. His pres-
ence has made it easy to attract guest artists of the caliber of
Rudolf Serkin, Isaac Stern, and the Budapest String Quartet.
The Festival Casals is, possibly, without peer.

In addition, under the great man's guidance, a conservatory
has been opened and Puerto Rico is attaining the status of a
musical mecca.

Recent years have also seen the growth of ballet. Somewhat uneven in performance, the Ballets de San Juan are nevertheless invariably interesting, for they are entirely original, using themes based on local folklore. Both the music and choreography are by native artists. During the Casals Festival they perform on off-nights, but they also appear at certain other seasons of the year (as, quite possibly, does Casals). Look at *Que Pasa*, the *Island Times*, or the *San Juan Star* (daily English-language newspaper) to see if they will be performing during your stay.

There is never any lack of activity in San Juan, and seeking entertainment is a simple matter of consulting the current calendar. Throughout the year, on Wednesdays, Fridays, and Sundays (and occasional other days), there is racing at El Commandante race track. You may be surprised to learn that Puerto Rico breeds race horses; many of them are to be seen here.

But you do not need to be a devotee of racing to find this a pleasant place to spend an afternoon; the grounds are beautifully landscaped with, of all things, a swan lake in the infield. Supposedly the racing strip is also unique, for it is composed of crushed sugar cane mixed with topsoil, which makes for especially springy footing, I was informed. You can test this by some pari-mutuel betting.

During the greater part of the year there is also cock fighting, should you be curious about this typically Latin American sport, but it is recommended that you go in the company of a Puerto Rican, who can possibly explain to you the intricacies of the betting, which is its vital concomitant. Some travel agents offer escorted tours; the fights usually take place on Saturdays and Sundays, from early morning to nightfall.

Waterfowl shooting, fishing contests, regattas, and tennis and golf tournaments are periodic attractions of specialized interest. Chapter 16 deals in more detail with some of these other attractions.

As explained in Chapter 1, the big hotels are an important source of after-dark entertainment. The Tapia Theatre, once almost exclusively given over to Spanish plays, now houses occasional English-language shows by the local Little Theatre.

The supper clubs of the grand hotels, although their shows are uneven, often present first-rate talent. The Condado Beach, Escambron, Caribe, La Concha, Americana Hotel, and El San Juan are all in competition.

So many additional night spots have opened recently, mainly in the old town, that it is difficult to give a complete list. Ocho Puertas, so named because of its eight doors, is an elegant club with Victorian décor, located in a restored Spanish colonial building. It's open from 5:00 P.M. till dawn, and features a guitarist, singer, or piano entertainment. Across the street, La Danza is open late for supper and piano entertainment. La Botella, on San Jose Plaza, has the informality of Greenwich Village in New York. Add to these The Owl, Al's Little Club, and La Carreta. A steel band night club—El Calypso, across from the Swiss Chalet (the latter has conventional dance music)—has made its successful entry in the field. Several

El Commandante Race Track.

restaurants, such as La Mallorquina, have added a combo and special act to their menus. In fact, there is a wide choice of music and entertainment in both old and new San Juan.

San Juan is a cosmopolitan city with a long list of restaurants and an infinite variety of cuisines. The Swiss Chalet serves fine European food in an attractive setting. The Rotisserie Castillo in the Caribe Hilton specializes in roast beef and shashlik on flaming spits. There are Le Rendezvous at La Rada, the Centauro, Eric's, Mario's in Isla Verde featuring seafood, and the Cotillon Room, across from the entrance to the Caribe, noted for its steaks. All of these are expensive restaurants. La Zaragozana, in a lovely restored Spanish colonial building in Old San Juan, serves traditional Spanish dishes.

Less expensive is the La Ronde restaurant in Santurce on Ponce de León, which specializes in seafood. If Mexican food appeals to you, Mexico in Puerto Rico not only is good and reasonable, but has an informal string orchestra whose programs often end in jam sessions. Under the Trees aptly describes that delightful informal restaurant in the Condado section. El Castillo Real, opposite the park on Ponce de León, has the uninspired look of an ice cream parlor, but its dishes are good and quite inexpensive.

It is impossible to discuss and catalogue all the restaurants, most of which are listed in *Que Pasa* and the daily paper anyway, but I would like to say a few words about Puerto Rican food. You will not taste it in the hotels, for here, as elsewhere, they cater to the common denominator. Very rarely does a Puerto Rican dish appear on their menus, and when one does, it is almost certain to be only a modified version of the real thing.

Two excellent restaurants in old San Juan—La Mallorquina and El Mediterraneo—are, as their names imply, in reality Spanish restaurants. (In one sense La Mallorquina is Puerto Rican, for it dates from colonial days.) Both of them advertise "typical Puerto Rican and Spanish dishes." This is not so far-fetched a claim as that made by places advertising "American and Puerto Rican food," because the Puerto Rican cuisine evolved from the Spanish.

Out on the Boca de Cangrejos road, just beyond the El

San Juan, there was a restaurant called Cecilia's, which was definitely and exclusively Puerto Rican, and extremely good. Unfortunately, Cecilia's burned down in 1962, and although there are no definite plans for rebuilding at the present time, this was such a popular spot that it is almost sure to be rebuilt sometime.

It is always helpful to have some idea what to expect in a place of this kind. Certain ingredients and, therefore, certain dishes constantly reappear on menus. Oddly, the staple is rice, although it has to be imported—mainly from California now, but Louisiana used to be its source. The popularity of rice undoubtedly dates back to the early colonial era, and since neither potatoes, wheat, nor to any great degree corn, thrive in Puerto Rican soil, it continues to be the poor man's fare. Various species of beans, on the other hand, do grow in Puerto Rico, and rice and beans are the mainstays of the peasant diet.

It is a generally accepted fact that sauces were invented by the poor to counteract their monotonous diet. In Puerto Rico, sofrito, a sort of basic sauce, is made up in quantity in advance, other flavors being added for various purposes. Its standard ingredients are salt pork, pork fat, green and red peppers, onions, garlic, and fresh local herbs, the most obvious one being a close relative of saffron, although not quite so pungent. To these are added tomatoes, olives, capers, lime juice, or whatever the chef fancies, and so considerable variety is possible. The sauce can be very good and delicate in taste. It can also, in inexpert hands, be greasy and over-spiced.

The most commonplace dish is asopao (pronounced a-so-pow'-o), which sounds like what it is—like soup. Here the rice, with chicken, shrimp, beans, or pork, is swimming in a diluted sauce which provides a mush that makes a meal. When, instead, the menu reads "Arroz con—" it should be rice only slightly moistened, which I find awfully good. Arroz con pollo, a chicken and rice casserole dish to which peas are usually added, is delicious. For an accompaniment to a broil or roast, arroz con gandules is highly recommended, even if the combination does sound strange. Gandules are a cross between beans and peas which everyone in San Juan glibly translates as "pigeon peas." This puzzled me, as I had never heard of them, and even the dictionary was of no help. Finally I was enlightened by a continental who had lived many years in Puerto Rico. *Gandules* are a native species, really untranslatable. They look like a bean but do have more of the soft consistency of a pea.

Chicken and pork are the two most plentiful meats, and it is these you will most often encounter on the bill of fare. Another meat, not so often found but distinctly regional, is kid. Sometimes it is roasted, sometimes made into a stew. It tastes somewhat like a very flavorsome lamb. Seafoods offer a huge choice—from small whitefish to snapper, pompano, and even dolphin. Turtle steak is considered a great delicacy. I ordered it and found to my amazement it *was* steak, of the same consistency and approximately the same taste as beef. Shrimp and lobster (rather, *langosta*, not the large claw type) are positively commonplace, as is crab, but crabs in Puerto Rico are exclusively land crabs, less fleshy than the sea variety. Ordinarily they are served in flakes mixed with rice and sauce. As the spawning season is not confined to the months without R's, shellfish appear at any season; whenever they are on the menu, you can rest assured they are safe to eat.

In case you are beginning to think that everything comes with a sauce, let me quickly reassure you. Broils and roasts are very much a part of the daily fare, and barbecued pork is one of the outstanding dishes. *Lechoneras*, which serve only pork, are a national institution. Have no hesitancy about ordering pork, even though you are in the tropics; it is immediately refrigerated, rapidly and hygienically handled, and at all times thoroughly cooked. Moreover, as Puerto Ricans will tell you with pride, there is no disease like *trichinosis* here.

For a very inexpensive but marvelous meal, drive out on the Bayamon Road (Highway 2). On the right, just before reaching the town proper, is Juan Roman's, also known as La Verdadera Lechonera. Their *lechon asado* is a work of art, full of subtle flavor and crunchy crackling. As an appetizer I suggest a plateful of blood sausage, cut up in tiny pieces, crisp and spicy, to nibble with a drink. The *lechonera* also sells roast pork to take home, and if you have housekeeping facilities, you can buy a pound already sliced that simply needs warming up.

Rice is no more inevitable with a meal than sauces. You will early run into plantains—which resemble and are blood brothers to green bananas—in one form or another, if simply as a replacement to potato chips in the hotel bar. Many people like these small-scale cold *tostones*. I like them better when they are mixed with herbs and used to make a dough or paste for *empanadas*, a sort of patty or fritter. The taste varies according to whether they are cooked ripe or green.

I prefer *sorullos*, a corn-meal dough rolled into small pieces the size of French fried potatoes and dipped in deep fat. (I have heard *sorullos* described as a kind of hush puppy, but I am not sure whether this is correct.) Puerto Ricans use a lot of garlic, much of the time subtly, but their garlic bread makes ours insipid, and garlic potatoes, French fried, have a marvelous tang.

In the final analysis food is a matter of individual taste, and the tourist can discover his preferences only by trying out various unfamiliar dishes. Many of the fruits and vegetables served here do not exist outside the Caribbean area and are impossible to describe properly. There is *chayote*, for example, with a white pulp which is mixed with milk and a little sugar and broiled on the half-shell. It also makes a delicious conserve. There is breadfruit, which is fried or boiled, and tastes remarkably like chestnuts. And, of course, there are also tomatoes, eggplants, green beans, and other vegetables with which we are more familiar.

Desserts on the whole are very sweet concoctions, but they are eaten in small quantities. For instance, sweet potato cake with white icing is like candy; however, it is cut the size of a double bonbon. Much fruit is used, such as fresh pineapple over grated coconut. The most common termination of a meal is *queso del pais*, a native cream cheese pressed so hard that it can be sliced. With it are served a jelly such as guava or mango and—if you are lucky—a piece of sweet potato cake.

Puerto Rican coffee is good, but strong. If you prefer yours black, you must be sure to say so, for Puerto Rican coffee is normally served mixed with hot milk, even at the end of the meal. In San Juan you are nearly always asked whether you prefer it or American coffee.

The beer is very good, the two outstanding brands being India and Corona. Each has its advocates, but neither one of them should disappoint you.

62

I have mentioned only Cecilia's and the *lechonera* in Bayamón as having exclusively Puerto Rican menus. Many other restaurants feature Puerto Rican dishes and are patronized by Puerto Ricans themselves. Some are quite good, but where there are rival cuisines within the same kitchen the choice may be limited. Look for something different in the next place you try.

The shops of San Juan are a trifle disappointing. There are a few very excellent shops and quite a number which are tawdry. Much that is offered is overpriced, and all too often the labels are marked "Japan," "Mexico," or "Haiti." Most visitors are interested in finding souvenirs and gifts that are typical of the country, and Puerto Rico does have some specialties. Unless San Juan is the only port of call, it is more sensible to confine yourself to these.

For instance, there are mahogany bowls and platters which are advertised as "Made in Puerto Rico," but this is an equivocal statement as mahogany is not a Puerto Rican wood. The mahogany comes from Haiti, frequently in a rough-hewn state. It is simply finished here. The Puerto Rican once did some delightful wood-carving, but there is very little to be had today. You may find a tray of native wood or run across some appealing figurines, most likely of a saint or the Three Kings, but the craft is nearly moribund.

Somewhat similar to wood products are the inexpensive bowls, goblets, and amusing children's banks of coconut shell. The dried, hardened shell is hand-burnished to a beautiful finish, its dark gloss reminiscent of mahogany or walnut. The shell is very tough, and impervious to liquids, hot or cold. You can find such items as these in the souvenir stores, but if you are going to Loíza Aldea (see next chapter), wait and make your purchases there, for these are their specialty.

Among the very best buys are articles of tortoise shell, which is both plentiful and quite reasonable. Timi's seems to be the chief concern specializing in tortoise. At least they have the most varied display of articles, ranging from attractive jewelry and compacts to chess pieces, boxes, fans, and lorgnettes. Timi's has three stores, one in the arcade of La Concha, one in the old city, and another at the airport.

Some of the embroidery is lovely, and the blouses and summer dresses are excellent values. Articles of straw and palm leaf are also typically Puerto Rican: handbags, baskets, table mats, and the glorified *jíbaro* hat which makes such an attractive wall decoration in an informal room or closed porch. (It is wise to shop around, for I have found the latter priced at $3.00 in one of the better-known stores and a mere $1.00 in an unpretentious little shop on the Plaza Colón). At Calle Cristo #257, easily identified next door to the Casa del Libro, is Dolphin's Court, specializing in woven straws (you can watch the hand-looming on the premises), with a diversified assortment of fiber articles at moderate prices.

Puerto Rican pottery is especially interesting, as it is a modern adaptation of ancient Indian designs in colors not usually found in clay products, such as turquoise and black. Go to the workshop itself, called the Puerto Rican Pottery, at 42 Paseo Covadonga on the edge of old San Juan, where there is not only a larger selection but you can see the whole process.

By no means to be overlooked is Puerto Rico's biggest product—rum. However, it is subject to federal excise tax of $2.16 a fifth, so that the standard bottle costs about $3.00. Many stores sell packaged bottles, the excise tax included. Otherwise you pay the difference at the airport—or dock—upon leaving.

Shops are open six days a week, but a number of them are shut from twelve to two and the normal closing hour is six, so plan your buying spree accordingly.

Cigarettes are so expensive in Puerto Rico that it is wise to bring all you can in your luggage. Non-filters cost thirty cents and filtered cigarettes thirty-five cents a pack, with an additional charge in the hotel shops.

In the Virgin Islands, on the contrary, they are an incredible $1.25 and $1.50 per carton, respectively. If you are going there you will find it a shopper's paradise. Both St. Thomas and St. Croix have free-port status, so if you are tempted to buy any items *that are not local products*, remember that they will be less expensive in the Virgin Islands.

CHAPTER 7

Two Short Trips in the Environs of San Juan

(Cataño, Isla de Cabras, a Seventeenth Century Chapel, and
Caparra Ruins—Loíza Aldea, Its History and Fiesta)

AT the marina, the wharf just below the main post office, there is a ferry which crosses at frequent intervals to Cataño, a slum and industrial sector recently incorporated into greater San Juan. The industry is new; the slum is old, and will doubtless need years to improve its aspect.

There are two valid reasons for taking this ferry trip. If you have no car, it is a means of treating yourself to the splendid sight of the commercial harbor and a perspective view of the old city. And, even if you do have a car, at the time of the *fiesta patronal*, the Cataño landing will give you a better vantage point for watching the regatta.

In the middle of July is celebrated the Fiesta of the Virgen del Carmen, the Virgin of the Carmelites, patron saint of fishermen. A number of seacoast villages (for instance, a little hamlet by the lighthouse at Arecibo) honor her, but the two largest and best-known celebrations are at Ponce and Cataño. Like most holidays of this sort, the festivities last about ten days. The plazas are turned into small fairgrounds, with merry-gorounds, Ferris wheels, refreshment stands, games, and dancing. There are also fireworks, and a fiesta queen is chosen and crowned—in Cataño, she is always a small child. The climax comes fittingly on a Sunday, when decorated barges arrive from San Juan, and a religious procession makes its way through the streets of Cataño to the wharf, after which the barges go out to sea for the traditional blessing. This is a spectacle quite worth the trip. The Tourism Information Booth recommends that visitors telephone them at 791-1014 for the exact dates and hours.

If you have a car, which I hope you do, Cataño is simply the first pause on a short (less than two hours) trip outside San Juan which I would like to suggest. At one point, this will take you through some completely bucolic scenery that will make you think you are many miles from the metropolis. Take Highway 2 to the first main turning-off (Route 24), which will bring you to the shore and a view of the bay. Then turn back one or two streets in Cataño to reach Route 165, which also clings to the shore as it passes a modest real estate development. The destination at this phase is the Isla de Cabras, and the first right-hand turn leads over the causeway to it. By the way, you pass the Carioca and one of the Bacardi distilleries en route, both of which welcome visitors.

A *polverin*, or old powder house, guards the entrance to the Isla de Cabras, today a pleasant picnic park with thatch-roofed summerhouses. Here you can look directly at the waterside of La Fortaleza and get a superb view of the old island settlement. On Isla de Cabras also are the semi-ruins of El Cañuelo (the Channel Fort), the one the Dutch captured back in 1625. It has since suffered further deterioration from abandonment. Enough remains, however, to be impressive, and although you cannot go close to it because it is situated on the Commonwealth Police preserves, you can see it adequately from the park itself.

Return to the highway and continue on it to the next road, Route 866; then turn sharp left. Drive very slowly. Quite near the corner is a farmhouse with outbuildings used as cowsheds. Wedged in the far corner, you will see the surprising sight of a black mortar cupola with a small squared-off stone wall beneath it. This is an early private chapel (1628 is the exact date), built by the Indians for one of the Spanish colonists. It is one of the oldest colonial buildings still extant.

Nothing remains of the settler's home but this tiny chapel, its roof extending outward from the sidewalls over the cattle stalls. Despite its use as a cowshed, it is in surprisingly good condition. The crumbling brick walls of the nave and the cupola, viewed from the interior, provide a magnificent example of brick masonry. The tiny transept probably once housed confessionals. The government is well aware of the chapel's existence and is discussing buying the property to preserve it as a national monument, but up to now few outside official circles have ever heard of it.

The remainder of this road, lined with flamboyant trees and hedges of tall bamboo and hibiscus, is simply lush countryside. For most of the summer, starting in late June, the flamboyants are in blossom, and the long rows of scarlet are overwhelming. The dirt side roads are also roofed over by a mass of red blossoms. Even when not in bloom, the flamboyant is a beautiful feathery-leafed tree, and the hibiscus is always in flower.

The road joins with Route 872, which leads back to the highway, and is equally ablaze with flamboyants and hibiscus. On the return to town, about three-quarters of a mile along the main highway on the left-hand side, in the midst of a modern suburb, are the ruins of Ponce de León's Caparra home. Strangely, they are all that remain of the original Spanish settlement—the bare foundations of what once must have been a luxurious home. A public monument, these remains offer little beyond an approximation of the number and size of the rooms.

Ponce loved Caparra, and neither wanted nor intended to move permanently to San Juan. He openly opposed the change of settlement, refusing to recognize the strategic importance of the island in the harbor. He believed that the fertile land around Caparra was a place where the colonists could better sustain themselves, for he felt there was little to fear from outside attack. The real enemy was the native Taino. Ponce's personal relations with the Indians had been excellent—he was an upright and honorable man—but upon the death of the chieftain who had befriended him and led him to San Juan harbor, a general deterioration in confidence had set in, fomented chiefly by the ruthlessness of the majority of Spaniards. After the Indians had tested the invincibility of the colonist and found it wanting (see Chapter 3), a general uprising ensued and Ponce spent from 1515 to 1521 subduing the rebellious Tainos.

This came after his first exploratory trip to Florida. When there was little more to be feared from the native Indians, he again set sail for Florida, never to return alive. That was the same year that the settlement was transplanted from Caparra to San Juan.

Have you noticed the Seal of State of Puerto Rico—a lamb recumbent on a book with the letters F and I overhead on either side? The letters stand for Ferdinand and Isabella; the lamb bears "a flag with a cross and banner as in the device of St. John," according to the words of the decree. (The entire island was called San Juan at this period.) The coat-of-arms was given to Caparra by royal grant in 1511, while Ponce de León was governor.

I felt, looking at modern Caparra, that one would have no suspicion of its historical significance if he did not already know its story. In fact, it seemed to me little short of miraculous that among the markets and suburban homes even these few stones mark the residence of the first governor. The ruins did not impress me nearly so much as the little chapel in the country, incongruously transformed into a cowshed. Abandoned and misused, it is still a recognizable entity. But of course it is over a hundred years younger than the stone foundations at Caparra.

About ten miles east of San Juan is the most unique and one of the oldest towns in Puerto Rico, with the melodious name of Loíza Aldea (Low-ee'-za Al-day'-a). It is unique in that it is the only completely Negro or, to be more accurate, Colored village on the island. The inhabitants are sometimes described as a semi-Indian race, and this is equally correct, for the great majority of them are a mixture of Indian and Negro. In fact, the earliest evidences of Indian life in Puerto Rico were found in a cave here—they date back at least 2,500 years—and if this is taken into account, Loíza Aldea can claim to be *the* oldest town in Puerto Rico.

A more advanced tribe of Indians was living on the banks of the Loíza River at the time of the settlement of Caparra, and with the almost immediate discovery of gold in that river, they were used as forced labor by the conquistadors. At the end of the century this Indian population was terribly depleted, but by that time there was a flourishing market in Negro slaves, who were bought as replacements. However, as the gold grew scarcer, the conquistadors turned to the planting of sugar cane. The slaves were concentrated in quarters on the nearby

St. Patrick's Church at Loíza Aldea, during Fiesta of Santiago. Costumed participants represent benevolent ones (Christian Spaniards) and devils (infidel Moors).

haciendas, but in the village were a few free mulattoes and Negroes, along with minor Spanish officials and a garrison of soldiers. Among the officials was a man named Mejías, himself a mulatto (his father was Spanish), who married the Indian chieftess Loaiza (another spelling of Luisa) for whom the new settlement was named. "Aldea" simply means hamlet. With the abolition of slavery in 1873, newly freed slaves joined this group. As the town was isolated, and even today is a good three or four miles from the main thoroughfare, the population has remained stable (around 8,000 inhabitants if one includes the neighboring *barrios*) and ethnologically unchanged.

Loíza Aldea is a poor town and, except as a curiosity, would be of no interest if it were not for the sixteenth-century Iglesia de San Patricio and for the annual Fiesta de Santiago, which is a fascinating, bizarre spectacle.

First, though, I should tell you how to reach Loíza Aldea. In this case I have to assume you have a car, which I hope is a small one. There is no difficulty with any car on the fast, direct route of the big highway, turning left at the modern town of Loíza (not Aldea) and following Route 185 to the shore. But if you have any spirit of adventure and take any pleasure in bypassing the beaten track, take the shore road one way. Not a good road, I admit. I hesitate to recommend it for large cars, but in a small one it is a slow, delightful drive. Start out on the road through Isla Verde to Boca de Cangrejos, and simply keep going. After Boca de Cangrejos it becomes a dirt road, but it goes through lovely forests of pines and palm. You will probably have it all to yourself, which is enjoyable, passing only an occasional *jíbaro* trudging along to collect coconuts. It ends in a clearing by the mouth of the Loíza River, with the town on the opposite shore. A flat barge will quickly put in an appearance and pole you, car and all, across. The ordinary fare is two cents a person; a car costs a dollar—but there is no charge for passengers!

To the left of the landing is a tiny restaurant and crab market, but better known is Richard's place, which can be found by circling the shore road. There are two exits from the town and he is on the farther one. If you feel lost, ask for directions at the gas station. Richard's is a simple restaurant, with picnic tables out under the trees. His menu is limited, but good enough to attract Puerto Ricans from San Juan. The most popular dish is *arroz con cangrejos*, a crab-meat pilaf.

Crabs, even if called land crabs, are found only by the shore, but they seem to be particularly abundant in Loíza Aldea. Richard's has a long shed housing them for take-home sale. Here you will see the crabs separated into a half-dozen cages as part of the long process of preparing them for eating. First they are starved, to rid them of all poisons; then they are fed cracked corn, both to fatten them and give them, presumably, their delicate taste.

Just back from the beach the hard sand is honeycombed with holes. Catching crabs is chiefly a matter of agility, as they cease-lessly scurry about. If none is in sight, a flashlight thrust down one of the holes will flush them to the surface via the back door. Light seems to daze them too, and the hunt resembles the catching of frogs. The truly professional method, however, is to set fire to the holes and make a big haul.

Before going to Richard's—if you do decide to eat there—you will have noticed the church, prominent on the square a few yards from the barge landing. A buttressed basilica with nail-studded heavy wooden doors and a sparcity of windows, from the exterior it gives less the appearance of a church than a fortress, for which purpose it was certainly used. Loíza Aldea is one of the few towns which was not only built on the coast but remained there; it was constantly under attack by either Caribs or pirates. Loaiza, the last known chieftess, and her husband, Mejías, were both killed by an invasion from Vieques. Loíza Aldea had been an Indian village long before the Caribs tried to invade the island. When the Spaniards moved in, they immediately established a small garrison and started the building of the church. Here the townspeople fled for security with each recurring attack.

Unfortunately the church underwent local ministrations prior to the establishment of the Institute of Culture, and its exterior is covered by an obviously recent coat of stucco. But the interior is in no sense spoiled. The original altar from San José, which was transferred here, is fitting in the sense of belonging to the era. Examine it, because it is a lovely panel of carved native hardwood. Among the saints on pedestals around the walls of the basilica is one black saint with a small black boy looking up at him, and a deer by his side. I wondered, but did not learn, who he was.

That the church is called St. Patrick's is one of many incongruities about Loíza Aldea. So much is steeped in folklore. For instance, the explanation given for the name St. Patrick (the tale is implicitly believed by the townspeople) is that once when a plague of insects descended upon them, it was decided to put all saints names in a hat and draw to see which saint to pray to. The first name drawn was St. Patrick, but there was a great murmuring, for he certainly was not Spanish and was therefore unknown to them. The name was put back, but was drawn again on the second try. Three times this happened (have you ever noticed that in folklore and legend, everything is repeated three times?), so they prayed to him, and when the epidemic abated, they recognized that he had been their protector.

The story does not say when this happened. Surely it was not during the Spanish occupation of the town, and certainly the church bore another name in the sixteenth century when it was built. It is not an unreasonable assumption that it was the Church of Santiago. St. James the Apostle had been the

Spanish patron saint during the wars against the Moors. "Santiago!" had been their battle-cry, and so it remained in their fight against the Indians, for the Indians too were not only enemies but infidels, whom they found nearly impossible to convert.

The Negro slaves, on the other hand, accepted Christianity readily, unconsciously interweaving it with their own African cults. Out of this fusion has grown the amazing and peculiar present-day Fiesta of Santiago, always beginning on July 25. There are several ceremonies of note during the traditional ten-day celebration. Even with the assistance of the Tourist Information Bureau it is difficult to ascertain the exact hour when these take place, for the religious aspect is so intertwined with the carnival that the celebration is a thoroughly undisciplined affair. In recent years it has become a tourist attraction, and on the biggest day both the plaza and the roads leading from it are jammed with cars and pedestrians. To my mind, it is not essential to be present for the climactic functions. Besides, many of the rituals take place early in the morning, with only the townspeople present. Go there any day, any time, during the celebration and you will find plenty of color and excitement.

For a large proportion of the males, both men and young boys, the fiesta is a ten-day masquerade party. There are two factions and two types of costume, the benevolent ones and the devils—the former representing the Christian Spaniards and the latter the infidel Moors! The benevolents dress as Spanish caballeros of approximately the eighteenth century, wearing tricorne hats and capes. The hats usually dangle ribbons of red and yellow, the colors of Santiago's pennant. Many have tiny mirrors sewed around the upturned brims, a jewel-like indication of affluence. The capes are made of any bright-colored material; several I saw appeared to be cut from plastic shower curtains. This group wears cheesecloth masks of the kind we are accustomed to on Hallowe'en, supposedly representative of kindly faces.

In contrast to those of the Moors, they certainly are benevolent-looking. The coconut-shell masks of the Moors are fearsome enough without the two, sometimes three, horns protruding from their brows. They have horrible mouths, eyes outlined in white, cheeks streaked with paint. Although each mask is somewhat individual, they all instantly remind you of Indian—or African—warpaint. To complete their terrifying appearance these satanic spirits wear a loose costume of gaudy fabric fastened at the wrists and ankles; when the arms are outstretched, the figures strongly resemble the outlines of a bat.

A number of these masqueraders are constantly milling about the plaza, particularly around the church, during the entire fiesta. They are not, however, permitted to enter the church in costume.

Inside St. Patrick's, in front of the altar, is the hallowed image of one or another of the Santiagos—compounding the

Spanish "caballero" wearing coconut mask during Fiesta of Santiago.

Evil spirits parading in street of Loíza Aldea during Fiesta of Santiago.

complexity of this fiesta, Santiago appears in three forms: the Santiago of the Men, the Santiago of the Women, and the Santiago of the Children. Only one of the small statues appears at a time in the church. The Santiago of the Men, about two feet high, wears a helmet and coat of mail and rides a white charger over the heads of fallen Moors. The Santiago of the Women is very similar, but that of the Children has a young, beardless face, and the forefeet of his horse are descending on only one Moorish head. By comparison, he does not look formidable at all. He is referred to as "Santiagito." Around the base of each of the images tiny charms are strung. These are given in thanks for miraculous cures, for despite the name of the church, Santiago is today the patron saint of Loíza Aldea.

Three different families, or rather the women of three different households, through inheritance, are entrusted with the housing and care of the images throughout the year. These women are known as *mantenedoras*. During the fiesta their homes, open to the public, are easily discernible, as streamers are stretched across the road in front of each one.

Each image of Santiago receives its separate devotional period, with a mass celebrated in its honor. The images are also placed on litters and carried through the town in a grand procession, with bells pealing and rockets being fired. At length all three images, with their followers, go to a spot near the seashore on the edge of town where, in the huge trunk of an old ceiba tree, according to legend the original image of Santiago was found. Then comes the traditional ceremony of racing with the pennants of the saint. "Caballeros" on horseback request from the *mantenedora* the privilege of carrying the banner of their favorite Santiago. At the end of the 800-meter course, they return and restore the pennants to the *mantenedoras*. The original procession re-forms for the return to town, with this time a different Santiago being taken to the church. So it goes. In the meantime there are dances in the plaza, the refreshment stands forming a wall about the dancers. This is a momentous season for the young people, who are allowed to intermingle regardless of sex, under the watchful eyes of their parents. Although the citizens of Loíza Aldea have retained many African customs, they are devoutly Catholic and most of their conventions are Spanish. One is the conserva-

Closeup of coconut-shell mask being carved for Fiesta of Santiago.

tive belief that a young unmarried girl should always be chaperoned.

On your visit to Loíza Aldea, be sure to stop at Ayala's Souvenir Shop. It is a small place, the only shop of its kind. In it is every conceivable thing which can be made of coconut shell, not the least being a selection of devils' or Moors' masks. Ayala has a primitive workshop nearby where he and two or three helpers make the masks and other articles. All are made by hand, and he insists the work cannot be done otherwise. This is a restricted field, his alone, for he supplies the occasional pieces to be found in San Juan. Here are salad bowls, trays, goblets, and coffee bowls. These are inexpensive but unusual souvenirs. I purchased some coffee cups—or bowls, if you wish, for they look like short-stemmed flower holders—with little pedestals instead of a saucer, the two pieces smoothly polished and gleaming like dark wood. I actually use them for flowers, but several friends have told me they make excellent receptacles for hot liquids, the use for which they were planned.

Return to San Juan by the main highway, which links up with Avenida Ponce de León in Rio Piedras. Shortly afterward you will pass the University of Puerto Rico, one of the loveliest campuses to be found anywhere. The central building, constructed around 1920, soft burnt-yellow inlaid with lovely ceramics, is one of the most felicitous examples of modern Spanish design. In the small University Museum there is a fascinating display of Indian artifacts from all over the island. It includes some very early Indian bones and skulls, as well as crude utensils of shell and rock which were taken from the cave in Loíza Aldea.

Nothing remains in the cave today; it is just another of the limestone grottos with which Puerto Rico abounds. Those early, primitive Indians were not like the later Tainos, who made fine utensils, nor even like their immediate predecessors, who cut designs in rocks and painted their pottery. But the artifacts collected by the university bear witness that Loíza Aldea can claim the earliest recorded history of the island, approximately 600 B.C.

*Campus of University
of Puerto Rico.*

CHAPTER 8

The Road to Arecibo

(Roadside Stands, Sugar-Cane and Pineapple Fields—Indian Caves—Arecibo—Sights to See on the Trip Back)

THE road to Arecibo is straight and wide. Its purpose is strictly functional, for it is part of the main highway which circles the island and links up the coastal towns. Therefore the accent is on efficiency rather than scenery. Yet to me it is a fascinating road, rich with the varied aspects of Puerto Rican life.

There are roadside stands, sugar cane fields, and pineapple plantations. There are also industrial plants, for *centrals*—sugar mills, rum distilleries, and packing plants—are located close to the fields. There is even a cockpit on this road.

Just off the highway are several lovely beaches. The new road, like the old, is built back from the sea, but a turnoff of a couple of miles takes you to either Cerro Gordo or Vega Baja, and an equal drive brings you to beautiful Dorado Beach, Laurance Rockefeller's superb development, which includes a vast park and golf course as well as the hotel and two miles of sandy shore. However, the main reason for driving to Arecibo is to see the nearby ancient Indian caves, with their pre-Columbian carvings in the coral rock. Arecibo itself has its own attraction in an old Spanish lighthouse, as well as a famous seafood restaurant for lunch.

From San Juan to Arecibo is fifty miles, and the sensible plan is to make an easy day of it, covering both the highway and the secondary but decent coastal roads. Often you will have to return to the highway and then come back to the coast again, as these are country roads and not a shoreline drive.

Study your map and decide how *you'd* like to do the trip,

but now, for the purpose of clarity, pretend that you are taking Highway 2 with me to just beyond Manatí. I have traveled this road many times and on each occasion I have made new discoveries. I implore you, don't drive too fast or you may miss something.

On the main street of Bayamon, for instance—a fair-sized city incorporated in greater San Juan—you may notice cars parked and people gathered about some glass-covered sidewalk stands. They are selling *chicharron*, or pork crackling, a specialty of Bayamon that, it is generally agreed, is unparalleled elsewhere. If you like the skin of roast chicken or goose, then this is your gourmet dish. One piece, incidentally, should do for the family, for it is sold in huge strips.

Pork is, after chicken, the staple meat of Puerto Rico. I must risk being repetitious and emphasize again that despite the warm climate it is completely safe to eat. In Chapter 5 I mentioned the famous *lechonera* at Bayamon. In driving about the island you will pass many others. Don't hesitate to go into any of them, unless you dislike pork. With the traditional touch of garlic and herbs, roast pork here is a superb dish.

Puerto Rican beef is almost entirely imported; the cattle one sees are mainly dairy cows. As the road pushes farther into the country and passes some pastureland, you will note something curious. Standing sentinel beside the cows are foot-high white birds, usually one bird to one cow, like good companions. These are cattle egrets, or aigrettes, first cousins of those birds whose plumage used to adorn grandmother's hat. They are known as "the cow's best friend" because they remove ticks and debilitating insects from the cow's hide. Unknown in the Western Hemisphere until a decade or so ago, they mysteriously flew over from Africa about the time Operation Bootstrap started, doing their bit for the health of Puerto Rico.

As the road moves closer to the shore, you may see men or boys standing by the roadside holding up strings of raw shrimp, still alive but strung together like a necklace. Or they may have land crabs, knotted and tied until they look as if they were in a net. There are also countless roadside vegetable and fruit stands, and the owners will smilingly welcome your interest, even if you don't intend to buy anything. Once, puzzling over the difference between plantains, which look like

Crab vendor. You may also pass shrimp vendors along the Arecibo road, and countless roadside vegetable and fruit stands.

green bananas but are actually another species, and the yellow ones we are accustomed to, I noted a third—a short stubby variety. The vendor plucked one off the stand and offered it to me. It was a *manzana*, or apple-banana, with a subtle after-flavor like apple juice. Another species is called piños, or pine-apple-banana. Delicious.

Noting my obvious pleasure, the owner motioned me to the back, where his house and small garden stood, and pointed out the different fruit trees. Naturally, he also had a coconut tree, and several coconuts lay on the ground ready to be opened. With a machete he slashed a huge nut open. A friend has told me, however, that I was treated deferentially as a tourist, since instead of handing me the nut with a straw through the opening, he poured the juice into a paper cup. I was aware, myself, of a grinning family circle of wife and children. As for the coconut juice (which is not the same as coconut milk), I found it somewhat insipid, warm. I have since learned that it is quite refreshing when chilled.

So many unfamiliar fruits and vegetables, with untranslatable names and flavors, are displayed that it comes almost as a shock to see an old stand-by like tomatoes. Actually, most of the fruits and vegetables we are accustomed to are in these stalls, but it was the exotic ones that usually caught my atten-

79

tion—the strange tubers, large and small, and fruit in shells rather than soft skins.

The display varies according to the season. Avocados come in August. It's an old wives' tale that if the crop is plentiful there will be no hurricane that year. Mangoes first appear in July, the pleasantly tart oranges in January, followed by grapefruit. Papayas are abundant the year around. So, too, are pineapples.

Farther along the road you will see these growing—a little beyond Manatí—neat rows and rows of them, some just sprouting and others holding the fruit aloft like strong-armed men. Good dirt roads crisscross the plantations, and it is permissible to drive through on your own inspection tour.

Before you reach the pineapples, however, you will have passed miles of ever-present cane fields. The lucky time to see them is during the Christmas season when they are in bloom, a beautiful white blanket of flowering tassels covering the landscape like the snows in the Christmas cards of the north. You may see some of them after the New Year, as the crops are slightly staggered. There is also a wild sugar cane that springs up in uncultivated corners and is likely to bloom at any time. I have seen it in midsummer, with tassels like swamp grass, the buds purplish and the open flowers a little off white.

Where there are cane fields there are sure to be rum dis-

Exterior of the famous Indian caves near Arecibo.

tilleries, and on the Arecibo road and its tributaries you will find a number of them. All have the welcome mat out for visitors and will show you the processing. Spring is the harvest season, but there is always some activity here. Personally, I can do without visiting the smelly molasses vats, but a cool bar awaits you at the end of the tour and you are offered your choice in rum drinks and usually given a small bottle of the product to take home.

The right-hand turn for the Indian Caves (Route 140) is less than a mile outside Manatí, which you simply skirt. They can also be reached by driving out from Arecibo, but it is more confusing coming from that direction, as there are no markings in town to indicate the way and the large sign at the entrance has its back turned toward the city. It may be that the turnoff comes before the pineapple fields, but no matter—you can see them on the return to San Juan.

Route 140, a secondary road of macadam, goes through pleasant countryside. When you reach a fork, take 681 to the left and keep on going until you see the large sign LAS CUEVAS INDIAS, a distance of about ten miles.

The rock carvings in these caves are remarkable evidence of a very early civilization. Archaeologists judge them to be close to 1,500 years old, which would date them as of the fifth century. Yet they are comparatively unknown. The caves are on private property, the owner of which seems to be something of an eccentric. He has built a park leading off the road with two large signs flanking the gate. These, translated, astonishingly read: "We do not admit young lovers unaccompanied," and "It is advisable that married couples bring their children." There was no one else about when I was there, and so I can't say how well his injunctions are obeyed.

A few feet inside, another sign advises: "After you buy the entrance ticket destroy it, but read it first." Just why you should destroy it is not explained, but the order to read it doubtless refers to the statement on the back that the proprietor is not responsible for accidents. This would seem to indicate some perilous sight-seeing, which is not the case. Of course you must wear low-heeled shoes, for the going is rough over the surface rocks leading to the caves, and you have to climb down a short,

81

but very sturdy, wooden ladder to reach them. They consist of two rooms; the first, which contains the carvings, is roofless, and so there is no danger of claustrophobia.

The ticket is bought at the refreshment counter for fifty cents a family. Then a small boy leads the way past some cages of assorted birds and three grotesque, fenced-in, dummy Indians, funnier than any wooden Indians of our continental past. They commemorate some obscure myth about a good Indian, a bad Indian, and the girl they both loved. The good Indian married the maiden, and they are supposed to have set up housekeeping in these caves, but the obvious fact is that the caves served as a temple to the gods.

You don't need to be an expert to be awed by these age-old intaglios. To refer to them simply as pre-Columbian is a gross understatement. Archaeologists estimate that the Tainos were on the island for close to a thousand years before Columbus made his landfall. They left ample evidence of far from primitive artistry. Their carvings were realistic, their animals accurate in design, their portraits—the stone-carved heads—showed such exactitude as to give a precise picture of tribal characteristics and their variations.

The Igneris, also Arawaks but precursors of the Tainos, on the contrary confined themselves to geometric patterns. Their utensils included rectangular hatchets and well-rounded cups. Their pottery, seemingly limited to bowls, bore simple designs of white on red. The coloring, by the way, has survived amazingly. The fragments in the University of Puerto Rico Museum are extraordinarily well preserved. Seeing these ranged beside the work of the Tainos, the layman is quite capable of grasping the differences between the two epochs. The caves outside Arecibo are unquestionably of the earlier era.

Erosion has undoubtedly wrought some changes, but the primitive outlines of the faces suggest children's drawings. Yet the fragments of geometric patterns similar to those on their pottery, resembling the classic Walls of Troy design, suggest the splendor of the temple before time took its toll.

It is regrettable that these caves are private property. At some future date they will surely come under the control of the Institute of Culture and be treated with the respect and care due such a rare monument.

Rock carving in the Arecibo Indian caves.

The farther cave, which is roofed over but not dark, is worth entering simply to see the blue sea framed in the natural window of the rock. Like the Igneris' designs, it is actually a rectangular window.

From here to Arecibo is a matter of minutes. The town, originally settled in 1566, suffered such destruction at the hands of pirates and Indians that nothing remains of the early days. Today it is simply an industrial center. Continue straight through to the beach. The square by the *playa* is dominated by a small replica of the Statue of Liberty beneath which is engraved: "Of the people, by the people and for the people," with no credit line to Lincoln. An esplanade, or tree-lined cement walk, leads to the sea. The area is called Victor Rojas Park, in honor of a citizen of the last century with phenomenal swimming endurance—he single-handedly rescued the entire crew of a foundering ship. Out on the point stands the old Spanish lighthouse, still doing duty after some hundred or more years. Such lighthouses are to be found in several parts of the island, extraordinary examples of solid construction. A U.S. Coast Guardsman who had been stationed in one of them told me that a few years ago our government decided to modernize it by replacing the incredibly thick, leaded panes with Miami windows. Along came a storm and the result was a

83

shambles, whereas the original heavy windows had withstood countless hurricanes.

Arecibo has an excellent seafood restaurant, the Aquarium. Ask anyone for directions, for it is well known. Scan the menu for the word *cetis*, although if it is the season for them they will no doubt be listed in large letters. *Cetis* are tiny, thumbnail-sized white fish of delicate flavor. In the mysterious manner of fishes, they visit a few choice harbors three or four times a year. Arecibo is one of their haunts, but their schedule is so unpredictable that when they appear, townspeople hurry through the streets calling, "The *cetis* have arrived!" They are caught by the simple expedient of lowering a large can into the water. Usually they are served in *empenadas*, the little fish being rolled into a soft paste of plantain and herbs, wrapped in plantain leaves, and baked. The other standard way of serving them is with a saffron sauce.

Take Highway 2 for the journey back to San Juan. If you have brought your bathing suit—and it is good sense always to carry one with you—a nice stop-off is the Playa de Vega Baja. For that matter, you can eat a light lunch there if you prefer. Road 686 leads to it from the industrial town of Vega Baja; immediately on the right when you reach the beach is a good, unpretentious luncheon place. The proprietor will set a table for you out on the sand in the shade of the palm trees and offer you fried fish, hamburgers, or hot dogs with beer. It is a lovely spot, one of my favorite beaches, with a coral cape jutting out protectively on the right and two islands of coral blocking the middle of the bay, assuring calm water and safe bathing. There are palm-thatched huts for dressing rooms, as this is a typically Puerto Rican beach.

Cerro Gordo, also a good sheltered beach, has modern facilities. If you prefer its conveniences, the road leading to it is the one after the road to Vega Baja.

You will pass Pennock Gardens and the Hydroponic Farms, located opposite the Vega Alta Corporation. Although situated next to each other, these two highly interesting projects are separate enterprises. The former is a commercial horticultural center with a fascinating collection of both known and little-known flowers and plants. The Hydroponic Farms are a government experiment station where vegetables are grown in concrete troughs filled with gravel and fed with chemical nutrients, producing something like twenty times the normal crop per acre.

Road 693 connects Cerro Gordo with Dorado Beach, without a return to the highroad. On the other hand, Laurance Rockefeller's beautiful development is worth a separate trip. With its own private air field, its own air service, and what is reputed to be one of the finest golf courses in the world, it represents the acme of luxury. It has a lovely wooded park through which one can stroll indefinitely without interfering with the golfers, as well as two miles of shore and an especially inviting swimming pool, and tennis courts, of course. Living costs average

The beach at Vega Baja, protected by a coral cape and islands.

The luxurious Dorado Beach Hotel has two miles of shore. Its golf course is reputed to be one of the world's finest.

$55.00 per person per day in season, and include breakfast and dinner. During the off-season, the rates are more than halved—as low as $15.00 or $20.00. There are accommodations in units separated from the main lodge, with the choice of either a beach porch or a balcony overlooking the sea.

Dorado Beach is an ideal place for lunch, or simply to stop off for a drink and a look at its magnificence. To stay there insures isolation for a rest cure with the distraction of a favorite sport. A new highway between San Juan and Dorado, Route 165, has shortened the trip to 30 minutes. The route skirts the Bay of San Juan and hugs the island's north coast, passing miles of still-undeveloped beaches and acres of sugar cane.

Should you travel to Dorado on a Saturday or Sunday and be curious about the national pastime of cockfighting, take Route 2 through Bayamón. You will find a pit situated on the highway not too far out of town. You will know it by the hubbub of noise and conglomeration of cars. Cockfighting is a peculiar sport not usually appreciated by us *norte americanos;* I am told that its main attraction is betting. This is so rapid and continuous during the fight that only an habitué can follow it.

I was curious to see the sport, but we arrived during the coffee break and, out of consideration for those of our party who stayed outside, could not wait for the show. Women can attend the fights, but preferably accompanied by male escorts. As my companion and I stood at one side looking at the crowd, a middle-aged man came up. With typical Puerto Rican courtesy, he offered his seat in the crowded bleachers so that *la señora* could better see what went on. He was somewhat hurt that we refused. I saw nothing but the animation of the crowd and heard nothing but the noisy birds in their cages somewhere in back. I did learn that often a cock lives to fight again; in fact the owner, conscious of his investment, prays that he will. There are frequent draws, as in boxing, and in many instances artificial spurs are barred. I saw proud owners returning homeward along the road, carrying their cherished champions upside down in cotton sacking.

There is another popular cockpit in San Juan itself, which has frequent fights during the season. Your hotel travel bureau will be able to give you exact information.

CHAPTER 9

East to Fajardo

(El Yunque and Luquillo Beach—Fajardo and Las Croabas)

To COME to San Juan and exclude El Yunque and Luquillo Beach is a bit like taking a first trip to Washington, D.C., and failing to visit Mount Vernon, or missing the redwoods on a visit to California. The half-day excursion is offered by the tour operators for $7.50. It is comfortably made in a Volkswagen station-wagon carrying a limit of eight passengers, and so the outing is more like a private party than an impersonal, conducted tour. In fact, there is no guide; an occasional comment is voluntarily supplied by the chauffeur. Few visitors fail to take this excursion or at least to visit these two nearby spots on their own initiative. Happily, the trip is as rewarding as it is advertised to be.

The road up the mountainside to El Yunque is full of sharp turns, so that many tourists take the reasonable, chauffeur-driven excursion rather than drive themselves. Of course, even the most attractive excursion does not leave you a free agent to browse around at will and dawdle where your fancy dictates. Some trips even skip Luquillo Beach.

The three major highways—south, west, and east—all commence in San Juan. The eastern one is Highway 3. It is a four-lane cement road as far as Carolina, and as dull scenically as most of this sort. It replaces a macadam road, which wavers about but can be seen parallel to Highway 3 from time to time. You might, if you are driving yourself, find it tempting to wander off on this road. Here you will see the old, almost untouched Puerto Rico that is behind the façade of modernity.

The small truck farmer, the poor, nameless hamlet, the roadside stand of the average Puerto Rican—not the display to catch the eye of the rich San Juan merchant—are to be found here. This old road is no longer marked on the map, but it is still used by local inhabitants. By either road, it is a trip of approximately twenty-five miles.

On the edge of Carolina, I believe it was, the friend who was with me spotted a snack bar. A woman was cooking *bacalao* (codfish) cakes in deep fat, a great favorite with the local population. She handed them out on paper napkins to be eaten with the fingers. If I recall correctly, one could also have *tostones*. A choice of coconut juice or coffee was available to drink. Farther along the route another stand had a selection of soft drinks, most of them entirely foreign to us continentals. I sipped something called *mabí*, made of the bark of a tree, and very pleasant it was, too. There is greater likelihood of finding these stands on a week end or holiday, as they cater primarily to the local inhabitant on his day off.

One comparatively pretentious establishment—that is, it is an entire building, not merely a stand—is a welcome stop, whether on the highway or the old road, for it dispenses thirst-quenching iced pineapple juice. This was situated on the right, not long before the turn-off for El Yunque—actually, on the old road, but a mere matter of feet separates the old and new at this juncture. The drivers of the excursion trips are familiar with this roadside stop; in fact, it was one of them who introduced me to it. The name of the place is Cardona's, and it is painted green.

On the old road you will find nothing of outstanding scenic merit, but it is more appealing than the main highway. The hamlets along it are shockingly poor, yet sometimes you will see, beside a shack, a newly finished, miniscule cement house. These do-it-yourself cement blocks are an integral part of the government's slum clearance program. In general, group enterprise is encouraged, but off the beaten track one often finds a single one of these houses standing in lone, or semi-alone, grandeur.

For as little as $400 the government supplies the necessary materials and the building instructions, giving a poor man the opportunity to erect what to him is a hitherto undreamed-of decent home. The difference between these cement-block houses and the flimsy huts is self-evident—especially during stormy weather—and each one built encourages a neighbor to do likewise.

Many of the new schools, even in remote regions, are fine new buildings, but the little frame schoolhouse continues to be the standard in the rural areas. Schools are in session the greater part of the year, as they open in mid-August and have but a brief Christmas vacation. You will doubtless notice the pristine white blouses and the red, blue, or green skirts or jumpers of the girls, as well as the uniformity of freshly laundered shirts and slacks of matching colors for boys. Uniforms are obligatory in some of the public schools (elsewhere the children themselves vote on the matter), a thoroughly sensible ruling which spares the pride of the youngster who would otherwise be in rags. They delight in conformity and are invariably spotlessly clean.

Parents are expected to supply the uniforms themselves but in cases of extreme hardship the government steps in. Today school attendance is close to 100 per cent, as against 67 per cent before the Commonwealth came into being, but facilities still fall far short of the need, and children attend only half-day sessions—which is why the holidays are so curtailed.

From the moment you leave San Juan, you can see El

New and old housing. The contrast is indicative of the progress throughout the island since Operation Bootstrap.

Coca Falls in the Rain Forest (El Yunque).

Yunque in the distance, rising abruptly from the valley like a pasteboard cutout superimposed on a backdrop. Clouds press down on this mountain range, obscuring the peaks. These ever-present clouds are why El Yunque is informally known as the Rain Forest.

The term is much more discouraging than the fact. I have heard tourists, primed for downpours, almost disappointedly inquire, "But where is the rain?" The showers here, though possibly heavier, are of short duration just as they are throughout Puerto Rico. There is an even chance you won't encounter one. Yet this National Park is exceptionally lovely for the very reason that it does have some rainfall every day. Take a sweater or light jacket with you, for the showers have a cooling effect and, besides, you will be climbing close to three thousand feet.

The beauty begins almost as soon as you turn off the highway. On the left is a stream which attracted prospectors as recently as twenty-five years ago; it is said that particles of gold can still be found there, but the mines which were its source were worn out by the Spaniards a very long time ago.

Shortly you enter the park itself, designated on the map as "The Experimental Forest of Luquillo." It is, in reality, a U.S. Federal Government Preserve, established as a National Forest

90

under President Theodore Roosevelt. Numerous types of tropical plants and trees are massed here with the lushness of a tropical jungle. The most outstanding is the fern tree, which frequently attains a height of thirty feet. A special species of orchid grows here also, but they are hard to find. They come in clusters of tiny yellow flowers resembling a swarm of butterflies, and hide beneath foliage or under the shelter of rocks. Their bloom is seasonal, so don't count on seeing them. Parakeets inhabit the forest, but they are even more elusive than the orchids. I did once spot the flowers, but I never saw one of the parakeets.

There are chameleons about, too, usually impossible to distinguish from the other little lizards which abound in this semitropical zone. Once, a bright green one crossed my path. Apparently as surprised to see me as I was to encounter him, he streaked part way up and around the nearest tree trunk. When I tried to find him, he was impossible to pick out, his quick-change coloring had blended so completely with the bark. I saw no snakes here, but in any case, the few which exist in Puerto Rico are non-poisonous. Their scarcity is sometimes attributed to the mongoose, which you will undoubtedly catch sight of on one of your excursions. This is quite possible, although the mongoose was imported to counteract a plague of rats, not reptiles. Success in that field is another influential factor in the present-day good health of Puerto Ricans. Now he, in turn, has become a minor scourge; with his diet of rats almost cut off, he has discovered that chickens will do as a substitute.

There are one or two strategically placed parking spots on the way up the mountain, permitting you to leave the car and wander on a nearby path for a closer inspection of the woods. The trip generally ends at the restaurant of El Yunque, but a little farther along the road on the right is the start of a trail to Mt. Britton. It takes about an hour to climb, but is not particularly enjoyable. Although the trail was partially cleared in the days of the CCC, a major section is still pretty rocky. Some visitors try it—there is even a sheltered bench on which to rest halfway up—but those I met were miserably demanding, "How much farther?"

To me, some of the short bypaths lower down are more

interesting. The goal of the climb is the watchtower on the summit of Mt. Britton, but the ascent can be made by car to within a couple of hundred yards. As the tower looms above most cloud banks, it does offer a bird's-eye view of the coastline and San Juan in the background, providing there is no haze. It also, naturally, overlooks the treetops, and I was enchanted by what at first glance resembled a giant dahlia tree. This proved to be a nest of air plants, distant relatives of the orchid family, which nestle mostly in treetops. These were huge, deep garnet flowers about the size of a Japanese chrysanthemum, with waxy petals. Although they cover some trees almost like a tent, they are not parasites, for they feed entirely on air. This is equally true, despite popular misconception, of other varieties of orchids.

The restaurant of El Yunque has the deceptive appearance of a northern hunting lodge, but its great stone fireplace is more decorative than practical. You climb down steps to reach its wide porch overlooking a portion of the forest, a very tranquil spot. Puerto Rican food is the specialty—to my mind just moderately good. As the proprietor used to live in the States—in fact, organized the waiters' union—you can, if you insist, procure a strictly continental lunch.

For those who drive to El Yunque in their own cars, there are several places with roofed-over picnic tables, in case of rain. However, if you like picnicking, Luquillo Beach seems to me to have stronger appeal. It is a very short distance away after the descent of El Yunque, and on weekdays the picnic grove is a heavenly, tranquil spot.

The fulsome description in *Que Pasa*—that Luquillo "has been ranked among the most beautiful beaches in the world"— is no exaggeration. To my mind it *is* the most beautiful—a huge crescent of fine white sand surrounded by a forest of palms. The tall coconut trees bring one question to mind: "Where are the monkeys?" According to the evidence in early Taino sculptures (some artifacts were discovered in Luquillo itself), there once were monkeys on this island.

The beach is huge, yet intimate, perhaps as a result of the protection of the palm grove. The water is blue, and the bay is so deeply indented that it is always calm. It is also so large that, were a hotel built, there would still be more than sufficient room for transient swimmers.

The most popular El Yunque-Luquillo Beach excursion does not allot time for a swim, but there is an all-day excursion which does. As the pride of Puerto Rico, Luquillo Beach is equipped with modern bath houses and showers. Parking is only twenty-five cents, lockers a mere ten. One word of warning: be sure to bring your own bath towel, as no amount of money will rent you one. Another reminder is not to visit the beach on a week end when it is jammed.

El Yunque and Luquillo Beach are on the road to Fajardo, which is only a few miles beyond Luquillo, but the Rain Forest-Beach excursion by itself offers a nice lazy outing. Fajardo represents an entirely different element, a completely different type of excursion.

If the idea of playing Robinson Crusoe for a day enchants

*"Huge, yet intimate"
Luquillo Beach, the
author's favorite.
El Yunque is in the
background.*

you, rent a sloop and go to one of the off-shore islands. The sloops are really procured in Las Croabas, three or four miles beyond the town of Fajardo, but for some unknown reason one generally says "Fajardo"; Las Croabas is not even marked on some maps.

This confused me so much that I insisted upon being driven to Fajardo Beach. My companion protested that it was a mercantile harbor, and as we approached it through a slum area, I began to realize it did not have the look of a pleasure resort. A Customs House loomed on the right of the *playa*; a strictly commercial bar and restaurant faced it. We would have turned around without delay, but for the unexpected sight of a steer in swimming with a number of men wading around him, shouting and gesticulating in a Chaplin-esque version of a bullfight.

It took some time, and several repetitions of this singular activity, before we comprehended what was happening. Anchored out in the bay was a sloop, and out of its hatch, one by one, steers were being drawn up by a pulley. The pulley carried them over the deck to the sea, during which operation the ropes with which they had been trussed were cut. We personally saw six steers taken from a small, certainly crowded, hold and deposited in the water, which was deep alongside the sloop. Great care was taken to keep the animal's head above water until, with the natural instinct of all beasts, he began to swim.

In a rowboat between the sloop and shore sat two or three men holding a rope attached to the steer's horns. Using this, they guided—sometimes tugged—him toward the beach. This same rope extended to the shore, where other men (those we had seen first) continued to pull the recalcitrant animal through shallow water to some hitching posts on the beach. It was at this point in the procedure that the outraged creature was likely to be balky.

We learned that the steers were from Vieques Island, destined for the slaughterhouse; they were eventually herded into a waiting truck. We were witnessing a commonplace means of transportation—rather primitive, crude, and a little cruel, but for all that, comic.

As it had become clear that the *playa* of Las Croabas and not

94

that of Fajardo was our destination, we moved on. The harbor at Fajardo was where United States troops made one of their major landings during the Spanish-American War, but unquestionably both the port and the town have changed a good deal since then.

Fajardo is neither somnolent nor dirty, but it is certainly not beautiful either. The inevitable little frame houses on stilts are in the majority, and only on the outskirts of town is there any suggestion of affluence. However, on the other hand, neither is there the air of extreme poverty still found in the remoter hamlets. Fajardo, in fact, is a thriving small city, with new industries starting up on its outskirts.

I read a memorandum written in 1765 and destined for the King of Spain, in which mention was made of the 474 inhabitants of the new community of "Faxardo." The Curate of Loíza, under whose jurisdiction the town was, had charitably but without careful consideration decided to apportion a miniscule area to each of the residents of this out-of-the-way community and "reduced conditions to those pertaining in the Danish Islands of St. Thomas and St. Croix," which were pretty bad at that period. The memorandum was written by Field Marshal Alexandro O'Reylly, who, despite the change of spelling, must have been a descendant of the original Don Alejandro, the Irish deserter from the British Navy who so successfully spurred on the defense against Sir Francis Drake in 1595.

The younger Don Alejandro—or Alexandro—was also remarkably outspoken, and his views must have sounded extraordinarily radical in that era. His economic theories were nevertheless both advanced and sound—a proper distribution of land sufficient to give a man sustenance, not an impractical small portion impossible to cultivate—in contrast to the established system which divided Puerto Rico among a few wealthy landowners with a mass of starving, dependent slaves and free men.

On the road to Las Croabas, a pretty one, you will see charming villas, but not homes of great wealth. You may, particularly on a Sunday, pass urchins selling baby egrets, or other live birds, along the road.

On the hilltop overlooking Las Croabas is the new eighty-room El Conquistador, a modern luxury hotel facing the sea and a series of small islands off the coast. The hotel has an Olympic-size swimming pool on the grounds, and also runs an aerial tramway, which carries guests to and from the lovely little beach at the foot of the hill. El Conquistador offers a complete range of water sports, including diving instructions, aqualung rental, water skiing, and sailing. Its American Plan rates average $22.00, single, and $36.00, double, per day.

A cabana-style fifty-eight-room hotel also has been built on nearby Lobos Island. A new marina on the *Isleta del Norte* off Fajardo caters to boating enthusiasts with modern pier, storage, and repair facilities. In fact, plans are being made toward developing the touristic potential of this whole eastern end of the island. This is a magnificent region for skin-diving and fishing. The Brown's Underwater Tours and the cruise from San Juan have recognized it as such for several years. (For more details on these sports, see Chapter 16.)

Sloops in Las Croabas harbor are working ships, built for commercial fishermen, but they can be rented at $25.00 a day for trips to the offshore islands. The number of passengers is limited by law to six per ship (children are winked at), so the cost amounts to only about $3.00 per adult. The harbor of Las Croabas attracts a certain number of yachters, but for less affluent visitors these local fishing sloops offer a delightful holiday. However, there are no appurtenances of any kind—you simply sit or lie on the deck. Lying down is a better position, since you must keep a sharp eye out for the boom when the sail is shifted, for the sailors do not warn you, flatteringly assuming you have sense enough to take care of yourself.

If you simply go out to Las Croabas in the morning there will always be a local fisherman on the beach who'll take you out. Or call 724-2604 or 722-7215 in San Juan for a reservation for a delightful day's excursion to offshore islands aboard a twenty-nine-foot sloop (see Chapter 13).

Several of the *cayos*, or keys, can be seen from the shore. The three largest—Icacos, Lobos, and Palominos—take about an hour to reach. Lobos and Palominos are private property, and although people do picnic on their shores, intruders are not welcomed.

I went for a day's picnic on Icacos with a group of fifteen spread out in three sloops. Some of the party slipped over the edge of the deck on arrival, but most of us rowed ashore with the provisions. The fishermen, having done their duty, went back to the sloops to wait patiently until we decided to return—around six-thirty at night. Several of the group had brought snorkels and other skin-diving equipment, and throughout the day conch shells, coral fans, and other sea treasures were accumulated. At one point a conch or two came to life and decided to crawl off. By then so many shells had been gathered that these were put back into the sea. We had an impromptu dish of small white fish cooked over charcoal, and examined with interest a weird, puffed-up, bright green creature with flounces of scalloped skin. This was a blowfish which I understand is prized for making lampshades.

Close to shore the sea was a gorgeous emerald color, with a definite demarcation line between it and the darker, deeper waters beyond. It was so incredibly clear that even without a snorkeling mask you could observe a good deal of marine life, but for skin-divers it was paradise. Close by was a submerged coral reef, always the happy hunting ground of snorkelers.

Wrap yourself in a bath towel, or in some way protect yourself from the sun on this trip, especially if you have recently come to the Caribbean. The rays feel marvelous, but they are insidious and can be dangerous.

CHAPTER 10

Off to the Mountains

Barranquitas—Treasure Island—Tobacco Country—
Aguas Buenas)

THE topography of Puerto Rico resembles an unblocked hat. It has a narrow brim and a high, unpressed crown, although the crown appears a great deal higher than it actually is. The mountainous interior averages only about two thousand feet, but there is no rolling country to blend it into the flatlands. Instead, the mountains appear to be superimposed like building blocks rather than growing out of the plain. Furthermore, there is scarcely a stretch of the contiguous coastline, including spread-out, sea-level San Juan, from which their sharp outlines are hidden.

The modest altitude of the mountains should be reassuring to drivers who flinch at steep roads. Of necessity there are curves and turns, but most of the roads—and certainly those mentioned in this chapter—are well graded. No mountain road is fast—but aren't you going to *see*, rather than break speed records?

I have heard such ridiculous exaggerations as that it was a half-day drive to Barranquitas. It would be hard for even the most timid to spend more than an hour and a half en route, even allowing for pauses to admire the view. On the whole, Puerto Rican roads are good, but most of them are not cement highways. A highway encircles the island and numerous roads traverse it. Both the highway around the perimeter and the fast route to Ponce are being straightened, and these have long stretches of cement. Most other roads are macadam. In certain remote regions the roads are narrow and incapable of absorbing

In Puerto Rico, the hills rise abruptly out of the flatlands.

any great amount of traffic, but this does not apply to the roads used on trips from San Juan.

The road to Barranquitas is a good one, demanding no particular driving skill. It is also a very beautiful one. Perhaps I should call it "they," for you can see on your map that there is a fork part way along Route 167 (which itself is a left turn from Highway 2 on the outskirts of Bayamon) permitting a circular drive. Keep to the right—that is, more or less straight ahead—to reach the hotel at Barranquitas.

Barranquitas has a dual attraction—the modern, delightful hotel outside of town, and the town itself. You can arrange to spend a day or longer at the hotel simply by applying to the Condado Beach Hotel in San Juan. The same company owns both places and runs two or three buses daily to the mountain resort.

The mountain hotel is excellently appointed, and has good food and a superb view. It is a quiet and restful place completely removed from town, not a spot for gambling, dancing, or staying up at night. There is a lovely covered terrace and a fine swimming pool with adjoining dressing facilities for transients.

99

Barranquitas is one of the nicest villages in Puerto Rico. It was the birthplace of Luis Muñoz Rivera, the great Puerto Rican patriot and hero and the father of Governor Luis Muñoz Marin, who was also born there.

Publisher of a great liberal paper, *La Democracia*, Muñoz Rivera worked for freedom and championed the rights of *all* Puerto Ricans. He fought bitterly and bravely for political emancipation under Spanish rule, and succeeded so well in arousing national consciousness that in 1897, after the failure of repressive measures (Muñoz Rivera himself was jailed), Spain reluctantly granted the island autonomy. Shameful to relate, when Puerto Rico became a United States possession, home rule was rescinded and Muñoz Rivera had to take up the fight again. At that time independence appeared to be the only solution, but Muñoz Rivera's tactics were moderate. He was long Resident Commissioner in Washington—where the present governor was educated—a lone but vociferous voice calling for justice in Puerto Rico. To him more than any other person goes credit for the Jones Act which granted United States citizenship to Puerto Ricans, but he died in 1916 before it was implemented.

Muñoz Rivera's home, recently converted into a combined museum and library, was a modest one. His parents were not

Barranquitas, "one of the nicest villages in Puerto Rico."

well-to-do, nor did he accumulate wealth. The museum has been admirably planned not to destroy the essential simplicity of the frame house. The furnishings, good but unpretentious pieces, are for the most part those which belonged to the great man—his desk, bookcases, wall clock, and the family pictures tacked onto the freshly-painted lathe partitions of the rooms. Even the library, properly lighted for study and research, has managed to preserve the qualities of a home, which makes it a very pleasant place to visit. It is always open to the public. In case it is locked when you stop by, ask anyone in sight to direct you to the keeper. (Take the street on the southwest of the plaza; the house is on the corner, one block beyond.)

In the graveyard, a short distance to the left on the next cross street, close to his tomb is a newly-built, combined monument and repository for Muñoz Rivera's papers. Some rather bad murals adorn the walls, and the papers can be of interest only to a student of Puerto Rican political history. I consider the house a far better memorial.

If you plan to return to San Juan from the town, go back to the neat square, with its light brown church of uncertain epoch but attractive appearance, and take 156, which leads into 167 and completes the circuit begun at the fork when you drove to the hotel. Scenically, this road is particularly delightful, with a stream running parallel through a deep gorge most of the route.

On the way, very shortly after leaving the town, is a plain and inexpensive but good restaurant called the *Union de Todos*. Here I ate *cabrito*, or kid, which I believe is a specialty of theirs. If it is on the menu, it is decidedly worth ordering.

There is more than a climatic change in the atmosphere of the mountains—you may notice that the people have a different appearance. A rather sound theory is that the mountain people are descended chiefly from Indians and are of decidedly less mixed heritage than the coastal inhabitants. The deeper one penetrates into the mountains, the more apparent this is. With the coming of the white man, the Indians fled to the security of the heights, where for a couple of centuries they lived more or less undisturbed. The Negro slave, on the other hand, had difficulty surviving in the cooler highlands (in winter the temperature may drop to fifty degrees at night), but thrived in the heat of the plains. Of course occasionally you do see mulatto faces, but fewer than in the coastal areas.

These are a lean, rugged people, a survival of the fittest. Life in the mountains, although improved, continues to be hard. Until recently, the water supply came from streams and springs, and people had to carry their own, sometimes a considerable distance over rough terrain. Puerto Rico's mountains provide an ample rainshed, but harnessing water for individual use has been a tremendous task. In some of the more remote sectors the problem is still not satisfactorily solved. A great innovation has been public water depots. Spaced not too far apart along the roads, these look something like hydrants and are generally, although not always, painted yellow. The respect the people have for this new convenience is manifest in the care they take to shut off the faucets. I have yet to see water dripping from one of them.

Treasure Island, the resort outside Cidra, is quainter than Barranquitas; the route to it is easier, and the return trip, although less spectacular, has more local color. Treasure Island was a development started by a continental, who still lives in the vicinity, but it is distinctly and typically Puerto Rican.

To get there, take Highway 1, which traverses the island, to the first right turn after Caguas, about seven or eight miles outside the town. Highway 1 is a fast four-lane road all the way to Caguas, and the trip takes less than an hour. After four miles on Route 172, turn right for a mile on 784, the only connecting road before Cidra.

In a large clearing are the main lodge and swimming pool, but a few steps off in the forest are a number of cottages, each separated for privacy. Several have front verandas looking onto a ravine and Lake Cidra. Families with children find this spot ideal. For tourists, it is a pleasant luncheon stop, but I would enjoy a restful week end here devoted to swimming in the pool, walking through the woods, or maybe taking a canter on one of the horses for hire.

The open-air dining porch has a thatched roof which fascinated me, as it was the first I had seen outside the poor quarters. Tiny lizards came out to look at the diners and scurried back after a moment of silent contemplation. These little crea-

Tobacco barns near Aguas Buenas.

tures are as much fun to watch as squirrels or chipmunks.

The luncheon was excellent, a crackling roast pork, French fried potatoes, and a *flan,* or cup custard, one of Puerto Rico's favorite desserts. There were other choices on the menu, but we took the waiter's recommendations. What the meal cost I do not know, but it was surely inexpensive; the charge by the day, with three meals, is only $10.00, including the use of the pool!

The return route via the back roads is thoroughly enjoyable. They are macadam and narrow, but almost empty of traffic. Drive into Cidra and take 173. Close outside the village is a branch, but keep to the right on 173, which will eventually bring you to Aguas Buenas. It is a lovely road, lined half the way with bamboo trees—tall, slim, packed together in high hedges and almost roofing the road.

On the trip to Barranquitas you may have spotted a few tobacco barns, but on Route 173 you will know you are in the heart of the tobacco-growing region. One after the other the barns loom up, with tin roofs and side walls of thatch to protect the tobacco until it is dried and ready for market.

The number and size of these barns indicate that this is a

comparatively prosperous region. In addition, the *camposinos* or *jíbaros* (the term *jíbaro* is generally used, but it translates as peasant; *camposino* is countryman) are invariably on horseback, with good, if well-used, saddles. The horses have the look of thoroughbreds, but this is one of the incongruities of Puerto Rico. Wherever you go in the country you will notice the fine lines of the horses. Often they show evidence of being underfed, but they have the look of aristocracy. They are descendants of the Spanish half-Arabian steeds brought by the conquistadors and have not been mated with lesser breeds. They hold their heads high, and sometimes their tails, and with a little proper grooming would not look out of place in a horseshow.

Aguas Buenas is certainly no lively marketing center, but in its quiet way is a nice mountain interlude. It is built on a plateau, and on departing you can look back across the valley at its outstanding building, the turquoise-green church on the plaza, with its cubic tower, the white cross on top matching the trim of windows and doors. The church dominates the neat square. It is neither new nor old, and belongs to no particular architectural school. It was the first green church I had ever

Camposino (*countryman*), *and his sturdy little horse.*

seen, and I found it a cheerful place, the red, green and white strips of its stained-glass windows beckoning through the entrance at the passer-by.

Only by looking down into the valley are you conscious of being on a mountain road, for this one runs on an even keel. On the right not far outside Aguas Buenas there is a short road—so short it has no number—but you will probably already have observed in the offing something resembling a small Eiffel Tower. This is the high-tension TV transmitter of *El Mundo*, San Juan's leading Spanish-language newspaper. In front of the transmitter is a natural parking space which affords a magnificent view of San Juan and the sea. If you have binoculars by all means take them along, especially since they help penetrate the heat haze.

Since this slight detour is dead-end, you must return to Route 173, which eventually connects with the highway back to San Juan.

CHAPTER 11

The Caribbean Side of the Island

(Route to Ponce—Jájome Highway—Salinas, Santa Isabel—
the City of Ponce)

PUERTO RICO is roughly a hundred miles long by thirty wide,
but these measurements only prove how misleading statistics
can be. The most direct route from the Atlantic to the Caribbean is fifty miles, and the highway along the northern shore
actually extends a hundred and twenty miles. Describing Puerto
Rico in square miles is surely more accurate, for although
there are no divergent points which are not within a day's drive
of each other, there are 3,000 square miles of diversified scenery,
customs, atmosphere, and even history, which make a sight-
seeing tour of the island a far lengthier proposition.

For instance, the circular drive down to Ponce, around to
Mayagüez and back along the Atlantic coast to San Juan,
without detour, is 236 miles. Allowing for intermediate stops
at least at La Parguera, San Germán, and Aguadilla, this is the
generally accepted Caribbean tour. One day is certainly insufficient; several are recommended, and a longer time is even more
rewarding. In fact, many people consider this southwest area
the ideal vacationland, preferring to spend their entire holiday
here rather than in San Juan.

You can fly to either Ponce or Mayagüez ($6.00 one way,
$11.00 round trip) and make car arrangements from there on.
But on the highway going down to Ponce there is a sudden
marvelous vista of the Caribbean which is lost when driving
in the opposite direction. Therefore it seems best to drive, going
first to Ponce.

By no means to be disdained, however, is the *publico* service.

106

Although only trips to the two big cities are advertised, the *publico* will drop you at any of the intervening towns. You can take the fast, direct route going through the center of the island. Call, or go to one of the lines, for full information. The *publico* is quite reasonably priced, averaging $3.00 to both Ponce and Mayagüez, plus an additional fifty cents or thereabouts to whatever destination you contemplate beyond. If you should choose this mode of travel, decide on one town as your headquarters and make short *publico* excursions from there.

The primary and fastest road across the island is Highway 1, the same highway you take to Cidra and Treasure Island. Beyond that turnoff is the bypass of the hill town of Cayey, picturesque in the distance, and a little farther along on a curve of the road is that first spectacular view of the blue Caribbean framed between twin mountain peaks. From there it is a quick, pleasant descent to Salinas.

Instead of continuing on Highway 1, there is an alternate route only a little longer which is well worth the slight extra time. It is the famed Jájome Highway (#15) to Guayama, picked up just after Cayey. This sixteen-mile drive is one of the most beautiful in all Puerto Rico. It adds only ten miles to the over-all trip, and although the road is mountainous, it is splendidly graded. Of course it is cut into the mountainside far below the high peaks. This road was originally built by the Spaniards, a remarkable engineering feat for the time, but almost as impressive to me are the substantial and by no means ugly brick barracks which were put up to house the road-builders. One of them has been turned into a summer residence for the governor. This is covered with white plaster and bears little resemblance to the original structure, but it is a pleasant, modern-looking summer home. Its entrance—since it *was* a barracks—is flush with the road, but it looks out toward the valley and a lovely informal flower garden covers the downslope.

High above on the mountaintops you will glimpse, from time to time, a white ribbon of road which from afar has the appearance of a well-worn footpath. This is the original Camino Real—*the* Royal Road—which connected the north and south of the island. It was built in the eighteenth century before the discovery of dynamite made the present highway a possibility, and in its way it is an even more awesome accomplishment. The actual construction was done by Chinese laborers, who were imported for this purpose and to strengthen and enlarge San Juan's fortifications. The Chinese were brought in on a transient basis, and presumably none remained after the work was done. Occasionally, however, an astute observer can note slant eyes in an otherwise typically Puerto Rican physiognomy. That the old Camino Real is still used by the peasants and still leads all the way to Guayama is a tribute to its fine construction.

The Jájome Highway passes streams and small waterfalls, not to mention gorgeous vistas across the valleys. The country people make practical use of the streams, washing and pounding their laundry on the rocks in the time-honored manner of peasants all over the world. You may see some of the women and wonder where they came from, for many of the shacks which pass for homes are hidden in the wooded mountainside. Quite a few of the *jíbaros* along this road, however, thanks to the sturdily built, brick barracks, are better housed than elsewhere on the island. Since the Jájome Highway is a road of outstanding beauty, there is also a community of summer homes belonging to well-to-do citizens of San Juan. Just beyond the governor's residence, on the opposite side of the road, is a charming shrine with a profusion of flowers in front. It is said to be a reproduction of the Grotto of Lourdes.

Guayama, at the end of the route, is a fair-sized town which has a nice square of magnificent trees trimmed umbrella shape. The small thick green leaves are like those of a privet hedge. It is not a town, however, that beckons you to lunch. Just a short distance away is Salinas, which boasts a renowned sea-food restaurant—Ladí's—by the beach.

Ordinarily Salinas' only attraction is for the gourmet, but it is also famed for its *paso fino* horse competitions, held in late August and early September. *Paso fino* refers to the gait, highly prized and cultivated in Puerto Rico, but although the horses vary in color (and include the palomino), they represent a distinct species—the Andalusian. They are slim-legged, with beautifully molded, heavy bodies—the type ridden by Spanish royalty in Velásquez' paintings. These horses are short-striding and trained to a single, excessively smooth gait, the test of

The plaza at Guayama, embellished with magnificently trimmed trees.

which is that a rider can hold a glass of water aloft without spilling any. *Paso fino* competitions are held in various parts of the island—in late October in San Juan, early November in Aguadilla, and so on—but the one at Salinas is particularly famous.

A little beyond Salinas, at Santa Isabel, is a recent gourmet rival of Ladí's, the Aquarium Restaurant. It is more attractive in appearance, but both restaurants are first-rate.

The *langosta*, or spiny lobster, is native to the Caribbean and is so plentiful as to be no longer a luxury. There are also several fine small fish to be enjoyed here. One of the differences between the Caribbean and the Atlantic is that the latter reaches enormous depth more quickly, bringing the huge carnivorous monsters like the barracuda and shark so near to shore as almost to exclude the smaller fish.

Whatever you order at Ladí's, look for the *sauce Ladí*, a subtle concoction which is a specialty of the house. At the Aquarium I had their marvelous broiled lobster, done a little differently from any I ever ate. After boiling, the meat was removed, cut up and mixed with a combination of melted cheese and butter, then replaced in the shell and grilled. If you plan a stopover at Ponce and are undecided about which of these restaurants to try, on this first day go to Ladí's, and retrace the short distance to the Aquarium in Santa Isabel on the morrow.

Ponce is not famed for its restaurants, but back of the Banco de Ponce on the Calle Mayor can be found the Lobster House, the premises being part of an old Spanish colonial home. Until recently, both good restauranes and good hotel accommodations were scarce in Ponce, but with the opening of the gorgeous Ponce Intercontinental the situation has changed at last.

The Ponce Intercontinental is built on El Vigia, a suburban hillside, and looks down on a green valley and across the city to the sea, which here is dotted with tiny emerald islands. It is a resort in itself, with casino, swimming pool, and a road under construction which will connect it directly with the nine-hole Ponce Golf Club. Its guests also may use the facilities of the Ponce Yacht Club, and as Ponce is one of the largest yachting centers on the island of Puerto Rico, this is a tremendous drawing card.

Even for those without a yacht, the club is enjoyable to visit, for it is built out in the bay on two islands joined by a causeway. The trip to it is via motorboat from the pier on the *playa*. *Playa* in this instance does not mean beach, but water front, and don't be surprised to drive several miles beyond the city proper, past *centrals*, distilleries, and refineries, for Ponce boasts a huge commercial harbor.

The departure point of the boat to Caja de Muertos (Coffin Island), a wonderful islet and decidedly worth a visit, is from the Ponce Yacht Club. Not only does the Caja de Muertos have an exceptionally fine—if small—beach and a farther area which is a joy to fishermen, but it contains a cave complete with skeleton. The latter is *not* a hoax; it was found there many, many years ago. Caja de Muertos, like so many Caribbean islands, was a hide-out for pirates. The trip to Coffin Island can best be arranged through the hotel.

For any extended stay in Ponce, the Intercontinental is unquestionably the ideal place to be. It is a delightful hotel, every room with a balcony and a view. The food is good, and there is just about every convenience. It is also a rendezvous for Ponceños.

110

For those desiring something more modest, there are two or three thoroughly decent small hotels in the center of the city. Largest is the Melia, modernized, completely air-conditioned, with privileges of the Ponce Golf and Yacht clubs. Nearby, just two blocks from the central plaza, is the San José Guest House. It serves no meals, but its ten rooms are air-conditioned. There is also El Castillo, with twelve rooms, and the recently finished Texan Motel (ten rooms) on the bypass of Highway 1. All four are in the same price range, averaging $6.00 to $7.00 single, $10.00 double. As you can see, costs are slightly lower in the south, but with such a scarcity of accommodations it is wise to reserve in advance.

Ponce is a booming, active city of well over 100,000. But it is said to be, in relation to San Juan, about what Boston is to New York. Like Boston, it is a conservative city with little or no night life, although it occasionally offers a good concert or theatrical attraction.

The most publicized curiosity in Ponce is the incredible Parque de Bombas, or firehouse, on the main plaza. Actually, there are two contiguous plazas—Degetau and Muñoz Rivera—which flank both the firehouse and the white cathedral on which it backs. Without equivocation, the Parque de Bombas is a unique architectural atrocity, sure to make one gawk and

The famous firehouse at Ponce, the Parque de Bombas.

wonder how it could have happened. Its shingles are painted in stripes of red and black, the whole surmounted by a pagoda roof with white lights trimming the already ornate overhang. As if all this were not a sufficiently bizarre mixture, above the windows there are fan designs of pale blue, yellow, and green placed against a red background. The muddy brown and white interior boasts a bright green, iron staircase. Naturally you will not really believe any of this until you see it.

The real, and only, explanation for such lunacy of design is that the building was put up as a pavilion for a fair. That was back in 1883, when tastes were considerably different from today, but the truly comic touch is that the motive of the fair was art! The Ponceños, however, have a great sentimental attachment for their Parque de Bombas, and every four years they scrupulously refurbish these fantastic colors. A modern firehouse has just been built, but the old Parque de Bombas will remain as a famed oddity and landmark.

History clarifies the reason for its preservation. It seems that until well in the 1900's, the fire department was not only a functional, volunteer organization but also an aristocratic social group. By some accident—presumably because they were awaiting other quarters—the pavilion remained as their headquarters. Then, in 1903, a terrible fire swept through Ponce. A powder house blew up, the fire spread, and much of the town was destroyed. The semi-social volunteer fire department, faced with a conflagration far beyond their control, performed magnificently, and the Parque de Bombas is kept as a monument to their extraordinary heroism. Funny and atrocious as it is, the citizens of Ponce see it with kinder eyes.

The other main sight-seeing attraction is the modern chapel at the Catholic University, the architectural antithesis of the Parque de Bombas. The university was established after the last war, and all its buildings are splendid examples of present-day design, but the chapel is inspired. As you drive up to it, you are likely to be momentarily startled by the use of a huge white cross as the side support of the portico. But shortly you will be absorbed by the beauty of the whole. The chapel is built in the form of a reversed U, in exquisite pastels, with blue-green tile pilasters placed against gray-green smooth stucco. Soft *bois de rose* covers the huge slanted interior but-

112

tresses. Opalescent stained-glass windows reflect the blue-green of the exterior, but square inset panes of red and pure blue vivify what otherwise might have been a monotony of undertones. One other highlight—the mosaic Madonna against a gold background skillfully blends modernity and the traditional primitive.

This lovely chapel and the unbelievable Parque de Bombas are by no means all that Ponce has to offer. The city is an excellent center from which to make short trips along the coast and into the spectacular, mountainous, coffee-growing country. Moreover, there is a good deal to see within the city limits.

At 70 Calle Cristina is a restored old mansion recently opened as the Ponce Art Museum. Its collection, to which additions are constantly being contributed, already includes Murillo, Van Dyck, several Teniers, Del Piombos, and Gainsboroughs, a representation of later artists like Gustave Doré, Burne-Jones, and Constable, and even an Epstein sculpture. These are simply random names; many other illustrious ones are represented here. There is also a room devoted to Puerto Rican painters from the great Campeche to the present.

The museum was begun as a civic enterprise by Luis A. Ferré, possibly Puerto Rico's most renowned private citizen. The Ferré industries have brought incredible wealth to an already wealthy family, but Señor Luis Ferré is both patriotic and philanthropic. A senator and head of the Statehood Republican Party, he stands in political opposition to Governor Muñoz. Nevertheless, he has taken an active part in Operation Bootstrap and, although he may have benefited in the bargain, has also made great contributions toward Puerto Rico's goal of prosperity. One of his most recent investments was in the building of the Ponce Intercontinental. He and the Commonwealth government each hold approximately a one-eighth interest. Like the other Intercontinental hotels, this one is leased to a subsidiary of Pan American Airways.

Ponce is frequently described as a very "Spanish" city. In fact, most of the old families here are more obviously of pure Spanish descent than those elsewhere. You will probably also be surprised to notice the number of blond and light-eyed citizens. Though the families in the upper social echelon compose a closely-knit group, they are by no means unapproachable. Like

New low-cost housing in Ponce.

Modern chapel at the Catholic University in Ponce.

Puerto Ricans elsewhere, they are both friendly and hospitable.

Many of the colonial houses still stand near the center of town, but they are for the most part modest homes. Wealth has come to the city in more recent years through its harbor activity and rapid industrial growth. There are a number of handsome properties on the ascent to the Intercontinental Hotel, but the larger residential districts of La Alhambra and, not far beyond it, La Rambla are where most of today's prosperous citizens live. A drive through these districts is most enjoyable. To my mind, La Alhambra has the most beautiful homes in all Puerto Rico.

On the other hand, the slums of Ponce not only rival those of San Juan but are more conspicuous in the open flatness of the city. Clearance continues here, but it has not kept up with the rapid growth of industry. To me, however, these and other slums on the southwest coast are less squalid because of the amount of bright paint splashed on the shacks. There are the usual incredible combinations, even gayer than the Parque de Bombas—light blue, with a sapphire entrance porch and red trim; shocking green, with pink porch and yellow trim—a kaleidoscope of colors as brilliant as flowers and as cheerful. The extraordinarily dry air of the region apparently preserves the paint, and the pleasant climate also doubtless moderates the discomfort of having to live in such quarters.

The great celebration in Ponce is the Fiesta of the Virgin of

Carmen in the middle of the summer, the same as in Cataño and several small fishing villages. From the church in the Playa de Ponce the image of the Madonna is carried to the wharf at the foot of the playa, where a barge sets out to sea to bless the waters for the fishermen. A splendid yacht regatta, best viewed from the Yacht Club, is also held in celebration of the festival.

The festival for Ponce's patron saint, Our Lady of Guadaloupe, comes in mid-December, with parades, masquerading, fireworks, and dancing in the plaza next to the Parque de Bombas. Patron saints' festivals, with few exceptions, are all celebrated in more or less the same way. One is sure to be taking place somewhere on the island during your stay, and a visit to one will give you a general idea of all such celebrations.

Far from the least of Ponce's unique attractions—and one which can be enjoyed at any season—is her famous market, situated just a few streets off the main plaza. What makes it different is that shops, not stalls, are partitioned off within a huge old warehouse, which is a full square block in size. Even the four outer walls of the warehouse are composed of cheap stores of every description, selling shoes, shirts, souvenirs, religious objects, toys, and kitchen utensils.

Inside the entrance on the Calle Union, the street leading from the plaza, are cages of live fowl and rabbits—it is a bit amazing to find chickens and rabbits crammed into the same cages. It is also surprising to see a housewife walk away with the head of a live chicken she has purchased protruding from a paper bag. Nearby is a place where chickens, pigeons, ducks, and rabbits are killed and dressed. There are fighting cocks and thoroughbred breeding fowl for sale here too. In fact, this part of the market smells a little like a zoo, but it is certainly an interesting place and quite unlike the markets elsewhere.

Ponceños, having grown up with the market, the Parque de Bombas, and the essentially unchanged center of the city, are for the most part unaware of its curious distinctiveness. Nor do they seem fully aware of its corners of beauty, of the fine new public buildings, of the parks and the charming residential sections. Ponce, nonetheless, vibrates with an appeal peculiarly its own—a mixture of old and new, a rich commercial center but also a city of traditions and continuity. It is a city that has never been properly publicized, but it is well worth a stopover.

115

CHAPTER 12

The Pirate Coast

(Guánica—La Parguera—Boqueron and Pirate Lore)

PONCE lies on the plain with verdant mountains behind, but arid flatlands sprawl on either side. Only occasional showers water this land (although in rainy May a tropical downpour may seem intent on submerging it), and the mountains which block the rainfall also all but dissipate the trade winds. This is dry, hot country, but the low humidity makes it not only bearable but enjoyable, except when you stand in the sun.

The road west from Ponce is never more than momentarily dull. Directly outside the city it dips to the sea and clings to it for quite some time. The water has a brilliant hue, and the number of islets is incredible, some only a few yards square. Surely nowhere in the world are there as many and as varied islands or *cayos* as in the Caribbean. Some, pure white coral reefs with only a pine or two finding root, shelter caves where pirates used to hide. Others look like jungles. Many of these actually are jungles of mangrove, the branches of which grow downward and root in the water to form an impenetrable maze. Oysters clung to several I passed, giving essence to the saying that oysters grow on trees..

Still other islands are thick with undergrowth but have a natural clearing of beach. Some are inhabited; many are free to the passer-by. Yacht-owners find it endless fun to cruise among them, finding a tiny continent here or there for a day. With the larger sailboats you can venture far out, but even the lowly, less expensive motorboat can make an exciting day.

116

These can be found easily farther along the coast, in the harbors fringing the so-called desert country.

The stretch of highway as far as Yauco is not, strictly speaking, desert. It is dry, but the ever present sugar-cane fields are huge and green. Ponce contains some of the biggest sugar *centrals*.

Many of the sugar plantations are serviced by trucks and power cranes, but the ox-drawn cart is still common. Oxen can be seen in all parts of the island, but they seemed to me to be more in evidence in this southwest section. They are not yoked together in the traditional fashion, but are held in line by a wooden bar slipped over their long horns. Evidently this is just as practical as the yoke, and these beasts of burden look no more put upon than any others.

By the time you reach Yauco the sea has disappeared from the horizon. Highway 2 dips to the south at this juncture, and just a little beyond town you can turn southward on Route 116 for Guánica. Then the dazzling blue or green water will be visible once more.

Guánica has just begun to prepare for tourists, and its delightful location in a deep inlet is sure to attract them. The Spaniards had already settled this spot in 1535; before that it was an Indian village, although no traces of either early settlement remain. It does, however, have a lovely little esplanade lined with casuarinas, graceful long-needled weeping pines. A large natural rock on the water front has rough-hewn lettering reading:

3rd Bat
1st U.S.V. Eng'rs
Sept. 1898

Surely the engineers themselves must have carved this simple record of their landing. Several other ports, notably Fajardo and Ponce, boast of being major landing points of American troops, but to me Guánica will always be outstanding because of this unpretentious, but eloquent, monument to our arrival on Puerto Rican soil. Out in the bay is another of the old Spanish lighthouses, which somehow have an ageless quality. It still functions.

The harbor at Guánica, where American troops landed in 1898.

The first hotel in Guánica, the Copamarina Beach Hotel, opened in 1961. It is a small-scale resort—twenty-four cabana-type rooms—but has the convenience of a bar, restaurant and swimming pool, plus a beach front.

There are two alluring beaches nearby. The easterly road on your left as you face the bay is a lovely scenic drive—a drive to nowhere except beauty and the beaches. The first *playa*, directly on the Bay of Guánica, is still without facilities, but in the next cove, out on a point, is Caña Gorda, which has dressing rooms and *cantinas* for food and refreshments. The deep bay of Guánica twists and turns so bewilderingly as to appear land-blocked, but at Caña Gorda, facing the open sea, are a couple of green islets seemingly close enough to stretch one's arms out and touch. The Caribbean water is very warm and, for those who like the shock of the cold North Atlantic, a disappointment; for the rest of us, it is the most relaxing and satisfying in the world.

From Guánica to Ensenada is a matter of minutes. Ensenada is a modern development of white frame houses and neat lawns for technicians of the Guánica oil refineries. From there to La Parguera, known as the "jewel resort," is less than ten miles.

Everything in La Parguera centers around the Villa Parguera on the water front. Otherwise the town is only a miniscule fishing hamlet, its public wharf just a step away from the hotel.

Of the thirty-two rooms in this charming little hostel, some are air-conditioned, some not, and there is a choice of private or semi-private bath. Prices range from $5.00 to $10.00 single, and $7.00 to $14.00 double, quite a big spread. Across the road is the new Casa Blanca Guest House, unpretentious but attractive, especially for those with young children, because guests are permitted full use of kitchen facilities. For adults, the Villa Parguera Restaurant is the equivalent of an annex. Seafood, of course, is the specialty, but you can order anything, including a sandwich. Dolphin steak, in season, is most highly reputed but I have never tried it. I was told that it is a steak similar to turtle steak, red-blooded and unlike seafood in general. Incidentally, you will notice "Escuela Hotelera" sewn on the waiters' sleeves, for this restaurant is one of the hotel schools. The personnel of Puerto Rican hotels, from the bell-hops upward, are specially trained. So few had ever before seen the inside of any hotel that this is a very practical scheme of vocational training. In the off-season, you can find these students mixed with the regular attendants in such top spots as La Concha, but the main school is in Ponce, and La Parguera—judging by the quite adequate service—supplies the post-graduate course.

The Villa Parguera looks out on a calm sea studded with yachts, smaller boats, and islets. Directly in front of the glassed restaurant is an inviting swimming pool, and a path to the left leads to the hotel pier. It comes as a surprise to discover that La Parguera has no beach, but there fortunately is a choice of nearby islands. For sea bathing the most popular spot is the Isla Mata de la Gata, an island owned by an eccentric gentleman known as Don Vicente Cotté. He has dressing rooms of a sort, but they're quite primitive and it is advisable to arrive already attired in your bathing suit. He charges twenty-five cents for the privilege of using his dock. The water directly around it is shallow enough for a child; it is unbelievably clear, and after a few strokes ideal for snorkeling.

La Parguera is well worth at least an overnight stop. Hiring a launch for offshore excursions will easily tempt you to a longer stay, and of course one evening you will take the excursion to Phosphorescent Bay ($1.50 round trip). More than likely, on your return you will be able to listen to an impromptu concert in the town square, where young suitors publicly practice serenades on their guitars.

The trip to Phosphorescent Bay is best taken during the dark of the moon. Then the wake and the ripples of water are luminous and opalescent. The effect is less marked when the moon is full, though there is the compensation of glimpsing the serene *cayos* along the way. If a bucket of water is hauled aboard and sheltered from the light, its iridescence is plainly visible. The phenomenon is caused by the peculiar algae in the water, which, even bottled, retains its unique quality for some time.

Waiting on the dock for the start of this trip is entertainment in itself, as there is a fenced-in segment of the sea where an incredible assortment of local tropical fish live uneasily together. I saw a small shark and a large crayfish there, both evidently fed amply enough to dull their appetites for the ordinary prey swimming around them. There were also starfish and anchovies, striped sergeant-majors, parrot and angel fish, and others as exotic as their names. These are so fascinating to study that no one minds the pilot's casual regard of the hour.

There is also a marine zoo on Maguey Island, which is so close as almost to touch La Parguera. Open to the public on

The calm waters of La Parguera harbor are dotted with islets, yachts, and small boats.

Looking offshore from the Villa Parguera.

week ends, it is serviced by motorboat. (Admission is twenty-five cents.) This is a comparatively recent endeavor, with new contributions constantly increasing its interest.

Beautiful lace fan-coral, both yellow and violet hued, emperor and conch shells, and other gorgeous treasures of the sea can be purchased here. If you have not yet taken up skin diving, you will certainly be tempted to now. For divers, it's finders keepers.

Boqueron, on the west coast of Puerto Rico, is another happy hunting ground for marine life. Unlike La Parguera, it has not become a tourist haven. There is a simple hotel (with baths, too) on the tiny square, so small that it has no designation, but it can be located immediately upon inquiry. There are also two restaurants, very reasonable and good, which are found by turning to the right at the foot of the main road. A stretch of water front, part of a 1,000-acre parcel, has been purchased for a modern hotel, and surely its ideal situation on a very fine beach will assure its success.

There is, or was, a Boqueron Yacht Club started by an ingratiating continental by the name of Fred Lee, who, to the deep regret of many, died suddenly before completing the installations. Several of the members are trying to form a corporation to continue the project.

For those who want to see an utterly unspoiled Puerto Rican seashore town, this is it. I spent three of the most fabulously interesting—and therefore exciting—days of my life there.

Boqueron harbor was once a haven of pirates. The most famous one in all Puerto Rico (as well known as Captain Kidd is to us) was a buccaneer called Roberto Cofresí. Of Italian origin, he was officially stated to be from Cabo Rojo, but Cabo Rojo is an inland town and Boqueron, a couple of miles distant, is its port. This whole coast—roughly from Ponce to Mayagüez —is filled with pirate haunts. The term buccaneer applies specifically to the corsairs of the Caribbean, and none of them was Spanish. In fact, they waged what amounted to an undeclared war against the Spaniards, primarily because the Spanish colonists were obsessed with trading solely with the mother country. At the same time, the homeland supplied the colonists with only a small portion of their needs in exchange for the exports, so that they were often dependent upon purchases from the buccaneers.

The word "buccaneer" derives from a French corruption, as the original outcasts were French Huguenots settled in Haiti, or Hispaniola as that entire island was then called. A "boucan" was a place where meat was dried, and these early settlers or "boucaniers" were harmless hunters who dried and sold meat and hides. The Spaniards forced them off Hispaniola, and together with some French Calvinists from St. Kitts, they took over and annexed the island of Tortuga, a few miles northwest of Haiti.

This was about the middle of the seventeenth century. They were joined by other outcasts, notably English, and they built a fort and set up a sort of pirate republic or freemasonry of freebooters. They continued to sell meat and hides, which they now acquired by raids on Hispaniola. They also preyed on Spanish ships and bartered the wares thus acquired for guns, gunpowder, and cloth from the English and Dutch. To the Spaniards, the Inquisition being still in full force, they were not only outlaws but heretics, and the Spaniards treated them without mercy when they captured them. Roberto Cofresí of Boqueron ended his days before the firing squad at El Morro in San Juan, but not before receiving an appropriate amount of torture.

The buccaneers, harassed on Tortuga, spread out through the Caribbean, wisely choosing islands with caves for protection. Puerto Rico is full of caves, and one is strategically situated near a cove in the Bay of Boqueron. I was taken there—a rough walk over three pastures enclosed by barbed wire and through a pitch-dark, bat-infested, terrifying succession of caves to—at last—a sort of shrine with a cross in the niche and an inscription beneath it stating that this was where Roberto (I think that was his name) Cofresí, the last of the buccaneers, perished in 1909.

The United States had taken strong steps toward ridding the Caribbean of pirates and is also credited with exterminating the last of them on the stronghold island of Culebra back in 1823. This more recent Cofresí (nowadays occasionally spelled Kofresí) was presumably a lone outlaw—a follower, to the best of his ability, of the family profession. He seems to have been a cattle thief, on the surface posing as an innocent farmer, behaving in genuine buccaneer tradition. Federal agents were sent to get him, and as he was running to the protection of the caves, they wounded him—as it proved, mortally. His body was found in the far recesses, and he was buried where he died, doubtless a filial gesture, with a little memorial over the tomb.

The Cofresí name has luster in Cabo Rojo and Boqueron, and the son, or possibly grandson—a mild, pleasant, respected, and law-abiding citizen—owns one of the two restaurants in town. It is called *Ruicof*, a combination of his partner's name and his own. You can probably watch the lobster catch being brought to the pier extending beyond the restaurant, or to the *Puerto Real* next door. You can eat very well in either, but they *do* have an affinity for a loud jukebox.

The cave at Boqueron is the only mainland cave identified to me as having served the purposes of the buccaneers. Quite likely there were others, but the small islands, especially those some distance out, were their strongholds. One fair-sized one, Desecheo, yielded buried treasure as recently as 1952. Another, La Mona, forty-odd miles offshore between Puerto Rico and Santo Domingo (here one always says Santo Domingo, not Dominican Republic), is a coral island rising two hundred feet out of the water, with two secluded harbor entrances and caves, natural pirate fortifications.

Tales of today claim it is haunted, that a hermit lives there, the incontrovertible evidence being a hut with unwashed utensils and a pallet; but few, if any, have encountered him. Wild goat and boar—the latter the particularly dangerous quill boar with a hump similar to that of the water buffalo—infest the wooded underbrush, and one sportsman tells a tale of seeing a male boar appear with a harem of five sows, at which frightening sight he dropped his rifle and fled to a tree (one must quickly choose a broad-trunked tree, for a boar can cut down lesser ones with his tusk), from where he watched them trample his rifle to pieces.

Game fishermen often pass this island, and a young Texan now living in Mayagüez spoke eloquently of a stop he and seven companions had made there. For some reason, he said humorously, Mona gives you such creeps that you manage always to be accompanied, whether poking your nose into a cave or merely walking a few steps away from the crowd. Stopping there for a few hours, the eight young men were sitting together on a rock jutting into the sea when they heard a rustle, saw an iguana—a mammoth lizard—and "eight brave men dove into the sea!"

Curiously, Mona Island must have been less fearsome centuries ago when Ponce de León came over from Hispaniola to look into the possibility of settling Puerto Rico. His ship was caught in a storm en route and took refuge at Mona. On it, at the time, was living a tribe of Indians, not hostile either, for the chief became so friendly that he and the great white man exchanged given names, a singular honor among these tribes. This same chieftain guided Ponce around the island and showed him the harbor of present-day San Juan.

But back to the mainland and Boqueron. It has a nice bay, fringed as usual with palm trees. Chugging about in a motorboat is fun, and in the shallow offshore is a wonderful coral reef, a skin-diver's kindergarten. Fred Lee of the Boqueron Yacht Club, then my guide, took me to it, first making me practice breathing standing in the waist-high waters and then submerging for minutes at a stretch. Below was a world of fantasy. To my great pride, I pointed out a yellow plant which I believe is tree, or live, coral. This he added to the collection in the huge saltwater aquarium adorning the Yacht Club bar.

Tranquil beach at unspoiled Boqueron.

Such an enormous choice was available almost outside the door that he amused himself by changing the scenic design frequently.

When I was there the exhibit included pale pink sea anemones, flame coral, a small sea urchin, a baby pompano no bigger than a thumbnail, a valuable little-finger-sized crimson fish said to be worth $40.00, and an equally tiny polka-dotted one (just $5.00), which enchanted me quite as much. The most extraordinary creatures looked like plants, but he informed me they were sea worms. More than anything else, they resembled minute variations of a palm tree with a brown trunk (the worm's body) and feathery little pinwheels of antennae above. One was almost white, another speckled brown, a third had a reddish tinge, and the last was a gorgeous royal blue. These blossoming tentacles are infinitely sensitive, and at a touch the whole works disappears within the stiff trunk. A second later they feel their way out again, unfolding and waving gently in the water. There is an unobtrusive ground cover to be found throughout the Caribbean area, along roadsides as well as in the woods, which shrivels when touched. This is the sensitive plant, and if you wait patiently the leaves will unfurl again after the danger has passed. These sea worms are the aquatic equivalent.

Boqueron without Fred Lee and his incredible store of folklore cannot be quite the same to anyone who visited there in his time. But the town can be fascinating in spite of its unprepossessing look. If the Yacht Club is revived, or when the modern hotel is built, a motorboat and guide will be easier to come by. Meanwhile, these can quite likely be arranged through one of the restaurants. There are a number of young men brought up on these shores, quite familiar with what to most of us is a fabulously different life, who can show you the mysterious marine world, assist you with snorkeling or even aqua-lunging, and lead you through the pirate caves with the aid of a torch.

As late as 1939, a woman visitor recorded that bathing suits were not permitted on the Boqueron beach. This conception of propriety is long outmoded. Shorts may even be tolerated on the street there now, although it is safer to assume that they have not yet become the accepted fashion.

CHAPTER 13

Enchanting San Germán and Quaint Hormigueros

(Desert Country and Salt Flats—San Germán—Hormigueros)

ALONG the tree-lined esplanade of the central plaza of San Germán, especially on Sunday evening, the young people gather to promenade—the girls, arm in arm, circling clockwise and the boys counterclockwise, primly flirting as they pass. On the stone benches sit the chaperones, watching with vigilant but tolerant eyes—for it was the same when they were young, and their mothers and grandmothers before them. In fact, it has always been like this in San Germán; the town is the oldest in traditions of any on the island. Lying beautiful and tranquil in the green foothills, it has a fascinating timelessness both in customs and appearance. It is a wonderful place to stay, and a fine jumping-off point for exploring the delights and curiosities of the coast, for you can return in the evening to the cool of the hills. The only unfortunate factor, from the visitors' point of view, is that accommodations are circumscribed.

Most of the intervening country between Boqueron and San Germán is what has been called the desert country; however, except very close to the shore, it is surprisingly non-arid. Some say that when you see cactus, *that* is the desert land. You see cactus here occasionally, but not to the extent that you see it in Mexico or in our own southwestern states. Large sections are lush pastureland with huge dairy farms, and the vicinity of Lajas is famed for its pineapples.

This *was* once the most poverty-stricken area of all Puerto

126

Rico; its dry, hard-packed earth made it impossible to make a decent living. However, long before Operation Bootstrap, the United States, which has been guilty and remiss about much in Puerto Rico, did try to give a helping hand to this desert area. The first efforts were made as far back as 1908, when it was recognized that without irrigation the land was untenable, like much of lower California. In recent years the area has received the close attention of the Department of Agriculture in an attempt at effective soil conservation. A large district is now designated as a Federal Agricultural Experiment Station. Even today, by our standards, the region is far from a land of plenty, but it has the look of prosperity. My most vivid impression is of well-fed, healthy cattle waiting in long, open sheds to give their milk.

Nevertheless, the region is still fringed with cactus and there are barren stretches near the sea. One spot on the southwest tip, Cape Cabo Rojo, is filled with salt marshes, and since the salt is commercially reclaimed, it is a rather extraordinary sight.

You will note on your map that Route 301, an offshoot of 101 leading to Boqueron, dribbles down to the Cape, first as a narrow macadam road, then a dirt road, and finally, according to the markings, disappears. Actually, it doesn't disappear, but the well-marked wheel tracks cannot honestly be recommended for easy traveling. At the very end is another one of the Spanish lighthouses, now serving the U.S. Coast Guard, but there is a broad, desolate spot at the turning before the tip of the cape which is dotted by a line of varied-sized stones, identifiable as the boundary of the path to follow. Woe betide anyone who strays outside them into the slimy marshes. The trip can be made if one watches carefully for the markers, but only in a small car.

However, the road is passable and any car can maneuver as far as the salt flats. In the inlet is a series of beds with sluices. The sea is slowly let in, sealed off, and the sun permitted to do the rest. When the process of evaporation is completed, men shovel out the residue. On the banks, awaiting trucks to cart it off, are huge pyramids of pure salt. There are no refineries; the salt is not prepared for human consumption, but made into cakes for cattle feeding. If proof were needed that the Caribbean is saltier—and therefore more buoyant—than the Atlantic, here it is.

To reach San Germán from this outlying spit of land, you merely need to decide whether to go by Cabo Rojo or Lajas, both of which are on short semi-circular Highway 4. Incidentally, this is truly hot territory with only the car top to protect you from the sun's infra-red rays, but the humidity is low and a soft breeze, the remnant of the northern trade wind, fans you.

In San Germán you will be completely comfortable. It is, as the name of its old hotel proclaims, "The Oasis"—green, comparatively cool, and so deeply imbedded in the foothills that, except for the core of the ancient city, its streets go sharply up and down. Above the town is the lovely, tree-shaded campus of the Inter-American University.

An estimated 30,000 people live in the area. The hilly outskirts are extensive and modern, but after the unexpected apparition of a new building in the downtown area, the citizens quickly passed a law that the heart of San Germán be preserved and protected against further incursions of modernity. It remains, therefore, an unblemished Hispanic colonial town. Unspoiled through the length of the two large plazas and the streets radiating off them, it exudes a charm quite surpassing any other community in Puerto Rico.

The main square of San Germán, with City Hall in the background.

Sangermeños, so proud of their heritage, sometimes innocently boast that their town is the oldest Spanish settlement in Puerto Rico. This is inexact, as there was not even a fort on the island until Ponce de León's advent. The need for a protective outpost on the western shore was recognized, and a military garrison was designated as the west-end capital in 1512 (four years after the settlement of Caparra). The following year King Ferdinand ordered forts built both at San Juan and San Germán. Originally San Germán was a coastal lookout; it was preyed upon not only by the fighting Caribs, but three times was burnt by French privateers. With each successive destruction the settlement moved farther inland until, in 1570, it reached the present site.

"G" in Spanish, as you probably know, has an "H" sound, and San Germán is pronounced Sahn-Hermáhn. The name is generally conceded to be in honor of King Ferdinand's French second wife, Germaine de Foix, whom he married in 1505 after Isabella's death. In the Iglesia de San Germán is a chandelier described as a gift of Queen Isabella, but it is not always explained that this was Isabella the Second, the nineteenth-century Spanish queen.

San Germán has an historical importance equaled only by San Juan. An eighteenth-century memoir remarks that the only two schools in Puerto Rico were in San Juan and San Germán! That San Germán is the second oldest settlement is indisputable, and the lovely church of Porta Coeli is regarded as the second oldest in the Western World. (The cathedral at Ciudad Trujillo preceded it.) As though placed on a pedestal, Porta Coeli stands on a knoll above the square back of the City Hall. Twenty-four ancient brick steps lead up to the Gate of Heaven (as the name so charmingly translates), and the brick and stone foundations of the building itself are covered by weathered plaster of muted beige, a wonderful hue achieved only by age. Once it was a combined church, fortress, and monastery. All that remains of the monastery is the arched wall and gate to the left of the church. Records show that the monastery was built in 1609, but the place of worship was undoubtedly constructed first, in deference both to the immediate needs of the devout and to the ever present danger of raids. An outstanding scholar and authority places Porta Coeli's con-

Porta Coeli (c. 1583), in San Germán, considered the second oldest church in the Western Hemisphere.

struction in 1583, within a few years of the foundation of the present town.

Its use as a fortress is patent in the impregnable walls, the heavy plank doors, and the narrow apertures. Porta Coeli is open to the public as a museum of religious art and its collection includes images carved by sixteenth-century *santeros,* ancient wooden statues, paintings and liturgical objects from Puerto Rico's historic churches. Despite much previous neglect, the church has remained in a remarkably fine state of preservation. The old wooden doors, beams, and posts are unravaged, and the lovely carved wooden altarpiece is the original. Because it has recently been cleaned the altar has a shining new look, but its fresh appearance is also attributable to the astounding properties of the native hardwood.

Backing the altar steps are exquisite Spanish tiles depicting biblical scenes in soft violet on white. Although not a large church, Porta Coeli has a rare beauty. Aloof on its rise of ground, its simple classical lines impart an aura of great dignity. It has been in disuse for many years, even centuries. It can be visited 9 A.M. to 5 P.M. weekdays, 9 A.M. to 4 P.M. week ends.

The large white church, the Iglesia de San Germán, on the neighboring plaza, which replaced Porta Coeli as a house of worship, was built some two hundred years ago. The elaborateness of its more recent design is in sharp contrast to Porta Coeli, but the fine Campeche paintings somewhat subdue the ornateness of the interior. These, and the magnificent but certainly not subdued nineteenth-century chandelier of Queen Isabella the Second, are its outstanding treasures.

The greater part of the old town bears the imprint of the late 1700's and early 1800's, from the charming old frame houses with their enormous balconies around the plaza (which bears the resounding name of Plaza Francisco Mariano Quiñones; the smaller one on which Porta Coeli is situated is the Parque de Santo Domingo) to the fine mansions filling the side streets.

The citizens of San Germán are something of a contradiction—they resist the idea of new hotels but at the same time welcome visitors. The Inter-American University may be partly responsible for their attitude. This co-educational institution, begun in 1912 and—though interdenominational—run by the Presbyterian Church, is what its name implies. Long before student exchanges became commonplace, it fostered the concept of mutual understanding through a student body composed of mixed nationalities and races drawn from the Western Hemisphere. These students are accepted as an integral part of the town and invited into the private homes.

The Sangermeño is, in fact, far from aloof. He is noted for his friendliness, and is inclined to address a stranger on the street and offer to show him the glories of the town. Lovely old private homes would be unknown to the outsider except for such kindness and thoughtfulness. One such friendly citizen has even been listed in brochures on San Germán: Señor Yamil Galub, owner of the Casa Antigua at 85 Calle Luna, is so delighted by a display of interest that he will conduct you through his home personally, pointing out the beautiful chandeliers and other exquisite Spanish furnishings, as well as the fine tiles and wrought iron which also adorn this splendid mansion. Like so many of the old homes, it dates from the affluent 1800's.

The quaint nineteenth-century Farmacia Dominguez on the edge of the plaza should certainly not be missed. Although it sells up-to-date pharmaceutical products, its original décor is scrupulously maintained. If you want additional assistance in your sight-seeing, the Fomento Organization includes a Department of Tourism.

San Germán is a town to roam about in, not one to be gulped in quick passage, and so it is unfortunate for tourists that there is not a hotel of adequate size. Costello Hall, on the university campus, is a delightful guest house. Rooms are $5.00 single and $8.00 double, all with shower and toilet.

In the old town is the 200-year-old Oasis, with agreeable dining under the colonnade in the patio. It, too, has rooms—ten to be exact; Costello Hall has eleven—but it is less tranquil than Costello Hall.

The desire to preserve San Germán unchanged is, of course, the chief reason for the hotel shortage. Obviously it would be unwise to plan on staying there without first making sure a room can be found. However, San Germán is well served by *publico* and is within easy driving distance of La Parguera (about eight miles), Boqueron, and other southwest points of interest.

Dining room of Casa Antigua, a private home in San Germán. The owner is proud to show his splendid old mansion to visitors.

Farther along on the highway to Mayagüez, but much closer to that city, is El Rosario, a modern, ranch-style hotel in a clearing on a mountain plateau. As it has a swimming pool and horses for riding, not to mention a bar and restaurant, it is conducive to a stay of several days. Besides—a persuasive feature for parents—it has a children's playground. Rates are $6.00 or $7.50 single, $9.00 or $10.00 double, with special arrangements on the American plan. For those who like the fresh air of the mountains, it is even cooler than San Germán and, like that town, a good base for sight-seeing.

Nestled in the foothills between Rosario and San Germán is Hormigueros. By either Route 343 or 103, it is only two or three kilometers from the highway, a slight but recommended detour. Hormigueros means anthill, from which you may deduce that the climb to it is not excessively steep. The road winds upward between the clean, neat houses of the village to the imposing cream-colored church crowning the summit. An infinity of steps leads up the green mound from the village proper, but the road will bring you to the rear entrance. The majesty of the Iglesia de la Monserrate is mainly attributable to its location, dominating a lovely valley. Its high tower tapers to a spire; a small porch shades the main entrance, and a wide stone terrace surrounds the unadorned edifice. Inside the nail-studded doors, the spacious, uncluttered interior is painted white, blue, and gold. The stone floor is well worn by the tread of centuries of worshipers.

The main chapel, naturally, holds the image of the Virgin of Monserrate to whom the church is dedicated, and on the walls surrounding her are small gold and silver objects—a tiny foot, arm, or heart—the *ofrendas* of the faithful. Her healing powers are considered great, and every year on September 8 the ill and devout make a pilgrimage to this shrine, praying for cures and climbing on their knees up the long, steep steps —a veritable Lourdes of lame, halt, and blind. Often their knees are bruised, sometimes bleeding, when they reach the top, but new *ofrendas* in the chapel testify to the Virgin's intercession on their behalf.

Her fame is widespread, and pilgrims come to the annual fiesta from all parts of Puerto Rico and from the neighboring Caribbean islands. During the week of celebration a special mass is held at seven each morning, and in the evening there is a religious procession for which the Virgin of Monserrate is taken from her niche and carried through the streets.

The first known visitation of the Virgin to this vicinity occurred back in the seventeenth century. It is on record that a well-to-do landowner—Gerardo Gonzalez, by name—had an eight-year-old daughter who became lost in the surrounding wild mountains. The search for her continued many days, and two weeks passed before she was found hidden in a hollow among the huge roots of a ceiba tree—safe, happy, and merrily singing. The ceiba, found only in Puerto Rico, is sometimes referred to as the West Indian cottonwood. Its distinctive feature is the enormous roots which grow high above ground, giving the appearance of flying buttresses supporting the trunk. Their extraordinary size makes it completely possible for a little girl to hide among them. (It was in just such a tree that the people of Loíza Aldea claim to have found the image of San-

The ceiba tree, found only in Puerto Rico, has enormous roots above ground.

Church of Our Lady of Monserrate in Hormigueros. Annually, on September 8, the ill and devout climb the long, steep stairs on their knees.

tiago. The ceiba lends itself well to legend.)

When Gonzalez' small daughter was questioned as to how she managed to stay so well, she replied that a lady with a dark face had looked after her, feeding and caressing her and making a light shine at night. With this description, everyone recognized that it was the Virgin of Monserrate who had saved the child. In the Spanish Pyrenees there was already a shrine to her, so named because a small ebony image carved by St. Luke had been hidden at that spot during the Moorish invasion.

The child's father decided to build a sanctuary on the highest piece of his property, to serve as a beacon to all in the vicinity. According to legend, other wonders quickly succeeded the initial one. The outstanding tale concerned a peon working in the fields who called upon the Virgin for aid when he was charged by a mad bull. Suddenly the bull doubled up and fell dead. This miracle is commemorated in an oil painting hanging inside the church.

Across the road from the church is a rather large and impressive house. This, too, was built by Gerardo Gonzalez—a hostel to care for the pilgrims who came to do obeisance. It had a fine tiled roof, spacious overhanging balconies, and an oversized kitchen with room for numerous charcoal stoves where pilgrims might cook their food. Today, somewhat renovated, it is the parish house. Should you find the Iglesia de la Monserrate closed, it is at this house that you should inquire.

The village, which grew up later along the winding road beneath the church, has no noticeable hostel. But when the faithful make their pilgrimage, any one of the small homes serves the purpose. Although the occasion is solemn and many come in hope that the Virgin will bestow her curative powers on them, this is also a joyous week, with blaring music and fireworks in the evenings. After all, it *is* a fiesta.

To Mayagüez and Back to San Juan

(Puerto Rico's Third City—Aguada and Aguadilla—
the Beach of Gaujataca)

"MAJAGUA" was the Indian name for a species of tree plentiful
in the vicinity, and the Indians named their village after it.
Like other coastal settlements of the Tainos, Mayagüez fell
victim to the conquistadors early in the sixteeenth century, but
they kept the original name. Today the city is the third largest
in Puerto Rico.

In 1916 catastrophe struck the west coast, and an earthquake and tidal wave all but wiped out the city. Almost no
vestige remains of either the early Spanish or Indian civiliza-
tions—not even of the trees which gave the city its name.

Nowadays, Mayagüez is a thriving, bustling, industrial port
—factories, warehouses, and modern buildings are its trade-
mark. Its greatest claim to fame today is that it was the birthplace of the great Pablo Casals' mother, but no monument or
house commemorates this distinction.

Few of the streets in this town named for a tree are shaded
by any trees at present. The great exception is the central
square, the Plaza Colón, which, in May and June, the glorious
blooms of the jacaranda transform into the most beautiful plaza
in all Puerto Rico. The square is a survival of both the tidal
wave and the rococo 1890's. It is dominated by a monstrous
statue of Columbus, surrounded by elaborate lesser statues of
incongruous Grecian and Egyptian maidens serving as lampposts—not to mention bronze Moors and Indians. The effect is
quite comic.

To me, the most exquisite tree in the world is the jacaranda appropriately termed *la Reina de las Flores* by the Puerto Ricans. Its purple blossoms not only roof the plaza but, as they fall, carpet it as well. It is a pity they do not last indefinitely, for the Plaza Colón is the center of the city's activities. As in other main plazas, the Alcaldía or City Hall is at one end, the church at the other. On week-end evenings, even in this modern city, the young people, chaperoned, meet and stroll within its confines. During the last week in January and the first in February it is taken over for dancing and other amusements, for the *fiesta patronal* falls on February 2.

The Mayagüez church is perhaps the only one named after the Virgen de la Candelaria or Our Lady of Candelmas, although the *Candelaria* is an important celebration throughout the countryside (see next chapter). But Mayagüez has the distinction of being the one city which marks the occasion.

On the outskirts of town is the Federal Agricultural Experiment Station, situated adjacent to the College of Agriculture and Engineering, an offshoot of the University of

Plaza Colón in Mayagüez, where incongruous statues of Greek maidens serve as lampposts.

Talipot palms at the Federal Agricultural Experiment Station on the outskirts of Mayagüez.

Puerto Rico. The FAES does invaluable work in testing the suitability of plant species for Puerto Rico's soil and climate. The Station grounds are very beautiful, containing such exotic trees as cacao, cinnamon, and ilang-ilang, and there is a greenhouse of orchids. I, personally, loved what someone called the "WPA era" main building, which is Hispanic architecture extravagantly covered with ivy. It looks like a livable, palatial home. Just beyond the principal building, on the drive, are some huge old palm trees, between twenty and thirty years old, which have the characteristic of blooming only once in a lifetime. At the time I was there, some of them bore tufts of blossoms like a topknot—a warning that soon they would all have to be replaced. Take time, if you can, to wander leisurely about the lovely landscaped park.

Right outside the gates is an India Beer brewery. Like the rum distillers, the brewers too are pleased to show you through and offer you a sample of their product.

Although the water front of Mayagüez is strictly commercial,

138

the coast south of the city is especially attractive. Since the mountains stop the east-west flow of the trade winds, the water is also calmer there than on the north shore. Highway 2, the major road linking San Germán and Mayagüez, runs inland, but Route 102, which begins just outside San Germán, crosses to the coast via Cabo Rojo and thence follows the sea into the city. The nearer you get to Mayagüez, the more boathouses and summer residences you encounter, until at last you come to the year-round suburban area. In the Bay of Bramadero, south of the Bay of Mayagüez, yachts ride at anchor. You will notice colonies of palm shacks on stilts—bath houses for the itinerant tourist. There is no apparent set fee for their use, simply the expectation that you will tip the attendant a quarter or so. Some of the beaches have soft-drink stands, and in the neighborhood are several decent small restaurants.

The very best of them—Bolo's—is close to town on the Playa de Guanajibo. They advertise seafood dinners, especially lobster, brought daily from Cabo Rojo (Boqueron). The food is delicious and the place is comfortably air-conditioned.

Mayagüez has but one recommended hotel—La Palma. It is in the commercial hub of the city, but some of its ninety rooms are air-conditioned and it has a pleasant roof-restaurant. Prices run from a mere $5.00 single to twice that amount, and from $8.00 to $15.00 for two. However, if you plan to spend more than a night in the vicinity, Rosario Mountain Resort mentioned in the previous chapter will have greater appeal.

Much of Highway 2, going north to Aguadilla, is delightful, but the towns of Rincon and Aguada are, to put it mildly, devoid of charm. (Near Rincon, however, is a delightful cottage colony resort, the Sea Beach Colony, which offers a choice of single or double units or housekeeping suites. At present accommodations are limited, but additional units are being built.) It was in driving through Aguada that I first noted the odd sign so often to be seen on branches of the Banco Popular, a government bank. There are branches throughout Puerto Rico, in the small localities serviced by a touring teller. The smaller the town, the fewer the depositors and the less time needed to accomplish services. In Aguada the sign announced that the branch was open only from 10:00 to 11:30 on Tuesdays and Thursdays. A little farther on, In Aguadilla, the branch was

139

open four days a week, proof of the town's greater affluence.

Aguada's other distinction was a marker by the sea, at the foot of the suitably named Calle Colón, commemorating the landing of Columbus. It appears that Aguada has usurped the honor which Aguadilla had previously claimed. Columbus planted the royal banner and a cross, which of course disappeared in a short time, but the argument as to his specific landing point continues unabated. There are even citizens of Mayagüez who insist he landed there.

The papers extant, however, give solid indication that his ships entered the Bay of Aguadilla, narrowing the likely claimants to those situated on its shores. Whatever the precise site, one of Columbus' officers described an Indian village located close to the shoreline. It consisted, he wrote, of "houses covered in thatch with miradors [windowed-turrets] made of intertwined canes. They were located around a plaza from which a road led to the water. This road was wide and straight, bordered with plants and flowers symmetrically arranged, giving a most agreeable impression of taste and of the fertility of the island. At the end of this lovely road a spacious mirador was erected on tree trunks and hung over the sea. It, too, was covered with flowers and vines like the roadside, just as in Spain the circles and garden paths are adorned."

The village Columbus entered had been hastily evacuated, and during that first two-day call the Spaniards encountered no natives. They were enchanted with the country, however, which Columbus declared had the very soft air "as of April in Seville, and it is a pleasure to be here."

The climate is unchanged and Columbus' statement might, in modern parlance, describe Aguadilla. Or, more specifically, the lovely Hotel Montemar on a bluff above the bay, only a short distance from Ramey Air Force Base. Luxurious, with a broad terrace overlooking the harbor, and also a casino, the Montemar well deserves a stop. It has the atmosphere of a clubhouse, and in fact was previously called the Aguadilla Country Club.

Should you be interested in a glimpse of the coffee country, it is not a long trip inland (Route 111) to San Sebastián, a regional center. More details are given in the following chapter.

140

Nun and students (note jumper uniforms) looking over Guajataca.

Around the bend on the Atlantic Coast is Guajataca, a beach with a tunnel cut into the rocky promontory on its left. I have heard it described as "an old Spanish tunnel." It is of Spanish construction, but it dates from the days when a railroad encircled the island rather than from the conquistador era. At the time of my visit a restaurant had opened there, and now modern bath houses have been constructed. Guajataca is being promoted as a rival to Luquillo Beach, although to my mind nothing can equal the beauty of the latter. Guajataca is less sheltered too, and so there is more surf. But it is a nice beach and the only decent one in this vicinity.

From Guajataca to Arecibo is as dull a stretch as any in Puerto Rico, but it is a fast road and only fifteen miles long. At Arecibo you can break the trip with a stop for coffee or— if the hour is appropriate—lunch at the Aquarium before the final run back to San Juan. On that last stretch, time permitting, you may want to explore some of the points of interest which you missed on an earlier trip.

CHAPTER 15

Going to the Island

(The Coffee Region—Interesting Out-of-the-Way Spots and Inexpensive Inns—the East Coast and Vieques—Coamo Springs)

WHEN a resident of San Juan is making a trip of more than five miles outside the metropolitan area, say beyond Carolina or the outskirts of Bayamón, he usually explains that he is "going to the Island." To "go to the Island" may imply Caguas, Fajardo or Mayagüez—any place, in fact, *except* San Juan.

To the mountain people, however, any town beyond the closest hamlet suggests a vast, unknown world. A peasant living near Adjuntas, nineteen miles north of Ponce, could nod that you were on the right road to Ponce, but if pressed for further detail might reply vaguely that he had a cousin who had once visited the city.

Looking for an Indian cave said to be between Lares and Utuado, I was assured that anyone in the latter place could direct us. This proved to be a gross overstatement. No one had ever heard of it. As we drove along the road linking the two towns, making numerous stops to inquire, we eventually learned that someone passing through had once mentioned it. Later another *jíbaro* declared that it was a few kilometers off the main road, but just where the turnoff came he couldn't state. It was not until we were within a radius of a few miles that we received any concrete information.

It is true that in this central, precipitously mountainous area —the coffee-growing region—you have the feeling of complete separation from the world at large. When I visited a coffee *finca*—the hacienda itself was a mile from the road—my host told me sixty families lived on the plantation, yet I only saw

142

A scene in the mountainous coffee-growing region.

one tenant house. (Most of them are hidden in the tree-covered mountainsides.) These families were so awkwardly distant from Jayuya, the nearest town, that the proprietor built a schoolhouse for the children on the property.

The coffee region is not ordinarily on the tourist's itinerary, but if you really want to know Puerto Rico, it is an area you will find rewarding. It extends, roughly, west from Jayuya—about the exact center of the island—to and beyond San Sebastian. Some declare it goes all the way to Aguadilla. All I can say is that if you are spending a leisurely holiday in Puerto Rico, by all means go into the belt. The roads are macadam, but it is not an easy drive. I suggest the Arecibo highway to Ponce. It is a good road, if winding, and I truly believe the most scenic route of all. In length it measures fifty-one miles, or eighty-two kilometers (the Puerto Rican, like most Latins, counts in kilometers, and you can always entertain yourself dividing kilometers by eight and multiplying by five to arrive at the mileage). The first half of the distance, to Utuado, is only slightly mountainous. You pass by beautiful Lago de Dos Bocas, where there is a hydroelectric plant, and not far beyond

Adjuntas reach the Alto de la Bandera pass, which represents nothing more than a summit, but from there on to Ponce is some of the most spectacular scenery you are likely to encounter.

Coffee flowers in September, the harvest comes in November; at other periods the land appears to be only verdant countryside. Never having seen coffee grow before, I was amazed that the beans did not come in pods or just drop off like dried berries. Actually, coffee commences as a berry which ripens in clusters in which it resembles cranberries. Processing is a matter of first stripping the berry for the core or seed (the outer husk is an excellent fertilizer), then washing and drying it. Puerto Rican coffee beans are tops, but the coarser Brazilian coffee is grown here too.

Our mechanical age has produced no alternative to hand-picking, which must be carried on up and down the sharply graded mountainsides. The harvest season requires double the labor of everyday care. Like grape vineyards, coffee plantations have certain requirements—sufficient hot sun, but also a cool altitude; the best coffee is grown from two to three thousand feet above sea level.

Ordinarily coffee plantations are inaccessible to the tourist but not long ago one of these *fincas*, near Utuado, was converted into a charming guest house. A visit to Hacienda Roses includes a tour of its 700-acre plantation. A package deal—arranged through any San Juan tourist agency—includes overnight visit, transportation both ways, lunch, dinner, and room for $18.00.

Deep in this mountainous area, you may suddenly find yourself sharing my feeling that history is inaccurate—the Indians were never exterminated. Here the faces are all markedly—frequently purely—Indian. It was in these remoter areas that they made their last stand.

Much evidence of the Indian civilization has been recovered in this region. The Utuado-Lares section was rich in marmol amulets with human figurine carvings. This brings me to the Indian cave or ceremonial grounds for which I searched.

It proved to be best reached by a separate trip from Arecibo to Lares. Take Route 129, a lovely drive, and at the junction turn right toward Lares on #111. Just before you reach the

144

town you will see a side road, #453, with a sign announcing "Entrada a la Cueva de la Pajita." The Indian word *pajita*, it appears, is difficult to translate, meaning anything from an eyelid to a flimsy curtain. In this instance, its meaning apparently indicates something like a stage curtain, for the cave is really a tunnel which looks like a Greek theater from the forefront. As it narrows toward the back, you can see trees

Stalactites in the cave at Lares, scene of Indian ceremonial dances.

framed in the exit. There are dark caves behind, but the *pajita* was where the Indians put on ceremonial dances, and today the custom is revived.

Despite a wooden dance floor and bar erected in one part, the natural beauty is undiminished. The roof sparkles as if studded with diamonds, but these are merely more or less evenly matched, tiny stalactites. Protruding at intervals from the floor of the cave, however, are five-foot stalagmites eroded into strange shapes resembling calcinated troglodytes. They are weirdly fascinating.

Although this *pajita* is privately owned, today it is under the supervision of the Institute of Culture. Previously, as the proprietor wryly admitted, souvenir hunters collected artifacts whose value he did not realize. The Institute reclaimed a few. At present .the owner and his son are trying to make a living from this playground of antiquity. It is commercially used for dances on week ends, but they would like to publicize its rare beauty and someday build a small hotel across the road—the site is tranquil and lovely. This is not to say that the owners do not love and respect their inheritance. They are very much pleased when visitors show a serious interest, and will gladly show you around. It takes little imagination to visualize the spot as it must have been when the Indians used it as a ceremonial ground.

The nearby town of Lares, by the way, has its own proud history. As far back as 1868, an insurrection was fomented here in a futile effort to gain independence from Spain. The town is picturesquely perched on a hill, a cool and delightful place for a quiet vacation. At present, however, the only accommodations are in the unpretentious but pleasant Hotel Quintana.

Along these roads at night there is only the cricket-like chorus of *coquis* to break the pervading silence, but these tree frogs— tiny, opalescent creatures—can be found all over the island, even including San Juan. Occasionally you may pass a *jíbaro* carrying his inevitable machete, but after dark he covers it with cloth as proof that he is an honest man. You may also see fires glowing on the mountainsides. Generally, these are smouldering mounds of brush covered with dampened earth to make charcoal.

146

Mountain family—father teaching son to play homemade guitar.

But should you be in the mountains during the first days of February, there will be glowing bonfires in celebration of the *Candelaria*, known in English as Candlemas. *The* night for them is February second, four weeks exactly after the Feast of the Three Kings. The *Candelaria* commemorates the purification of the Virgin Mary when, according to custom, she presented the Infant Jesus in the Temple. As far as I was able to ascertain, the building of bonfires throughout the countryside is distinctly Puerto Rican, its particular significance being due to the fact that the date coincides with the inauguration of the sugar harvest.

Religion, in any event, plays an integral part in the life of the mountaineers. Often the church is an impossibly long distance away, but *rosarios* are held in the homes, not only for the ill and recently deceased, but to ward off such impending tragedies as hurricanes. Candles remain lighted in the window, and for a period of five to nine days the neighbors join in prayer and chanting.

Closely associated, although not necessarily allied with religion, is the music. Homemade stringed instruments are common, accompanying songs recognizably derived from Arab dirges—a curious holdover in the New World of the Moorish influence in Spain. In addition to these, there is a distinctly Puerto Rican type of music which scholars declare lacks form, although they admit is sweet and plaintive. Worth listening to are the decimal singers, participants in contests wherein each composes his own words and music, playing and singing by ear.

In the hinterland, life continues almost unchanged from a generation or more ago. The government pursues its vast effort to improve conditions, but the difficulty of reaching these hill dwellers makes progress slow. Bit by bit, through the patience and encouragement of government workers, they are persuaded to join forces in such communal efforts as laying pipe up the sheer mountainsides to bring water within closer reach.

In planning a drive into the coffee region, it is inadvisable to take the availability of a *publico* for granted. Unless your Spanish is fluent, the obstacles may be overwhelming. It is difficult to make connections and often impossible to arrange a return trip, and you are likely to find yourself in a hamlet with no sleeping accommodations for visitors. The Victory Line, for instance, runs one *publico* per day to and from San Sebastian—but the one from San Juan leaves at three in the afternoon, and the one from San Sebastian goes at six in the morning. The Choferes Unidos also lists *publicos* to San Sebastian, as well as to Jayuya, Lares, Adjuntas, and elsewhere, but make sure of your return reservation before ever leaving San Juan.

In addition to the accommodations at Lares, there is a nineteen-room hotel at San Sebastian. Jayuya has two tiny, simple, and clean hotels. Adjuntas also has a small one. I know of none elsewhere.

Other parts of the island covered in this chapter are far more accessible, although they too, for various reasons, are off the beaten track. The east coast of the island of Puerto Rico, for example, is being developed in many respects, but at present the highway below Fajardo and on down the coast is badly in need of repair. Coming north from Guayama to Naguabo is a gorgeous but strenuous drive (on what in reality is a secondary road) through the mountains—with streams, boulders, and glimpses of the sea. But the towns are without attraction and the beaches negligible to nonexistent.

At the Playa de Naguabo this condition is reversed. Not only is there a nice beach, but yachts fill the harbor. A fishing village similar to Las Croabas, Naguabo is untouched by changing times and remains both unspoiled and inexpensive. Corsino's restaurant is superb.

You can reach Naguabo and its *playa* via Caguas as well as Fajardo, turning on Highway 30 and, at Juncos, proceeding on Route 31. Along this latter road, just west of the hamlet of Rio Blanco is a small guest house called Matricardi's, which offers the best value I've heard of anywhere. It is on the south side of the road at K. 10 (these kilometer markings are often used as designations). At the moment, it consists of only three cottages, but in the expectation of eventual enlargement, it already has a swimming pool. Señora Matricardi does the cooking. All meals included, the week-end charge for a *couple* is $25.00! And it is, of course, just ten kilometers from Naguabo.

Off Puerto Rico's east coast is Vieques.
Vieques is an island some twenty miles long, the eastern tip of which is restricted to the U.S. Marines. They use it seldom, and then only for landing maneuvers. The rest of the island, mainly agricultural, is hilly, and its south shore is indented with bays. Above the town is the fort, begun during the days of Isabella II but never finished. Until recently it served as the civil prison. Now it is being meticulously restored,

An attraction off the beaten track: spectacular limestone cliffs near Ciales, a small town south of Manati.

using wooden pegs, old timbers, even bricks made according to formula in the original kiln. From it there is a striking view of the outlying islands, including St. Thomas in clear perspective forty miles away.

For those less interested in grandeur than expense, there is a nice sixteen-room hotel in the town. Immaculate but thoroughly unpretentious, The Carmen has neither private baths nor hot water (nor, indeed, cold—for water at best or worst is tepid in this locality), but rooms rent for $3.00 single and $5.00 double. A drawback, recently rectified, was the impossibility of securing a decent meal. The hotel itself has no restaurant, and the only available one would have adorned no recommended list. Now, the Tropic Isle, opened by a nice continental named Hilton, provides good food at moderate prices.

Vieques is an attractive and distinctive island. Its inhabitants like to be referred to as Viequesans and even pretend not to be Puerto Ricans. It can be reached easily and cheaply by charter plane from Isla Grande airport, just across the bridge from old San Juan, or by the regular ferry service from Fajardo.

There are more small inexpensive inns and guest houses in Puerto Rico than is generally realized. Frequently the limited accommodations make advertising scarcely worth while; sometimes there is not even a sign to indicate a hostel's existence.

At Yauco, inland but near Guánica, is La Casa Roig, a Spanish colonial house built around a flowering patio, with eight rooms; meals are available if you wish. The cost of the rooms is $3.00 and $6.00, single and double respectively. It is an ideal place for families with children.

Hacienda Roses is a coffee plantation guest house between Utuado and Florida on Route 140 at Km. 30.7. It has seven rooms, and a feature of a visit here is a tour of the plantation, Indian caves, orchid garden, and nearby lakes. American Plan rates are $10.00 to $12.50 single, $20.00 to $25.00 double.

I have tried, to the best of my capabilities, to cover all sections of Puerto Rico, marking their outstanding features, but no book of this kind dares claim to be complete. Any one of the innumerable roads crisscrossing the island can take you on a voyage of discovery.

CHAPTER 16

Yachting, Fishing, and Other Sports

(Boats and Fishing—Other Aquatic Sports—Beaches—
Golf, Tennis, and Riding)

UNTIL quite lately Puerto Rico had but meager facilities for either yachtsmen or game fishermen. Today all that is changing, but the number of pleasure yachts for hire is still so limited that it is advisable to inquire well in advance. The recently opened marina off Las Croabas-Fajardo (half-mile ferry service to shore) promises to be well equipped for renting boats as well as for mooring those privately owned; the Intercontinental Hotel at Ponce has arranged exchange privileges for its guests at the Ponce Yacht Club.

On the other hand, facilities and conditions for just about every type of fishing are ideal. Puerto Rico is renowned for the deep-sea fishing off its coasts, but also offers bone-, shallow-water, and even lake (black bass) fishing. The very best deep-sea fishing is off the northern and eastern shores—that is, on the north out of San Juan and Arecibo (which however is less accessible in winter), Fajardo, Vieques, and on down the eastern coast as the various new projects are completed. On the south, the top port is Ponce, although La Parguera is almost equally good. On the west coast Mayagüez, facing the Mona Passage, boasts of virgin territory (true, also, of the southeast coast) and better climatic conditions. Advocates of the northern and eastern shores claim that the Mayagüez vicinity has swells, if less

153

stormy weather, and that it is a two- to three-hour run to the open sea, whereas it takes but an hour from San Juan and Las Croabas. Nevertheless, Mayagüez holds well-attended tournaments (light-tackle) in November and in January. Ponce, too, has several bill and light tackle tournaments.

The various categories of fish include:

1. Deep sea—blue and white marlin, Allison's and black fin tuna, sailfish, dolphin, wahoo, mackerel, barracuda, bonito, and kingfish.

2. Spinning, etc.—tarpon and snook.

3. Bottom fishing—snapper and permit.

4. Light tackle—bonefish.

There are more, but not being a fisherman myself, I have had to accept the listings from others. I do know that world records are being broken constantly, and that fishing contests are almost continuous, for Puerto Rico has all-year, all-around-the-island, and all types, of fishing..

The best people for specific information are:

Captain Art Wills, Box 1133, San Juan, who has charter

A haven for boats on Puerto Rico's eastern shore.

boats that rent for around $75.00 a day, including crew, tackle, bait, and gasoline, as well as outboard motors on a "drive-yourself" basis for something like $2.00 an hour, $6.00 a half-day, and $9.00 a full day. He can also inform you on conditions prevailing elsewhere throughout the island, with especial attention to Fajardo and the environs. His San Juan office and telephone number is listed in *Que Pasa,* or you can communicate with him through the travel bureau handling your arrangements.

Carlos Quiñones at La Parguera is extremely well-informed on that area, particularly in regard to bonefishing, light-tackle fishing and spear-fishing, which are popular along the south coast. Address him at Villa Parguera. A twin-engine cabin cruiser is available for $60.00 a day, other boats less. The price includes experienced guides, tackle, and bait. Rates are moderate, too, for light-tackle and spear-fishing with a guide, but bring your own equipment.

You can also address the Commodore of the Yacht Club at San Juan, the Ponce Yacht and Fishing Club, or the Club Náutico del Oueste at Mayagüez. The Club Náutico at Boca de Cangrejos, outside San Juan, is accessible only to small boats.

Around the entire perimeter of Puerto Rico are bays and harbors, but the above-mentioned locations are the best. Aguadilla is huge and open, Santa Isabel and Salinas are possible anchorages, and Boqueron can accept shallow-draft ships, but none of these offer facilities.

Spear-fishing, of course—I am tempted to make a pun—is a different kettle of you-know-what. Call it snorkeling or skin-diving, there are few who don't want a try at it. Bill and Shirley Brown of San Juan provide an ideal short course. They make daily trips—leaving the capital at 9:30 and returning around 5:30—with parties of six to the Icacos group, those *cayos* or keys off Las Croabas, furnishing equipment and instruction and guaranteeing identification of the underwater life, at the modest fee of $15.00 apiece without lunch, but arrangements can be made with the fine restaurant at La Rada to fulfill that need.

Another service out of Las Croabas makes no pretext of

being a school, but simply takes you for a cruise where you can swim, snorkel or laze on deck or on an offshore island, as the spirit moves you. You set sail from Las Croabas in the morning in a twenty-nine-foot sloop, equipped with cabin, ice-chest, and cockpit for six, returning about sunset. The charge is $35.00 for six people for the day, not including lunch and beverages, although you will find that they are available from a waterfront restaurant in Las Croabas. For reservations contact Hal Underhill at 724-2604 or 722-7215 in San Juan.

Don's Restaurant (very good, and reasonable for seafood, by the way) in Caparra Heights, close to the center of San Juan, specializes in aquatic services—renting aqualungs, filling and repairing your own, and renting underwater cameras. Moreover, he's a nice person to whom you can bring any allied problem. His address is P.O. Box 10481, San Juan, and his phone number is 782-0072.

Another aquatic sport of San Juan is water-skiing. For some time this sport has been featured at La Rada, which fronts on a lagoon.

If you are in Puerto Rico for any length of time, you will almost certainly take up skin-diving and end up by buying your own outfit. Carry it with you whenever you travel, just like your bathing suit. If you should be heading for a beach without conveniences, wear the suit under an easily removable shirt and skirt. (A man's trunks present no problem.) Similarly, when motoring, wear shorts for long hot drives; during the heat of the day, in the privacy of the car, shorts are certainly more comfortable, and a loose skirt will conceal them when you step out.

Here is a partial list of good public beaches:
San Juan:
Some sea-front hotels, notably the Escambron, the Intercontinental, and Coral Beach at Isla Verde, accept transients at a daily charge. In San Juan, besides, are long stretches of shore fronting private residences and apartments, with sand and open-sea bathing free to all comers. Many guest houses are within a block or two of them. In addition, there is a cove on the island of old San Juan, next door to the Reserve

156

Officers Club off Avenida Muñoz Rivera and opposite the downtown end of the park, which is somewhat unprotected but has sand and good surf bathing. In the other direction, farther out at Ocean Park on Route 37 going to Boca de Cangrejos, is an extraordinarily nice beach, with a refreshment bar and terrace across the road. It is at the foot of Calle Tapia and can be reached by the Loíza bus if you have no car; ask to be let off at the Tapia stop, which leaves you a walk of approximately three streets to the sea.

NORTH SHORE:

Luquillo—best of all. Full facilities.

Cerro Gordo—natural breakwater of rocks; all conveniences.

Vega Baja—even more sheltered than Cerro Gordo; charming, but only palm-thatched huts for dressing rooms. Has luncheon place, however.

Mar Chiquita—with a few householders on the hill to share it. Pretty, lonely, somewhat protected bay.

El Guajataca—facilities, restaurant on beach. Nice; but some surf.

WEST COAST:

Bay of Bramadero-a few miles south and adjoining Mayagüez. Long stretch of fine beach; simple but adequate shacks for changing. *Cantinas* on beach, restaurants nearby on road.

Boqueron—good beach, no facilities. Excellent restaurants in village.

SOUTH COAST:

Guánica—there are several beaches in the vicinity, but Caña Gorda, on the outer bay, is by far the most beautiful. This beach has full facilities.

EAST COAST:

Playa de Naguabo—beach club, narrow strip of sand. Otherwise no recommendations at present, except the island of Vieques and the keys off Las Croabas.

Every big hotel has tennis courts, and both the Caribe Hilton and Dorado Beach hold international tournaments. In San Juan —or rather, Rio Piedras—there are public courts.

The golf course at Dorado Beach designed by Robert Trent Jones is so famous as scarcely to need mentioning. This is

157

twenty miles from San Juan, but the Berwind Country Club near El Commandante race track has an eighteen-hole course. Even nearer at hand is El Morro, officially known as Fort Brooke, which has nine holes and is open to visitors. Ramey Air Force Base has an eighteen-hole course also open to the public. On the Caribbean side, the Ponce Golf Club offers a good nine-hole course. The Arecibo Country Club is planning to build a course soon. Meanwhile, tourists are welcome to use their fresh-water swimming pool, tennis courts, and very excellent restaurant.

Most mountain resorts have horses to ride, notably Treasure Island, Barranquitas, and Rosario Mountain Resort near Mayagüez.

From the middle of December to the middle of February is the season for shooting waterfowl. Those interested should get in touch with the Department of Agriculture and Commerce, 652 Avenida Hipódromo, Santurce; the Department of Tourism at 666 Fifth Avenue, New York, or its other office at Dupont Plaza Center, Miami, Florida.

San Juan has two bowling alleys. Fencers can pursue their hobby at the Escambron Beach Club. For bridge and chess—if these are considered sports—there are clubs which visitors may join on a transient basis. Even Ponce has a chess club.

Life in Puerto Rico is certainly not somnolent. One can go sight-seeing, take in the amusements, participate in the sports, or—biggest luxury of all, perhaps—just enjoy laziness. The choice of activity is up to the individual, but surely everyone will agree that the range is wide.

SECTION II

The Virgin Islands

CHAPTER 1

Introduction to Our Virgin Islands

THE Virgin Islands snuggle close to Puerto Rico, but they are as unlike her as children of different families. Yet the flight from San Juan to either St. Thomas or St. Croix is more over land than sea. It is as if the ocean, like a sharp knife, had sliced into the earth at short intervals. One feels that somewhere, deep beneath the sea, these contiguous islands of volcanic origin must be joined together in a fair-sized continent. The plane flies low, skimming over one green isle after another, among them Culebra, lying about halfway across to St. Thomas, and below her, athwart the course to St. Croix, Vieques—both part and parcel of the Commonwealth of Puerto Rico.

It is an amazing sensation, winging across these little mounds of green, then abruptly descending on St. Thomas or St. Croix. Suddenly there is a different look, a different feel, which is one of the hoped-for ingredients in travel.

All plane flights and ships direct their course first to San Juan, except for Pan American's once-a-week non-stop jet flight from New York to St. Croix. Pan American also has a once-a-week jet flight from Miami. The mainstay of both St. Thomas and St. Croix, however, is the shuttle service run by Caribair,

159

and, in the case of St. Thomas—the smaller of the two islands but the bigger tourist resort—it is the only airline. Alcoa, the primary regular cargo-passenger line, makes runs every ten days to St. Thomas and St. Croix, but the first stop of course is San Juan.

Among the few remaining American "possessions," the Virgin Islands are the most easterly outpost of the U.S.A. The term generally is applied to three—St. Thomas, St. Croix, and the tiny, underpopulated St. John. In reality, there are over a hundred islands (or so they say, but it is uncertain if they have ever been properly counted), of which about fifty are American, the remainder being under the British flag. Some are claimed both by England and the United States! In any case, except for the aforesaid three islands, they are tiny and mainly uninhabited; the British ones, without exception, are poor and primitive.

Their much-joked-of name is attributable to a decidedly humorless Christopher Columbus who, on his second voyage in 1493, before reaching Puerto Rico, made a rather cursory survey and piously named them after St. Ursula and her 11,000 martyred virgins. He himself was apparently confused by the quantity of isles and islets and quite definitely did not set foot on all of them.

Prior to this, the quiet Arawaks had been living on them, but by 1493 the ferocious Caribs from the south had pushed their way so far along that the poor Arawak was all but exterminated. That Columbus and his fleet did not linger long is understandable, since they were immediately faced with evidence of an unpleasant Carib custom known to us as cannibalism, a distortion of the Spanish word *caríbal*, or Carib-habit. Some pleasanter discoveries, however, were the practical Indian hammock, which the white man quickly adopted for himself; tobacco—possibly an unfortunate find; many tropical fruits and vegetables, and exotic herbs and spices which greatly enriched the culinary enterprises of Europe.

Though the Virgin Islands share with Puerto Rico the distinction of being discovered by Columbus quite a few years before the white man encountered the continent of America, their history is singularly divergent. Spaniards uninterruptedly occupied Puerto Rico, but the Virgin Islands saw the arrival of numerous nationalities, and—especially in the case of St. Croix—the succession of conquerors resembles a comic opera. To some extent, each island has its unique history, but by the eighteenth century St. Thomas, St. Croix, and St. John were all united under the Danish flag, where they remained until purchased outright by the United States as military outposts in 1917, simultaneous with her entry into World War I.

That the native tongue is English is one of the first surprises. Despite their long occupation, the Danes never forced their language upon the people. On the contrary, they discouraged the slaves from learning it. Moreover, St. Thomas was an international harbor with a medley of languages where first Dutch, then English, was paramount. The plantation managers of the other two islands were very often Scots. At any rate, the English language took the lead, and if the melodic tone and turn of phrase is pleasantly alien, the speech is recognizably our own.

Throughout the Caribbean, as a result of the very active slave trade, there is an admixture of African blood. In Puerto Rico, combined with Indian and Spanish strains, it has evolved into a type of its own. But in the Virgin Islands the heritage is amazingly unadulterated. Intermarriage existed and is recognized today, but with the exception of half a dozen old merchant families still remaining and the present influx of tourists and new settlers, the society is Negro. Statistics give the following apportionment: approximately 70 per cent pure Negro, over 20 per cent mixed blood, and less than 10 per cent white. The Indians were extirpated, and the native Virgin Islander is, in most cases, the descendant of slaves. The slave-owners were usually absentee landlords, but the overseers kept the slaves in strictest segregation. As elsewhere, of course, there were some free colored, usually indicative of a mulatto heritage.

Since the capital of St. Thomas was the most important slave market in the whole Caribbean area, and the local merchant and plantation-owner naturally had first choice of the auction block, the Virgin Islander can claim with some reason that his forefathers were the most distinguished of the captured—tribal chieftains and those of outstanding intelligence, as well as the best physical specimens.

The Virgin Islander is a quietly proud man, and being in the majority and not subject to the indignities of the continental Negro, he lacks racial bias. Indeed, one charming elderly gentleman confided to me that colored visitors from the States frequently distressed them with talk of racial problems. *"Here,"* he said, *"we have none."* This commendable state of affairs has not been mentioned in anything I have read on the Virgin Islands, but it is quite as significant as their natural beauty and Danish architecture. So important does it seem to me that I believe it is best explained in terms of personal experience.

It happens that I had met only a few Negroes on a social basis, and although I like to think myself devoid of racial prejudice, I found little common ground with those I had encountered. Secretly I had felt self-conscious, as if I must prove my sympathy for them. In the Virgin Islands this subconscious reaction was nonexistent.

Prior to my visit I had been told that the population was "mainly colored." But I was still not prepared for the impact of a society composed of an entirely different race. It had not occurred to me that this referred to all social stratas, and that the most cultivated group I would meet would be men and women of color. I went open-minded, but knowing no one. By the time I left, I had formed several cherished friendships. I met a number of white residents, but for the highlights of my stay I am indebted to the true Virgin Islander, with his kindness and courtesy. What I most appreciated was that they made no distinction about me, or the shade of my skin. We met on the common ground of mutual interests. They assisted me in the garnering of facts, lent me rare and precious books for historical research—greatest of all, they opened their homes to me and accepted me into their midst.

Theirs is a life completely lacking in racial hostility. You will get to know the Virgin Islanders and enjoy them much more if you accept their unbiased attitude. It was an atmosphere that I had never before breathed, one which gave me confidence in the brotherhood of man.

CHAPTER 2

Gay St. Thomas

(A Practical Guide to Hotels, Restaurants, and Shopping)

A BROWN promontory looms in view, and minutes later the plane lands in a sparsely vegetated area. This is a momentary shock to anyone coming from lush Puerto Rico, but those brown hilltops are symbolic of St. Thomas, which receives practically no rainfall.

Here is a land with humidity so low as to be almost non-existent, a perfect haven for sufferers of sinusitis, asthma, and other respiratory miseries. It has just about a perfect climate. Moreover, those outlying mounds are almost instantly forgotten, for although the air is practically pollen-free, there *are* trees and there *are* flowers—all the tropical foliage and paradisiac colors which make the Caribbean so enchanting. Above all, you are aware of the exceptionally brilliant coloration of the sea against the dead-white coral sand of the beaches.

During the short drive from the airport near the extremity of the island to the capital and only city, Charlotte-Amalie (the A's are soft and the accent is Ah-mahl'-yah), hibiscus, bougainvillea, poinsettias, and other flowers, flamboyant, golden shower, the handsome tamarind, and mahogany trees appear. Huge-leaved, graceful sea grapes shelter the beaches instead of the anticipated palms; strangely, only the small tyre palm is indigenous to the Virgin Islands.

On that first drive you may be puzzled by what look like up-ended cement tennis courts pressed into the hillsides. These are really rain catchments feeding underground reservoirs, for water is precious here. This lack of water to some degree accounts for the high cost of living, equivalent to that of any large continental city, for although the newly-opened plant for the conversion of salt water to fresh has greatly eased the situation, additional water must still be imported.

Taxis are plentiful on this island where the motor car is the sole means of conveyance, either standard five-passenger models or station wagons performing a semi-jitney service. The charge is based on zones, and theoretically the price schedule is affixed inside the car. Actually, it is often missing, and it is well to consult the rate listings in *St. Thomas This Week* and *Here's How,* both give-aways. No tip is expected, but the charge is per passenger. For instance, from the air terminal to Charlotte-Amalie is $.60, but a couple must pay $1.10—a slight reduction for the second passenger. On the other hand, if you are alone and decide to ride downtown, say, from the Virgin Isles Hilton or Yacht Haven, you may find yourself in a station wagon with several other hotel guests, and although you will be dropped at your specified destination, there will be no discount for your having shared the car. One further item: a round trip is only one and a half times the one-way fare.

Offshore view from the Virgin Isles Hilton on St. Thomas. The rectangular object on the foreground hill is a water reservoir.

Drive-yourself cars here, as in Puerto Rico, are naturally the most convenient means of locomotion. Three agencies—Hertz, Tropical Motors, and Maguire—supply them at just under $10.00 a day, everything included. (This means *gas* as well as insurance.) Vying in popularity with the small European car is the Jeep Gala. This specialty of the island has foam rubber cushions and a canvas top trimmed with a fringe; it comes in such unconventional colors as shocking pink, aqua, and sky blue.

One lone bus line is in operation, going as far as Yacht Haven on the east side of town to beyond the golf course near the airport on the other (cost is ten cents; bus runs at quarter-hour intervals).

Be sure to wait for the bus on the left-hand side of the road and when driving your own car, keep the left-hand flow of traffic in mind. The Virgin Islands are the unique bit of American soil where this custom prevails. Presumably it dates back to the days under Danish rule. After the American flag was hoisted, a futile attempt was made to reverse the procedure.

St. Thomas makes no pretense of being an inexpensive vacation ground, but costs nevertheless vary enormously according to one's demands and requirements. At such de luxe hotels as the Virgin Isles Hilton and Bluebeard's Castle, you should count on rates ranging from $25.00 to $35.00 single, $40.00 to $55.00 double MAP (Modified American Plan) in season; rates are slashed as much as a half between May first and December first. Smaller places like Smith's Fancy, Harbor View, Trade Winds, and the Island Beachcomber are about a third less, in and out of season. The Island Beachcomber, Morningstar Beach Club, and Mafolie Apartment Hotel, among others, also have efficiency apartments at reasonable daily rates.

Conveniently located in the center of town are several small hotels and guest houses where one can find good accommodations with year-round prices of approximately $8.00 to $15.00 including breakfast, depending on single or double occupancy; by no means all rooms have private baths. A complete and up-to-date listing can be secured from the Virgin Islands Tourist Office, 16 West 49th Street, New York City.

Few hotels are on the water front, and fewer still have pools, but this is no deterrent to enjoying good swimming and skin diving. Many of the hotels are built up the steep hills which form the topography of St. Thomas, having sacrificed sea front for gorgeous panoramas.

Some of them own, or have arrangements at, beaches, and supply transportation to these for their guests. Several beach clubs—notably Water Isle, Morningstar, and Sapphire Bay—welcome transient members at a modest fee. Russell Tours on the water front runs a jitney service to the latter at the low price of 50¢ each way. For further information on beaches see Chapter 6.

St. Thomas is rich in restaurants of every description. Special mention should be made of the Petite Pump Room and the Left Bank; the latter is a splendid Haitian restaurant. Hagan's House has a charming café terrace on the waterfront; Sebastian's, nearby, is a long-time favorite. Several restaurants are particular gathering spots on specified nights during the week. A communal spirit pervades them, and local café society joins the visitors at the designated place. For instance, The Gate serves a spaghetti supper on Sunday evenings; Galleon House has curried dinners on Tuesdays; Caribbean Hotel and Beach Club has barbecues on Tuesdays, Thursdays and Saturdays.

Since the dates and popular meeting places are more than likely to change, it is wise to check with the local publications. *St. Thomas This Week,* the size of a high-school newspaper, is helpful and up-to-date. The older *Here's How,* a semi-annual publication also offered *gratis,* is an invaluable aid, with fuller information on many things. In addition, there is *Caribbean Vacationlands,* that very useful general guide to the entire Caribbean.

These published guides are equally helpful as to places of entertainment. As of this writing, the Black Patch and the Fallen Angel are two of the night clubs, but hotels and restaurants, although not specifically night clubs, also offer entertainment. There is dancing at the Bamboushay, a steel band every night except Tuesday at The Gate, nightly dancing at Bluebeard's Castle, and soft music at Sebastian's. Thursday nights are the time to watch, of all things, tortoise races at the Virgin Isles Hilton.

There is definitely no dearth of entertainment or restaurants, and the hotels which do serve meals also accommodate transients. On the whole the cooking is good, though not particularly gourmet. American cuisine prevails. St. Thomas offers few Virgin Islands dishes, and these are to be found only in poor, strictly native establishments.

To some extent, recommended spots for luncheon are entirely different from the evening places of rendezvous. Unquestionably one of the pleasantest light-luncheon spots is the Coffee House, where sandwiches and salads predominate. Go through the small indoor restaurant to the long, narrow outdoor terrace, which has tables under cover from the hot noonday sun.

The Grand Gallery, in, of course, the Grand Hotel diagonally across from the post office, is a lovely, cool balcony facing toward the water front. It offers both snacks and luncheons ranging from $.75 to double that amount. It is also where the habitués, café society, or what you will, meet from noon onward at reserved table 19 for a "bullshot." A bullshot is vodka and beef bouillon, said to be remarkably appetizing and fortifying.

In a different category is the $2.50 smorgasbord at the magnificently situated Bluebeard's Castle. The buffet choice is excellent and copious, and more than one person has left there so replete that a mere sandwich suffices until the next day.

Looking down on the harbor of Charlotte-Amalie is especially fascinating because the many islands within it make the geographical layout as difficult to solve as a Chinese puzzle. One of these islets—Hassel's Island—has a lovely old inn known as Goodheart's, reached by a motorboat supplied by the restaurant. Get this in front of Sebastian's. Goodheart's is understandably popular, but the seating capacity is circumscribed and one should telephone in advance for reservations. If the motorboat is not already against the pier, it will be shortly.

Beyond Hassel's Island is Water Isle, which, small though it is, happens to be the fourth largest of the Virgin Islands. On it is a lovely hotel with cottages, a great favorite with people seeking a tranquil resort, but it is also a delightful place to spend a day. Water Isle has a launch at the submarine base that leaves almost every hour, returning on the alternate half-hours. The all-inclusive charge for the boat and bus trip to Water Isle beach, dressing room, lunch, and use of snorkeling

*View from Fort Christian, looking down on the water front
of Charlotte-Amalie.*

equipment or small boats is a modest $3.50. It is well to tele-
phone in advance for reservations.

Telephoning, by the way, is something you should ask the
hotel or a native St. Thomian to carry out for you. The procedure, as I experienced it, is to ask for the person rather than
the number. The operator gives you a running account, similar
to the old village service, of your party's door-to-door progress
through town until, possibly a half-hour later, you surprisingly
find your connection. It may turn out to be in a shop or a
restaurant, whereas you had started on the assumption of calling the home address. Many people somehow never achieve
listing in the telephone book—a situation the St. Thomian
regards as normal and of no consequence. This system has its
compensations, the greatest of which is that there is no charge
for calls. Evidently phone rentals are among the least expensive
of necessities.

Another recommended luncheon spot is Mountain Top
Hotel, which has a view on a clear day—that is to say, not
hazy—of countless islands. The Mountain Top specialty to
precede the meal is a much-publicized banana daiquiri. It is
presumably an unwritten law that every hostelry have its distinctive drink. Smith's Fancy goes in for a pineapple daiquiri,

the Hotel 1829 for Planter's Punch, the Grand Gallery and The Gate for bullshots, and the Water Isle fittingly for water islanders. Favorites there are bound to be, but all of them are an invitation to experiment.

Summer clothes and summer clothes only are called for here, with a light wrap for emergencies. Over a five-year period the registered extremes of temperature were a low of 63 degrees and a high of 91, with a year-round average of 78.

Shorts are acceptable attire—with reservations. In the streets of Charlotte-Amalie a woman in shorts—even Bermudas—is subject to passing comments from the Virgin Islands equivalent of the drugstore cowboy. Men, on the other hand, are deemed correctly dressed in shorts no matter where or at what hour. Many dinner and night spots require a tie and jacket, but white shorts and long socks predominate below the male waistline also after dark, with a cummerbund sometimes added for flair.

As in Puerto Rico, during the Season there is more of a trend toward evening dress, but even then the afore-mentioned masculine attire and a low-cut cocktail gown for women will usually pass muster.

Light materials and sleeveless dresses are all-round favorites. St. Thomas promotes its own line of fashions, easily and quickly acquired, with the accent on exotic prints and trimmings, perhaps better suited to this environment than transplanted elsewhere.

In the days of colonization, buccaneers, and the slave trade, the fine deep harbor of Charlotte-Amalie made it the most bustling port of the entire Caribbean. Here pirates came to trade or sell their loot, a term today applied by the shops to their honestly acquired wares. The word is believed to be derived from the Danish *lods*, meaning pilot, the person who after all was responsible for the safe arrival of the goods. Some of the prices are so ridiculously low compared to those in the States that you are inclined to feel your purchases *are* loot.

Even a casual bit of window-shopping is enough to turn the worst miser into a spendthrift. Visitors should plan in advance to put aside a certain sum simply for the joy of spending. The concentrated displays (the shopping district is fairly compact) represent a kind of enticing global cut-rate. There are beautiful and rare bargains from Siam, India, and Hongkong, and practically every country in Europe, for Charlotte-Amalie not only was, but continues to be, a free port. This was a stipulation of the Danes when they sold the islands to the United States. In actuality, it means there is an over-all 6 per cent duty; things cost slightly higher than in their port of origin, but a great deal less than in any other region under the American flag.

A misconception fostered by the St. Thomians is that the free-port status applies only to their island. This is categorically untrue. A strong feeling of rivalry persists between St. Thomas and St. Croix, but the same shops, the same wares, and the same prices prevail on both. Therefore it is more convenient, and less weighty and costly, to do your shopping at whichever is your second port of call, provided you are visiting both islands. Misinformed, I lugged my quota of liquor to St. Croix and paid the airline for excess poundage, only to discover the same choice and price list in Christiansted. I even found cigarettes there ten cents cheaper a carton, but you can shop around for reductions on either island. It is said, for example,

Rooftops rise in tiers in Charlotte-Amalie.

that liquor is less costly in Frenchtown, on the outskirts of Charlotte-Amalie, but make sure that the package is prepared for long-distance haulage.

Because of the free-port conditions, returning citizens are required to fill in a customs declaration. Should you be returning to San Juan, the formalities will be taken care of there rather than at the continental port of entry, and since the inter-island planes have a small passenger load, will be accomplished with dispatch.

The Virgin Islands are the only place in the world where the U. S. Government permits a $200 exemption. Amazingly, you need only journey over for the day from San Juan and this exemption is allowed. Moreover, if you have been on a Caribbean cruise you are still allowed the $100 extra quota for purchases here, plus any unused portion of the normal $100 allowance, so that, if you spend $75.00, for example, in the foreign islands, you may still make purchases free of duty up to $125. Federal law also allows you to receive a gift by mail up to $10.00 in value per day, which is handy if you are over your quota or prefer paying postage to excess weight in luggage.

One gallon, or five standard-sized bottles of liquor, is duty free. With Scotch costing $2.50, liqueurs averaging $3.00 and $3.50, and the excellent native rum $1.00, paying duty on an excess may be worth consideration. The stores will give you full' information on duty and the regulations pertaining in various states.

Cigarettes, on the other hand, may be purchased without restriction, provided they are not for resale. Moreover, arrangements are customarily made for staggered shipments up to a one-year deadline. This is so astonishing that one wonders if or when that law will be amended, since the standard cost of non-filters is a mere $1.25, filters $1.50, the carton—a price, to the best of my knowledge, unobtainable in any of the fifty states or Puerto Rico.

A favorite saying in the Virgin Islands is that "necessities are expensive, luxuries cheap," the latter referring to the bargains in the stores and the former to the importation of food, water, and building materials. The cost of land has risen sharply with the boom of popularity, but the cost of building is even higher compared with Stateside standards.

In spite of the discount, many of the articles in the shops remain expensive. That is to say, Danish and English china, Swedish and French crystal, Georg Jensen silver, Swiss watches, and German cameras are all remarkable, but circumscribed, buys unless you have an unlimited expense account; however, small items such as souvenirs, knickknacks, and inexpensive gifts are harder to come across. They are there, nonetheless, and *Here's How* has a very helpful listing of purchases under $5.00 —articles which may be overlooked among the costlier displays. The perfume bottle, though, is as much in evidence along the shopping thoroughfare as the liquor bottle, and the famous French brands are as staggering bargains as the other alcoholic concoctions. Mahogany, mostly from Haiti, provides handsome salad forks, spoons, bowls, and platters at reasonable prices.

In planning your shopping outing, bear in mind that the stores are closed not only on Sundays but on Thursday afternoons. They do keep open all day Saturday.

Mail home the heavier purchases, provided they are under $10.00 in value, and fit the others into your customs' allowance. Goods of Virgin Islands origin, with the exception of rum, are not subject to duty, but about the only native craft is weaving straw. Some of the baskets are pretty, and the high-crowned Virgin Island hat—useful on the beach—becomes an amusing souvenir back home. Be prepared, in any case, to commit a few extravagances, for the shops are laden with temptations.

CHAPTER 3

St. Thomas – Yesterday and Today

(History and Government)

LETTERS to residents usually carry the bare inscription "St. Thomas, V.I.," for Charlotte-Amalie, the capital, has the only post office on the island. Mail delivery is carried out with the same direct simplicity as telephone calls. Everybody knows everybody and where he or she can be found—so why bother with a street address any more than a telephone number?

St. Thomas is a tiny island, a mere twelve miles in length and three miles across at its widest point. Although it does not approach the size of St. Croix, it has a greater density of population. The last (unofficial) census estimated that about 15,000 people are permanent residents, four-fifths of whom live within the boundaries of Charlotte-Amalie. With the addition, besides, of a floating population of a couple of thousand, the island is not exactly sparsely settled.

The figures—impossible to check—may have been similar in the late eighteenth and early nineteenth centuries when St. Thomas or, if you prefer, Charlotte-Amalie was the richest and most active commercial center in the Western Hemisphere. The old city remains so essentially intact that even the least imaginative can visualize that earlier heyday.

At that period the town, which is baptized Charlotte-Amalie in honor of a Danish queen, was generally referred to as "Tappus," or "Taphouse," a most descriptive name. Because it was the trading post of buccaneers and the world's largest slave market, it was a tough seaport in those days. Seafaring New Englanders sailed here with their wares, exchanging them for rum, of which they were inordinately fond, and the Spanish, French, Dutch, and English who had colonized most of the

Caribbean were, even when not on speaking terms, at least able to secure from one another the goods they lacked. Besides, the fine deep harbor was perfectly suited to servicing ships on the long run to or from Europe. It was a free port in every sense of the word, and the warehouses extending along both sides of the main street as well as along the water front, despite conversion, are so well preserved as to be recognizable monuments of the thriving merchants.

A little farther back on the steep streets the beautiful homes of the well-to-do still stand. There were some sugar plantations on St. Thomas, but not as many as on St. John and St. Croix, and the aristocracy was chiefly one of new-rich shipowners, wholesalers, agents, and foreign consuls. Even bookkeepers and clerks were so highly esteemed that their position as a favored class persists today.

Along the wharves and in the streets was a babel of tongues in which the merchants, of necessity, were well versed. Their fabulously decorated homes presented an international aspect, with Oriental tapestries and rugs, Danish crystal, dishes of Spanish gold and silver, various types of European chandeliers, and hand-carved native mahogany furniture. On the tables were vintage wines and liqueurs to accompany the exotically spiced dishes served by a retinue of slaves. For the upper classes it was a magnificent life, gay and carefree, inflationary but without a worry about collapse. Prices were so exorbitant that doctors charged $100 for a visit. Alexander Hamilton, a seventeen-year-old boy on his way to the States, reported, "Gold moved through the streets in wheelbarrows!"

St. Thomas was a Danish possession and, except for a brief interlude of English occupation, knew no other flag until sold to the United States. Though Columbus gave it its biblical name, he did not land there. During the sixteenth century when all Europe seemed bent on securing possessions in the New World, tiny St. Thomas continued to pass unnoticed, except for sporadic settlers. Entirely mountainous and without resources, it did not appear a tempting prize. Even the Caribs did not settle there permanently.

Not until the middle of the next century did the island receive any attention. An unsubstantiated story is that the Dutch laid claim to it in 1657, but in 1665, when the Danes

Looking up a side street in Charlotte-Amalie. Houses appear to be piled on the steep hillsides.

decided to enter the race for New World colonies, they established a foothold on St. Thomas without so much as token opposition. It seems likely that Dutch settlers had staked individual claims rather than made any concerted attempt at nationalization. Certainly many Dutch did live on the island and continued to throughout those days of prosperity. They were so numerous, in fact, that the Dutch tongue actually superseded Danish among the inhabitants, even though in commerce England soon gained the ascendency.

The Danes quickly put up forts, installed a garrison, and chartered the island to the Danish West India Company, which two years later began the profitable importation of slaves. The top officials were Danish, but the various business enterprises were conducted by other nationalities. It was almost a hundred years before the Crown bought all three islands—St. Thomas, St. John, and St. Croix—and took outright possession.

Throughout the seventeenth century the various sovereignties jockeyed for positions in the West Indies. Europe's constant state of war was reflected in the taking and retaking of many of the islands. The sinking of the Spanish Armada did not end hostilities between England and Spain, and soon the English were also fighting the Dutch. Later, in an about-face, they became allies against France. When the French Revolution exploded like a bomb over Europe, the Dutch found themselves on the side of France. But all three powers were ever ready to unite in their enmity against Spain.

The Danes with their minor but, as it proved, profitable possessions managed to stay more or less outside the conflicts. In fact, the Danish West Indies—St. Thomas in particular— offered a haven to whoever was being harried at the moment. Above all, the Danes were religiously tolerant, though being Protestants, they were somewhat wary of Catholics. French Huguenots fled from the islands belonging to the motherland, Spanish (or Dutch) Jews escaped from British conquests, and *marraños*—those of the Jewish race who embraced the Catholic faith during the Inquisition—uneasy under Spanish rule, sought asylum. Regardless of religion or race, other groups flocked to St. Thomas simply because the constant wars had cut off their means of support. St. Thomas shone as a land of opportunity.

During the Napoleonic Wars, England at last turned her attention to the Danish islands, blockading St. Thomas and, in 1801, briefly occupying it and the two sister isles, but she returned them to Denmark before the next year passed. Again, in 1807, the English retook the strategic harbor of Charlotte-Amalie, returning it to Denmark finally in the spring of 1815.

Denmark was not only late in entering the slave trade—in fact, was the last country to do so—but was among the first to end it, following the example of the Americans, who ceased their importation in 1808. Actually the British occupations had caused a natural cessation of a once profitable market, but the plantations already owned hordes of slaves and by the normal course of propagation were assured of free labor for generations. The great revolt of 1848 achieved freedom for slaves through-out the Danish possessions, spelling, as in our South, the economic decline of the islands.

However, quite some years before this—on March 3, 1823, to be precise—a steamship flying the Stars and Stripes put into

176

the port of Charlotte-Amalie, an event forecasting the end of her maritime prestige, for with the use of coal her importance as a supply center was doomed.

When we bought the islands for what worked out to an approximate $285 an acre, Herbert Hoover, then Secretary of Commerce, remarked that we had obtained "an effective poor-house." A very few years later when the Prohibition Amendment became law, we condemned the Virgin Islanders to an even worse fate, for the only paying industry they had left at that time was the distillation of rum.

A forgotten outpost for many years, today the Virgin Islands, like Puerto Rico, are booming. Unlike Puerto Rico, they remain a U.S. possession and, despite a few irritations, would not want it otherwise. Both for the prosperous tourist business and the steady sale of rum, they are dependent upon us and glad to be under the U.S. flag. In the present era of de-colonization their chief protest is that they live under an appointed governor.

In 1946 President Truman appointed Judge William Hastie to that position. Judge Hastie is able, affable, and well-liked, married, moreover, to a Virgin Islander, but Truman's good intention backfired somewhat. Judge Hastie is colored, and the sensitive Virgin Islanders felt his appointment was a political maneuver which put unnecessary emphasis on their racial derivation. The present governor, Ralph Paiewonsky, as well as his immediate predecessor, are members of well-known white island families. Having a native-born governor matters far more to the Virgin Islanders than mere racial extraction, and they are delighted that nowadays one of their own represents them. They have, besides, local self-government. Their only remaining regret is that they have no voice in national affairs.

CHAPTER 4

Touring Charlotte-Amalie

(History, Buildings—Jewish Colony—The Impressionist
Painter, Pissarro—Carnival)

SURELY every one of us as children dreamed of being transported on a carpet, like the fabulous hero in the *Thousand and One Nights*, to a far-off, fascinating land. As grown-ups, we discarded the idea as manifestly impossible, but the short plane hop from Puerto Rico to the Virgin Islands is reminiscent of that bit of fictional magic. Whether the first stop is St. Thomas or St. Croix—and the two islands are dissimilar in many aspects —the tourist finds himself transplanted into another country. The scenery is different from Puerto Rico's, the people and the language are different. And the stage setting—that is, the architecture—is as far removed as the countries of Denmark and Spain are from each other. In a sense it is like crossing a frontier where the passport formalities have been dispensed with— and a very relaxing sensation that is, too.

The visitor here suddenly finds himself surrounded by the charming, unadulterated beauty of a Danish colonial town. Moreover, Charlotte-Amalie is so compact, and its appearance so little changed from the old days, that he has the feeling of being transported in time to its earlier era of prosperity.

Kronprinsens Gade, which is the water front, and Droningens Gade, the main street, are lined with warehouses. They are beautiful buildings, not what the word "warehouse" usually conjures up in the mind, with lovely arched interiors, stone walls three feet thick, and massive mahogany doors fastened by heavy black iron bars. Mostly, these doors are hooked open, and the old warehouses are used for every purpose—banks, restaurants, apothecaries (a designation still in use here), and, of course, stores. Beretta Center, once a beehive of small warehouses, is a showplace today. As you enter off the main street, several flagstone walks lead to the small shops, mainly of artisans and fine craftsmen, and also to the Virgin Islands Museum.

This two-room exhibit is honest and unpretentious. For early Indian history the one at Christiansted on St. Croix is superior, but such displays as old coins marked "20 francs 4 Daler," dated 1879, or "20 cents Dansk," minted in 1904, are interesting. Back in 1849 the Danish West Indies adopted our monetary system, but for reasons of trade the money often bore the equivalent in French francs. One of as late as 1907 stipulates "2 francs 40 cents." This museum also has books under glass with early accounts of the slavery on the islands. Upon request, you are permitted to look at these more closely. Of the most general interest, however, are the examples of colonial furniture, fine carving, and cabinet work of native mahogany, which are similar in design to our colonial pieces and quite as fine.

The old warehouse doors are usually gaily painted, which in no way detracts from their original beauty. In fact, the bright colors are a welcome touch there just as they are on numerous buildings, such as the green bank and the red hotel. The Virgin

Dronigens Gade, main street of Charlotte-Amalie, lined with shops in converted warehouses.

Islands are not as rampant with color as Puerto Rico, but the preference is for far more somber tones.

Unquestionably the oldest building on the island is Fort Christian, constructed as stated in large black letters on the tower in 1671, within five years of the original Danish settlement. These numerals and the superimposed tower, however, are later additions. The fort is used today as police station, prison, and legal chambers, a slight variation of its original purposes. A narrow, airy section enclosed by chicken wire faces the courtyard. Behind its padlocked screen door, I could see two far from unhappy-looking prisoners when I went through. In the old days, prisoners were thrown in the dungeon beneath, and on request, you can visit the cells and subterranean torture chambers.

In the paved courtyard there is a well-worn tombstone, so worn that the name and other information are obliterated, with the exception of the skull and crossbones carved in each of its

Fort Christian, the oldest building on St. Thomas.

Bluebeard's Castle, originally a watchtower.

four corners. Buccaneers enjoyed a more or less respectable position in the early life of Charlotte-Amalie, and so this tombstone should not necessarily be construed as marking the grave of a condemned criminal. One of the very early governors of St. Thomas (1684–86), for instance, is described as "a soldier of fortune," in other words a pirate or privateer, and his descendants as a matter of birthright today represent one of the socially outstanding families of the island.

Since the fort was the earliest solid construction on St. Thomas, it also served for quite a long period as the local church and burial ground. You will notice in all the old churches of these islands that a large part of the aisles and general paving consists of flat gravestones.

The free port of Charlotte-Amalie was never a walled city like San Juan, but defensive precautions were naturally taken. Fort Christian directly overlooks the harbor, and two lookout towers, Blackbeard's and Bluebeard's, were built higher up on the hills. As you stand in front of the fort, Bluebeard's is to the east and Blackbeard's can be seen directly back and above the town, close to a handsome white house.

The names of these two towers resound of legend and romantic history. The hotel called Bluebeard's Castle, on the grounds of which that tower still stands, was built on the ruins of the home of St. Thomas's first governor, Erik Smidt. Some of the eleven cannon which fortified it still decorate the upper drive. In the middle of the nineteenth century the stone tower underwent restoration, and the pristine white plaster which walls the sturdy iron circular staircase has an appearance of even later vintage, but Bluebeard's, or the *Tour de Barbe Bleue* as it is sometimes called, actually dates from 1689. Its exact history is deeply shrouded in mystery, but any St. Thomian will vouch that at the time of its restoration an ironbound chest filled with mildewed manuscript was discovered next to a rusty broken sword. The manuscript contained the memoirs of one Musa Ben Hassen, who, according to the name, would appear to have come from the Barbary Coast to join the corsairs of the New World. When translated, it told essentially the same story as the one told by Perrault, the French fairy-tale writer who immortalized Bluebeard and his seven wives. This coincidence is further fortified by Musa Ben Hassen's identification of himself as "known to all men as Bluebeard." It is fairly well authenticated that a manuscript *was* found, and belief in its contents was strong enough to give this name to the tower and castle. The story of Bluebeard has cropped up in the folklore of many countries, and the model for the chief protagonist has been variously identified, but Charles Perrault wrote the best-known version in 1697. Therefore, the conjecture that a witness or near-victim escaped to carry the story to France is an entertaining one. In keeping with it are the headstones which form part of the hotel's cocktail terrace, but a closer scrutiny of them reveals they are marked with crosses, carry the names of Stakeman and Simmons, and bear nineteenth-century dates. In any event, there is ample evidence that pirates were prominent in the early life of St. Thomas, and they probably were more powerful than the history books would tell us.

The numerous cannon of old Fort Christian have been removed and now form a decorative border to the drive leading down to the U.S. Coast Guard station below it. On the other side, or to the right upon leaving the fort, is a green brick building which today houses the islands' legislature. Once it was white and served as garrison for Danish troops, later for American soldiers. The choice of green paint seems a pity, for it is a fine example of Danish colonial days.

Between the fort and the Grand Hotel is a small park called Emancipation Gardens. In it is a replica of the Liberty Bell, presented by France in recent years, with a tablet fittingly inscribed: "Dedicated to you, a free citizen in a free land." Just beyond is the main square, with the modern post office, the only new building I recall in the middle of town. Yet it is not an eyesore, but an attractive structure which blends into the local scene. Inside, some quite nice murals decorate its walls.

Opposite and up the steps from the square stands the Hotel 1829, a patrician mansion in the nineteenth century. It is not necessary to be a house guest in order to see it; Mrs. Maguire, the owner, is only too pleased to show you about. She will take you into the music or drawing room, the floors of which are covered with very worn but exquisite French Moroccan tiles. Similar tiles face the patio through the central archway, with steps leading to the white frame slave quarters, converted into guest rooms, beyond. Built into the hillside, behind the

*Government House
at Charlotte-Amalie.*

hotel, a small flower garden forms a landing on the steep staircase which winds upward. The hotel bar is an excellent conversion of the original kitchen, retaining the old fireplace and the basic brick stove, which is used as a mantel. The outer brick and stone covering of the stove have been removed to the courtyard, which serves today as an outdoor kitchen.

The driveway from the square to the hotel continues as part of the street running parallel to, but above, the shopping center. Two lovely old balconied houses and a street of steep steps leading to another still higher street separate Hotel 1829 from Government House.

Government House I find completely enchanting—unpretentious, livable, but with cachet, its brick masonry and iron scroll balcony alike painted white. Two old gas lamps guard the entrance flush with the street. It is so unpretentious and typically a part of St. Thomas that anyone may walk through it freely, both the main and the second floor. Replicas of the Danish furnishings adorn the reception hall and State dining rooms, for the originals were removed at the time the islands were turned over to the United States. Today these interior walls are painted a cool and inviting white; to some this may

183

appear to be a desecration of the basically fine mahogany paneling.

The Danish Government built the house in the middle 1860's, and during the two years of its construction the Governor resided at Blackbeard's Castle, the impressive mansion which now houses the Danish Consulate. Many Danes retained business interests on St. Thomas, and their consulate is still quite as important as it looks.

The flight of stone steps beside Government House offers a nice view from halfway up; at the top you are rewarded with glimpses of other colonial homes. Everywhere there are steps, the pedestrian's short cut to the circuitous streets. All of Charlotte-Amalie—in fact, most of the island—is built on hillsides where the ascents are steep. The only way really to enjoy yourself is to browse around these back streets and alleys and climb the steps. The most famous flight is known as the 99 Steps, a misnomer by someone who couldn't count. I believe they number 107. Wider than some, these steps are the photographer's delight for recording vistas. Actually, I was always confused as to which set of stone stairs these were, for the others seemed to me quite as productive of local color. However, I do know they come in at right angles to the top of the flight by Government House. One of the curious topographical

Street of stone steps next to Government House.

Entrance to Charlotte-Amalie's synagogue, which dates from 1833, although the history of the Jewish colony goes back much further.

aspects of Charlotte-Amalie is that the hills are also well-rounded, and so the visitor is always finding a pleasant surprise around the next corner.

Using Hotel 1829 as a landmark, you will find a lovely walk to the left and slightly back from it, which takes you past other old homesteads. Here are mostly smaller houses which appear to be piled one above the other in a pretty but somewhat crazy fashion like the superstructure of a huge wedding cake. Here too is Smith's Fancy, with its white frame galleries, and just beneath it the six-sided red-roofed synagogue protected by a high iron fence.

The synagogue is quite old, dating from 1833, but the history of the Jewish colony goes back much further than that. They were Sephardic, or Portuguese-Spanish Jews, the first of whom emigrated from St. Eustatius, a tiny dot in the Leeward Islands. It was (and again is) a part of the Netherlands West Indies but was a flourishing free port when sacked by the British fleet in 1781. Although the English did not mistreat the Jews, there was greater tolerance among the Dutch. But the primary motivation for the exodus from St. Eustatius was the destruction of the port, which meant also the destruction of their means of livelihood, for most of these people had been skippers and merchants, who at the time were supplying the American Revolutionary Army. This, naturally, did not endear them to the English and was sufficient reason for the attack on St. Eustatius.

The first group of Jews that settled on St. Thomas was a small one, but within a few years they had built a synagogue. In 1804 a terrible fire swept through Charlotte-Amalie and destroyed much of the town, including the synagogue. The Jewish colony had meanwhile been augmented by new arrivals from St. Eustatius and from other islands as far off as Curaçao, even from England. About five hundred of them were living on St. Thomas when the present synagogue was built, representing approximately a half of St. Thomas' total white population at that period.

These Jews were quickly assimilated into the life of the colony. They were very active in the commercial affairs of Charlotte-Amalie, and were designated by their country of origin rather than by race or religion; that is, they were considered Spanish, Portuguese, or Dutch, as the case might be. Anti-Semitism did not exist in the Danish West Indies.

The finest tribute one can pay to the Virgin Islanders is the recognition of their complete religious tolerance. From 1660 (before the Danes took formal possession) to 1680 the religious life of St. Thomas was divided between two closely-knit Protestant groups—the Danish Lutherans and the Dutch Reformed. French Huguenots—Calvinists—arrived about fifteen years later and soon merged with the Dutch. Meanwhile, in 1685, an edict permitted all sects the right of private worship, particularly applicable to Jews and Catholics.

Mafolie and Frenchtown, suburbs of Charlotte-Amalie, were settled later by French arrivals from the nearby islands of St. Barts and St. Martin. These French were not Huguenots but Catholics, and the reasons for their emigration are still unknown today. Presumably the cause was economic, but, curiously, none went to St. Croix, St. John, or any of the neighboring British Virgin Islands. They all came to St. Thomas. At any rate, priests' diaries of an earlier epoch give ample proof of the complete lack of hostility among the different religious groups living in such close proximity.

At that date all who practiced Judaism were strictly orthodox. The Jewish population later declined, and the present small colony no longer adheres entirely to the traditional rites, but the synagogue of St. Thomas clings to one ancient custom—sand is spread on the floor to commemorate the passage of the Jews out of the desert.

Among the earlier members of this Jewish colony were Abraham and Rachel Pizarro, who had a gifted son named Jacob. The father, a Portuguese Jew married to a Creole, was himself of French background, and so it was natural that he send the boy to France for his later education. Jacob returned to St. Thomas within a few years to take up a business career, but his mind and instincts leaned always toward painting. At twenty-five, he left Charlotte-Amalie to return to France for good. Today he is known to posterity as Camille Pissarro, one of the great Impressionist painters. Although he is regarded as a French painter, especially since he substituted a Gallic first name for Jacob, not to mention adopting the French mode of spelling his surname, it is a curious fact that Pissarro never relinquished his Danish citizenship.

Although no plaque commemorates it, Camille Pissarro was born on the main thoroughfare of Droningens Gade in the building which now houses the offices of Alcoa Steamship and Sears Roebuck. Walk into the courtyard and you will get a better idea of his original home. Its situation as well as its size would indicate that Pissarro's father was a prosperous merchant.

Grand Hotel, facing main square of Charlotte-Amalie. The Grand was once owned by the father of Impressionist painter Camille Pissarro.

He was also interested in real estate and was the owner of several other buildings in town, among them the Grand Hotel, which was opened on May 6, 1841, when Camille was eleven years old. The Grand Hotel, therefore, is not just the oldest hotel on St. Thomas but probably was the first "modern" one.

Only a short distance from the onetime Pissarro home is the market, at right angles to the main thoroughfare. An open-air shed with display tables, it is as colorful as the surrounding buildings. The market is devoted exclusively to fruits and vegetables, many garnered from neighboring isles. They are not only beauteous to the eye but often fascinatingly strange— melons, papayas, tomatoes, and pineapples making familiar and unfamiliar bright spots against the multitudinous greens, some of which, like dasheen leaves, are as foreign to us as their names. Equally so are the tubers and native fruits. Women in native headdress add an exotic note. It may be just a bandana, but more than likely the bandana will be surmounted by a flat-crowned, broad-brimmed hat, which is excellent for shade and for carrying a basket.

The Virgin Islands woman, unlike the tourist, protects herself against the sun. Many of the older generation also wear hats after sundown to ward off the dangers of night air. The chambermaid in my hotel, herself hatless throughout the day, carefully put on a black felt before making her evening rounds. She gave me the impression that not only diseases but goblins were likely to be wafted in with the welcome cool breezes of night.

The mass of the people, uneducated, are simple and superstitious. Like children they are also joyous, and so the St. Thomas Carnival has great spontaneity. This outstanding event of the year, held annually the last week in April, is unique in that *everybody* takes part—tourist, recent settler, old families, rich and poor alike. Everyone dons at least a fancy hat, but most of the merrymakers spend a great deal of thought, time, and sometimes money on their costumes. Prizes are given for the best such as a group last year meticulously dressed in eighteenth-century attire with wigs and knickerbockers.

The adults elect a king and queen, and the children are represented by a very youthful prince and princess. Naturally,

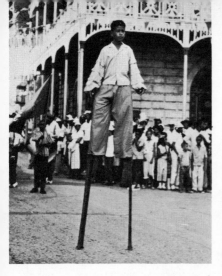

"Mocko Jumbi," St. Thomas Carnival.

Blithe spirits at St. Thomas Carnival.

there is dancing in the streets, impromptu and otherwise, calypso contests, limbo (that curious stunt which is the reverse of vaulting a bar), steel bands, and parades. The grand climax comes at the end of the week—Friday and Saturday—the revelry ending abruptly at midnight Saturday, for the people are deeply religious. During these latter days come the biggest parades, with floats, stilt-walkers, and frequent reference to "Bam-bou-shay," "Roas'-A-Time," and "Mocko Jumbi." Since these terms are probably as unfamiliar to the reader as they were to me, I hasten to explain that "Roas'-A-Time" is merely a slurring of "Rousing Time." "Bam-bou-shay," on the other hand, is a corruption of a Haitian word meaning "good spirits," and "Jumbi" are the local equivalent of the opposite—gremlins or zombies. The costumed participants on ten-foot stilts are make-believe zombies—those at which the people can laugh.

The celebration of this carnival is distinctively St. Thomian. If you are able to be there, you will certainly enjoy it. Above all, be prepared to enter into the festivities. Actually, it's next to impossible not to.

189

CHAPTER 5

More About the People

(Their Antecedents, Character, and Way of Life—Slavery
and the Moravian Missionaries—Churches)

THE Virgin Islands has a very special distinction in that it is
the only place in the world (at least so far as I know) where
asking for a key to your room is bad manners. I stayed in two
hotels in St. Thomas, neither of which produced a key. Moreover, the doors of one did not even have keyholes. When I
inquired, the whole matter was shrugged off—Why do you
want a key? That I continued to lock my valuables in my suitcase was considered a quaint old-fashioned habit.

Apparently crime in all its phases is moribund. There is no
thievery, no arson, no murder, no—well, fill the list out for
yourself. When I asked an elder citizen about this extraordinarily idyllic state of affairs, he declared that occasionally there
was trouble with a teen-ager or two, although gangs did not
exist. In regard to the two quite contented inmates sharing the
sunny cell of Fort Christian, I was unable to learn the causes
of their incarceration, but possibly they were panhandlers, too
lazy to work, for there is no unemployment in the Virgin
Islands either.

Such a state of affairs might incline one to think that the
Virgin Islander would be the most outgoing soul in the uni-
verse. On the contrary, he is likely to be somewhat reserved.
One reason for this attitude is the fact that many Virgin
Islanders consider the average continental rude. We do not
speak as we pass by. Obviously, in the center of town nodding
to everyone is impractical, but beyond the main stream of
traffic a friendly recognition is quickly reciprocated.

190

On my second night in St. Thomas, when I was staying at an outlying beach hotel, I walked over to the nearby airport restaurant at dusk. Two cars halted—one was going in the opposite direction from me—and the driver in each instance inquired if I'd like a lift. I was frightened and refused. On my return walk to the hotel—it was fully night by that time—an employee from the airport offered me a lift. By then I understood that the offer was merely a kindly gesture, a commonplace, everyday courtesy which I continued to encounter wherever I went. The driver went out of his way to deliver me to my exact destination.

Like most inhabitants of a semitropical climate, the Virgin Islander takes life easily. His requirements for comfort, over and above the beneficence of the weather, are minimal. Slums as such do not exist, but the houses of the poor are pitiful structures, though by no means so bad as a generation ago. Above all, hygiene is excellent and disease at a low ebb. The Virgin Islander is naturally clean and neat—an astonishing thing considering the degrading poverty in which the majority of them lived at the time we purchased the islands and the even worse conditions prevailing for long afterward.

Though he does not believe that work in itself is a virtue, the Virgin Islander is a reliable employee. After the repeal of Prohibition and, later, the start of the amazing tourist traffic, there was such a shortage of labor that help was imported from the British Virgin Islands. Today that has been halted, and our Virgin Islands are self-sufficient as to labor.

From the monetary point of view there is no upper class, no new rich. There is a cultivated, better situated group, but no class cleavage. In this concentrated locale everybody knows everybody.

However, the mass of the Virgin Islanders are poorly educated. No facilities exist for instruction beyond high school, and the majority do not attend classes after the eighth grade. The ambitious, exceptional ones must come to the continent for college degrees.

This situation goes back to Danish days, and was even worse then. Free colored, which meant favorites or mulatto offspring, were given the opportunity for private education, and it is

191

Virgin Islanders delight in colorful celebrations and music. This parading steel band is adding to the gaiety of the St. Thomas Carnival.

interesting that today the Danes still offer a few scholarships in Copenhagen for Virgin Islanders of demonstrable ability. The slaves, however, were not *permitted* education. They had been captured from various African tribes, each speaking a different dialect, sometimes an entirely strange tongue, and it was an advantage to keep them from communicating with one another. The Danes were the least prominent plantation owners. A good percentage were Dutch, French, or English. Besides, they were mostly absentee landlords.

As a further precaution against their acquiring a common tongue, the controlling churches—the Danish Lutheran and the Dutch Reformed—refused to allow the slaves to attend services. It was a group of Moravian missionaries who eventually penetrated this wall of isolation and ignorance behind which the slaves were held. Because of this, even now the Moravians are venerated, no matter to what church the present Virgin Islander adheres. The story of these missionaries is inseparable from the history of the islands.

It all began in a village called Herrnhut in Saxony, which had given refuge to a new sect called Moravians. One of them, an aristocrat by the name of Count Zinzendorf, received an invitation to the coronation of the Danish king, and after careful consideration, it was decided that he should attend the affair. During his stay in Copenhagen, he made the acquaintance of a slave whose owner had brought him along from St. Thomas. The slave told the Count many things about the condition of his people, especially that they were forbidden instruction or to attend church. Furthermore, he declared, no one could help them, for they were impossible to reach unless one belonged to the same despised, low estate.

Returning to Herrnhut, the Count reported his conversations with the slave, and the devout Moravians felt they had received a divine call. Two of this group, a potter and a carpenter, set off to investigate the situation, arriving at St. Thomas early in December, 1732. Unobtrusive toilers, they were able to communicate with the slaves. One of them returned to Herrnhut to report, and came back with other equally lowly members of his faith. Semi-clandestinely, the Moravians began drawing the terrified Negroes to them, offering religion and a modicum of education. They were also practical medical men, binding wounds and treating ills. These Moravian missionaries brought the first solace and kindness many of the slaves had ever received, and it is not surprising that they were held in such high esteem. The slaves fondly called them "Boss," a corruption of the Dutch word Baas, with which they were acquainted.

Just east of Charlotte-Amalie is a landmark known as New Herrnhut. It was here that the Moravians eventually—in 1777, forty-five years after the arrival of the carpenter and the potter —built a combined church and school. It has a new roof but is otherwise intact and still used for Sunday services; in the eyes of many Virgin Islanders, it is their finest monument.

The Moravians worked so unobtrusively, living little better than the slaves themselves, that the inroads they achieved— what proved to be an effective alteration in the life of the colony—were in reality an accomplished fact before the overseers were aware of them. These Moravians ministered only to the slaves, and in the Virgin Islands *no white man was admitted into their faith*.

Early in the nineteenth century the Danish Royal Government took a hand in the matter, passing a school ordinance legalizing the instruction of slaves. The Dutch Reformed Church then became active and approached the Moravians. Together they printed a "Negro Dutch Creole" Bible and hymnal, which can be seen in the library at St. Thomas. Creole, in this reference, had another connotation. It referred to the local patois, which showed a remarkable similarity to Afrikaans, its basis being an esperanto of tribal languages primarily influenced by Dutch. Some Danish and a little English, French, and even Spanish also found their way into the Virgin Island dialect as the slaves evolved a means of communication among themselves.

West of Charlotte-Amalie is another early Moravian church, called the Nisky Moravian Mission; there is a later one in the town itself. Many other Protestant groups are represented on the island, and in more recent years a flourishing Catholic parish has grown up. After the Emancipation of 1848, the Catholics drew many converts with their tenets barring racial discrimination.

The oldest church in town is the Frederik Evangelical Lutheran Church. The first Lutheran pastor arrived on the ship with Captain Erik Smidt, the original Danish governor, but for a long time the services were prudently held in the fort. By 1789 it was both safe and advisable to have a separate house of worship, construction of which was completed four years later. This Lutheran church is situated on the main street, below and a little to the left of Government House.. It is austere in appearance, except for the angels which ornament the fine chandelier hanging in the transept and the 200-year-old ecclesiastical silver still in use. There is a fine gallery at the back of the church, a distinctive feature of most of the churches on the islands. Some of these galleries may have been built for the slaves, but this is uncertain. In many cases they were indisputably planned for the choir. Incidentally, the adjoining parsonage is an excellent specimen of late-eighteenth-century structure.

In view of their history, particularly the important part

religion played in their reconstruction, it is not surprising that the average Virgin Islander is extremely pious. On Sundays the melodic sound of church bells, followed by the muted voices of the choirs, is wafted on the clear air throughout the town. The shops, needless to add, are all shut tight.

They are a dignified, unpretentious people. In a society where all have the same antecedents, there is an entire lack of self-consciousness. Intermarriage exists here, but is of no great consequence to them. In truth, it is viewed with slight disapproval.

The Virgin Islanders are, of course, aware of the integration controversy in the States. They deplore it, but they feel they set a fine example of banished bugaboos. Their emancipation, although not the first, came early. At the time Lincoln was signing our Emancipation Proclamation, the once downtrodden Virgin Islanders had not only enjoyed a couple of decades of freedom but were demanding—and soon granted—their first Colonial Council, their earliest voice in government.

CHAPTER 6

Pleasures Outside the City Limits

(Harbor Cruise and Glass-Bottomed Boat Trip—
Beaches—Magens Bay—Mountain Top)

It is safe to assume that the principal thoroughfare leading
from Charlotte-Amalie to the airport will quickly become
familiar, not simply as the route to town on arrival and to the
plane on leaving, but for a number of attractions in between—
possibly to go for a swim or to join an off-island excursion,
maybe to take a trip in a glass-bottomed boat, or to have a game
of golf, or just to pay a visit to Frenchtown. Sometimes you
will start via the water-front route out of town; at others you
will follow the bus circuit along the main street past the Jewish
Cemetery, where Pissarro's parents are buried, and the adjacent
Christian burial ground, both with more or less the same distinctive markers—a mound over each plot, walled in by native
stones in the center of which flowers are usually growing.

Not far beyond comes the turnoff for Frenchtown, where
the two roads join. Slangily known as "Cha-Cha Town,"
Frenchtown is a late settlement of emigrants from St. Bartholo-
mew—St. Barts, in everyday usage. An isolated group, on
friendly terms but rarely mingling with the other Virgin
Islanders, Frenchtown is an unexciting colony of modest homes,
a simple church, and cheap shops. You can pick up a few
bargains and delicacies, particularly in food and drink, and
there is a simply magnificent pastry shop (with tables for on-
the-spot enjoyment) opened by a fairly recent arrival from
France. Not many years ago he was pastry chef at the fabulous
Château Madrid on the French Riviera. After a professional
sojourn at the Virgin Isles Hilton, he decided to branch out on
his own.

Here, too, at the end of the promontory, is the Villa Olga, today a popular restaurant but once the Imperial Russian Consulate. A very narrow stretch of water separates it from Hassel Island, with a view of the inner and outer harbor to the left and right. A lovely situation at any time, it must have been truly glorious in Czarist days when a Russian cruiser put into port each winter. Offshore in the evening, the portholes of the cruiser twinkled like a multitude of fallen stars, and the Consul's home itself was a blaze of lights. Throughout the ship's lengthy stay the Consulate was filled with guests, and, outside, the uninvited gathered to watch and listen, for night after night there was music—deep, rich Russian voices blended in splendid choral singing. One St. Thomas native, himself a fine musician, declares that these evenings are the outstanding memories of his youth.

Back on the highroad, a left turn leads you toward the pier of the Virgin Islands Pleasure Boats, the nine-hole public golf course, and the most convenient public beach.

Virgin Islands Pleasure Boats, which offers a harbor cruise and five daily trips in a glass-bottomed boat, is a very short walk from the highway. That is to say, it is close to the bus stop, but it is also only a fifty-cent taxi fare from the center of town. The VIP—for short—also has a nice combination arrangement of harbor cruise and glass-bottomed boat trip, with a fifty-cent, or one-way taxi fare, saving.

Every day at sunset a cruise is made around Charlotte-Amalie's harbor, that jigsaw puzzle of tiny islands and jutting points of land. The cruise is somewhat of a party, for cocktails are offered on the house—or rather, on the boat. The entire delightful excursion costs a reasonable $3.00. (The luxuries *are* cheap.) Take binoculars with you, if you have them; spotting landmarks is as much fun as weaving among the islands.

The one-hour, $2.50 trip in a glass-bottomed boat, lost among so many cays that again you are confused about where you are, is fascinating. The fish confuse you, too, because the extraordinary clearness of the water serves as a magnifier—what looks, literally, like a sardine you are told is a four- or five-pound fish. Actually, the minimum depth at which you begin studying the submarine life is thirty-five feet, later it goes to fifty, and eventually to a hundred feet. Blue rudder with their brilliant-

197

Yacht basin, St. Thomas.

hued tails scuttle by; then come sergeant-majors done up properly in stripes and droves of tiny anchovies. On the ocean floor are numerous sea anemones, beautiful plants but so small you have to look sharp to catch a glimpse of them; baby sea urchins adhere to rocks and driftwood, but the biggest display is the vast variety of coral (according to the very instructive captain, five hundred species are extant and three hundred of them are represented here), including tree coral, flame coral— not named for its color, but because it is the only poisonous species and sears like a burn when touched—and brain coral, as well as an enormous number of sponges. What fish you see depends to some extent upon circumstances. For example, when many anchovies are in evidence, it is indication that the larger fish have had their fill and are dozing under the rocks, sponges, and coral. The peak of the trip comes when you reach the sunken Portuguese fishing trawler. It has been here since a gale in 1924, and now is the home of much of this marine life.

Reservations for either of these excursions can be made most easily through the Virgin Islands Tours, and the two can be handily combined into one big outing by taking the late afternoon trip in the glass-bottomed boat and returning in time to transfer leisurely to the sunset harbor cruise. Boats of various descriptions can also be rented through VIP, as well as skin diving equipment. (Details are given in the chapter on sports.)

The office on the pier, incidentally, is also an interesting shop. In glass cases are specimens of fossils and all types of shells, from the standard conch to small sea snails which look as if they had been dressed up with water colors, for yellow and black stripes outline the humps and there is something resembling a painted eye, either black or gray-blue, in the center. White coral can be bought in paperweight size for ten cents, or large specimens for $2.75 or thereabouts, not to mention lovely yellow and violet fan coral.

At the fork in the road is a bus stop and ordinarily, after a momentary halt, the bus continues straight ahead as far as the golf course. Beyond the Trade Winds Hotel the road is only partially paved.

The nine-hole golf course is open to all. For guests of member hotels, it is free; otherwise the fee is $2.00. Don't expect too much of it, for the greens turn out to be sand—victims of the water shortage.

But to return to the fork in the road—on Thursday afternoon when the shops are closed and business is at a standstill, the bus makes a deviation in its schedule, taking the left turn toward the beaches. Just beyond the Island Beachcomber is a stretch of public beach. The Caribbean Hotel Beach Club, on the opposite side of the narrow cape, welcomes visitors at a slight admission charge.

A vast amount of gushing copy, liberally sprinkled with superlatives and exclamation marks, has been expended on St. Thomas' beaches. However, face to face with actuality, I believe it is almost an impossibility to overstate their beauty. The sea and sand are the lushness of St. Thomas. The sand, a gleaming, finely ground white coral, is as richly soft to the touch as pulverized sugar, and thanks to the reflection from the equally white sea-bed, the green and blue tints of the water attain something akin to an incandescent quality, contrasted against the beaches, with sea grapes framing the whole. There is an utter unreality about what, miraculously, is reality.

This is true of the entire coastline with all its private and public beaches. Morningstar and Sapphire Bay, to the east of Charlotte-Amalie, are the most celebrated "admissions" beaches. That is to say, they are run as clubs but arrangements are made for tourists. (Unlike them, Bluebeard's Beach is limited

199

strictly to members and hotel guests.) There are also several smaller, less-known beaches, and if you are stopping on St. Thomas for more than a few days, it is fun to investigate them for yourself.

The most beautiful of all is the public park situated on Magens Bay (once pronounced Danish-fashion as Mahgens, but today rhyming with the month of May). But then, the huge, deeply indented Magens Bay on the north shore is a sight-seeing must whether you swim or not.

Arm yourself with a map, not only to assist you in finding out-of-the-way spots but to avoid the narrow roads which are as likely as not to end up as goat tracks. Some of the dirt roads, beneficiaries of the dry climate, are possible, but others simply disappear into uncleared land.

If you rent a drive-yourself, of course, a map is provided, but the non-driver who would nevertheless like an idea of the general layout can secure from his hotel, upon request, a folder containing maps of both the city and the island. The maps not only show roads but identify sightseeing interests, shops, and places of entertainment. Many estates are also indicated on the island map. You hear frequent reference to Rosendal Estate, Van Dyke Plantation, Contant Estates, for instance, but nowadays these are more likely to be geographical or real estate terms, for the great sugar plantations are non-existent.

Fishermen's nets drying on the beach at Magens Bay. The huge, deeply indented bay "is a sight-seeing must."

Most of these estates have changed hands many times and been parceled off in sales. One which is essentially intact is Rosendal Estate, purchased shortly after World War I by a wealthy American named Fairchild, whose home received the name of "Fairchild's Castle." Consisting roughly of the land from the top of the hill to the shores of Magens Bay, the estate cost Fairchild $10.00 an acre, or a pittance of $14,000 for the entire property. (The present average is $5,000 to $6,000 an acre!) He erected thereupon a fabulous home for a few hundred thousand dollars.

Fairchild was a man of wide cultural interests, possessor of a fine library, an excellent collection of paintings, and he had a great appreciation of music. He also had a deep love of the island and an affection for the native population. To any who showed talent in music or the other arts, he was quick to bestow a scholarship and early became a legendary philanthropist to the St. Thomian.

Nevertheless, he was a misogynist who lived alone, refused admittance to women, and resented trespassers in general. He did, on the other hand, possess some sense of humor and was the perpetrator of the myth of "Drake's Seat." This cement bench near the entrance to his castle was an outcome of his annoyance with a couple of young lovers who singled out his property as a trysting spot. He built the bench as a subtle hint, and, since it faced on the channel of water which bore the appellation "Drake's Passage," remarked jokingly that this was where Sir Francis had sat while planning his strategy. To the untutored, there seemed no reason to doubt this statement, and what was intended as a joke gained credence. That the bench was not of stone did not discourage the legend—as witness the souvenir chips removed from it—let alone the historical fact that Sir Francis Drake never set foot on St. Thomas.

The joke, in the end, was really on Mr. Fairchild, for the bench was placed in far too unsecluded a spot for a lovers' rendevous and his wooded grounds continued to have greater appeal. The view from here, however, looking down on Magens Bay, is superb and the tourist at least can be grateful to the unsentimental Mr. Fairchild.

The visit to Mountain Top Hotel is easily included on the

same run as Magens Bay. It can as well be reached directly from Charlotte-Amalie, but it and Magens Bay are the two outstanding attractions outside the city limits.

Whichever way you approach Mountain Top you will pass through the area known as Mafolie. Like "Cha-Cha Town," Mafolie is inhabited by French emigrants from St. Barts and neighboring islands. Both groups are Catholics and should not be confused with the earlier Huguenots, who became so integrated with other Protestant sects that they no longer exist as a separate group.

Like the other Caribbean islands, St. Thomas is dependent upon the trade winds from the Atlantic for such rainfall as it receives. The mountains effectively block these winds from southerly-situated Charlotte-Amalie and its environs. The people of Mafolie, with an inherited knowledge of fine cultivation, industriously made use of the northern slopes, carefully terracing them to catch every last particle of water. As a result, they supply the best local produce to be found in the markets.

Mountain Top Hotel is on nearly the highest elevation of St. Thomas. From this almost 1500-foot unobstructed vantage point the long-distance view is an extraordinary one. It is exciting to have the islands under different flags pointed out, often as much as forty or fifty miles away.

The hotel has made the very best use of its situation, and its glassed-in cocktail lounge with sunken bar is surrounded by windows. Go there for a drink, if not lunch, and remember that it calls itself the "Home of the Banana Daiquiri." You should try it at least once. The many acres of the hotel grounds are beautifully landscaped, too, and include a permanent orchid exhibit.

On your visit to St. Thomas you should not fail to take a day's trip to nearby St. John. There are three offered, any of which can be arranged through your travel agent. One is simply an excursion to the gorgeous Caneel Bay Plantation, Laurance Rockefeller's pre-Dorado Beach enterprise, including a buffet lunch, changing facilities for swimming, and the boat and taxi fare each way. The cost is $12.50.

Another is a coastal excursion around the island by the yacht *Grey Gull*, which affords a visit to Estate Annaberg, the best preserved of St. John's once-numerous plantations, and allows

View of beautiful Magens Bay from Mountain Top.

a long stop for lunch and swimming at magnificent Trunk Bay. The charge for this leisurely day is $14.00.

The most popular excursion, however, is the long-established, comprehensive Island Safari, also $14.00. You are picked up at your hotel, driven to the ferry at Red Hook Wharf, and met at the end of the 25-minute crossing by covered jeeps (they remind you of surreys with the fringe on top) with foam rubber cushions. Call it an informal trip rather than a rough one, because these jeeps are astonishingly comfortable. They also navigate over roads which ordinary vehicles could not negotiate and take you on an extensive tour of a great part of the island—that which is today a National Park—ending with a leisurely stop at Caneel Bay Plantation. The price includes not only a very adequate picnic lunch but Thermos bottles of rum cocktails. These are served on a beautiful, quiet beach, with plenty of time out for a swim. In fact, the entire trip is cleverly spaced for ease of travel, and the continental guides are extremely congenial and informative. Indeed, the whole trip is an extraordinarily fine value; these safaris are so popular that reservations cannot always be secured on short notice. Many visitors actually make their arrangements before arriving in St. Thomas. The informality of the trip demands equal informality of dress, and for this occasion shorts are ideal.

Details about St. John itself are given in the next chapter.

CHAPTER 7

St. John, Tropical Retreat

(History, Slavery—the Island Safari—Caneel Bay
Plantation—Other Accommodations)

ACCORDING to the 1960 census, St. John's nineteen square miles
holds a population of 900, and though the rate of transient
visitors has increased amazingly, the number of permanent
residents has been augmented by no more, perhaps, than a
hundred. This is a primitive island of idyllic natural loveliness
and, with the exception of Caneel Bay Plantation, few conveniences.

When Laurance Rockefeller first saw it, he is said to have
exclaimed that it was this side of paradise, and he proceeded
to purchase 5,000 of the 12,000 acres, most of which were
given to the U.S. Government for a National Park. The rest,
meaning Caneel Bay, became one of those financial intricacies
wherein Jackson Hole Preserve (a part of the Rockefeller set-
up) is the nominal owner of the hotel and grounds. Any in-
come derived goes to the Jackson Hole Preserve (which also,
for example, owns Grand Teton Lodge, Grand Teton National
Park, Wyoming), but it is whispered that it is impossible to
make a commercial success of the development here. This is
not for lack of guests, as Caneel Bay is very popular, but the
cost of importing every item of necessity and luxury is terrific.
In any case, nothing has been done that detracts from the
island's beauty, and the Rockefeller improvements (whether
feasible or not) have put St. John firmly on the map.

Today, despite the drawbacks of insufficient electricity on
much of the island and the more rugged demands of the
simple life, there are less expensive colonies than Caneel Bay

Caneel Bay Plantation, famous resort on St. John.

catering to those who are willing to forego modern conveniences for the sheer joy of beauty. Here and there, too, well hidden and difficult of access, are small homes constructed in defiance of ordinary twentieth-century expectations. On this roster are well-known names, attracted by St. John's quite obvious charms and fleeing what some consider the slavery of the machine age.

St. John rises sharply out of the ocean to over 1,200 feet. The waters surrounding it shade from pale turquoise to a rich deep blue, and the mountains are covered by a luxurious green. Yet it was more lush when Columbus, on that famous second voyage of his, stopped here briefly following his landing on St. Croix. It was he who christened it St. John, or San Juan as he named all his discoveries after biblical figures. This San Juan, or St. John, was baptized in honor of St. John the Apostle, whereas the larger island of Puerto Rico was named for St. John the Baptist.

At that period, St. John the Apostle did not suffer from a water shortage. This began during later days, when it was so intensively cultivated for sugar cane that the hillsides were terraced and the trees, whose roots had absorbed and held the water, were destroyed. One small stretch in a valley is today covered with a new wild growth, the trees bearing green leaves brighter than those of arid origin. They may, over the years, prove to be a restoration of St. John's original fertility.

Once the island was occupied by Arawak aborigines from the Orinoco delta of South America, but here as elsewhere in the West Indies there were incursions by the Carib tribes. Inland, unapproachable by road, are petroglyphs—stone picture writings—which some believe prove pre-Columbian occupation. Many archaeologists dispute this opinion because, along with other doubtful symbols, the Christian cross is among the stone carvings. In fact, much evidence indicates that the Caribs never lived on St. John, merely encamping here from time to time during their ceaseless warfare.

The white man took a great liking to St. John, and throughout the sixteenth and seventeenth centuries the Spanish, English, Dutch, and French successively controlled it. The Danes did not move in until the beginning of the eighteenth century. They established their first settlement in 1717, but both St. John and St. Croix were acknowledged French possessions then. Seventeen years later, the Danes bought the two islands.

By that time St. John was under intensive cultivation, almost completely covered by sugar plantations. The slave population was enormous and their living conditions ghastly to contemplate. They were whipped for the slightest offense, and a second offense brought a mandatory lopping off of the ears. Runaway slaves, if captured within a week, received a punitive 150 lashes; if captured after three months, they lost a leg, and

Beach rimmed by sea grape trees, near Caneel Bay Plantation.

after six months, their lives. Leaders of runaway slaves were always hanged, but not before being pinched with a hot iron. The hot iron was also used if so much as a hand was raised against the white man. You can read about these and other atrocities in the local archives.

It is certainly not surprising, therefore, that in 1733—the very year of the Danes' purchase—there was a terrible slave insurrection on St. John. This, I believe, is the earliest slave revolt on record, fifty-eight years before the more successful Haitian revolution. The story of this uprising is a remarkable and terrible one.

The characteristics of the numerous African tribes from which the slaves came, varied enormously. One was recognized as so unruly and impossible to control that each individual from the tribe was kept separated from his fellows—usually on an entirely different plantation.

Six of these tribesmen—all in the vicinity of the great fort on the east coast—managed nevertheless to communicate and unite in a carefully planned movement. They asked other slaves to join in the plot but the latter were afraid, although they agreed to join in should the six succeed in overcoming the fort.

Thereupon, these six intrepid black men managed to sneak into the fort with machetes and exterminate the entire garrison. This was the signal for a general uprising which so terrified the white managers and overseers that they fled to what is known today as the Caneel Bay Plantation. It was then called the Peter Durlieu (sometimes spelled Durloe) Estate.

An appeal for help was sent to St. Thomas; the British rushed reinforcements from Tortola, but it was the French from Martinique who finally saved the white man. According to legend, the ringleaders of the revolt, when they saw their situation was untenable, joined hands and jumped over the cliff into the sea. In actuality, they mercifully killed each other with machetes, one bullet being preserved for the destruction of the last man, rather than face the unbearable punishment that would await them.

Strangely, when Emancipation at last came in 1848, over a hundred terrible years later, the slaves accepted it calmly, although they did raze some estates. But many manor houses had been in partial ruins ever since the eighteenth-century rebellion.

After the abolition of slavery the planters left, and St. John reverted to bush. No building of that era remains intact, but the ruins of the Peter Durlieu sugar mill, part of the present Caneel Bay Plantation, are very revealing. You can see the flat roof where the wheel was placed and the horse trod until the sap ran below, funneled into vats where it was boiled for molasses. It was a seasonal occupation, doubly grueling in the intensity of the heat. The slaves were housed in minute quarters attached to the mill. Throughout the harvesting season work was almost unceasing, with a bell tower to call the slaves when the wind was good.

There are many ruins on St. John, all of them now under the supervision of our government. Despite the destruction, wonderful examples remain of the fine masonry of that era. But these sights are incidentals on the Island Safari.

More fascinating, perhaps, is the guided nature tour. Many of the trees found here grow on St. Thomas too. On this trip, they are identified and you learn interesting details on their

Ruins of Peter Durlieu sugar mill, part of present Caneel Bay Plantation.

uses. There is the bay tree, for example, responsible for that second great industry of these islands—bay rum. You learn that sea grapes are too tart for raw consumption, but make a jelly that is a marvelous accompaniment to duck. There are purple and yellow cedar (the latter the state flower), no relation to what we know as cedar, and something called a false almond, which the natives use for relief of pain—placing the leaf on the forehead for a headache, or on a burn or aching limbs. The calabash tree grows a hard fruit similar to a gourd, which comes in a variety of sizes and shapes and is made into bowls and dippers. The West Indian gooseberry, apparently the same as the Puerto Rican *acerola*, is hailed by scientists as the world's most concentrated source of vitamin C. Mamey apples are a fruit, but unripe they are cooked as a vegetable.

The trip terminates at Caneel Bay Plantation, which has cultivated gardens as enchanting as the wild mountain land. Here experiments have been carried on with hibiscus, producing hybrids of many colors, sometimes double in size. Here too I saw what was shrugged off as a common, easy-to-grow tree called Poor Man's Orchid, but I found it lovely, its branches covered with miniscule flowers exactly like orchids.

There was already a hotel on Caneel Bay before Rockefeller bought the land, for in 1930 the Danish West India Company had built a rest home there for its employees and their families, who came over from St. Thomas for a holiday. Many of the outbuildings are part of the original construction. The present property is, of course, a magnificent and fabulous development. It boasts of ten separate beaches (one of which is public). There is accommodation for yachts, and other sailing craft, charter, and glass-bottomed boats are for hire. There is an alfresco restaurant, weekly barbecues are held, steel bands entertain. You can choose rooms in the main building or in cottages at $38.00 a day and up, double occupancy, including meals, during the winter; summer discount is approximately $10.00.

Caneel Bay Plantation is, naturally, run on a completely self-sufficient basis, with shops and a commissary which is a great boon to the other island dwellers. It is not, however, the only vacation spot. But it and Cruz Bay, next door, are the

209

only two places where there is electricity, except for a few private generators.

Outside of Caneel Bay Plantation the accommodations on St. John are limited. There is a small guest house called Lille Maho on the slightly cooler north shore which has six rooms and a reputation for its food. One visitor reported the following luncheon there: "Roast turtle, curried whelks, and custard apple ice cream." This menu may sound a trifle exotic and was certainly an exception to the everyday fare, but Mrs. Thorpe, the proprietress, is a Frenchwoman who knows about cooking and combines a European cuisine with native dishes and seafood.

Nearby, at Gallows Point, the mystery writer Richard Ellington and his wife run a small cottage colony. This seems assured of continued expansion, especially as its open-air bar is a favorite gathering place of the islanders. These excellent redwood cottages can be rented usually for between $125 and $175 a week, but rent for about half that amount in summer.

In addition to these there are a couple of rooms and cottages to be had in the tiny—and only—village of Cruz Bay.

Up until a dozen years ago even Cruz Bay had to be content with six hours of electricity, and the only roads were donkey trails. There has been a vast improvement in conditions—all of the above-mentioned places have electricity—but the genuine beauty and simplicity of St. John remain unchanged.

Trunk Bay in Virgin Islands National Park, St. John.

CHAPTER 8

Lovely, Bucolic St. Croix

(Practical Guide for Hotels, Restaurants, Clothes, Shopping,
Beaches—Christmas Festival and Jonkey Races)

ST. CROIX is not really one of the Virgin Islands.

What we call the Virgin Islands is our own arbitrary designation. When we made our purchase from the Danes, St. Croix came in a package at that time labeled the "Danish West Indies." It is forty miles south of St. Thomas and extends slightly east of it too, so that, literally—to paraphrase Alice-in-Wonderland—it is "the nearer then to Europe."

St. Croix, also, was the first bit of present-day American soil which Columbus discovered. Here he definitely made a stop. Although he paused in passing St. John, whether any Spaniard stepped off the ship's deck is problematical.

The flight from San Juan to St. Croix takes ten minutes longer than that to St. Thomas, and from Charlotte-Amalie to the larger island is a mere twenty-five minute run. On St. Croix, however, a great deal larger airfield was possible, and so Pan American can service it on runs from New York. For inter-island hopping, Caribair has numerous scheduled flights. Otherwise there are the inexpensive charter planes, common throughout the Caribbean.

Incidentally, there has been a great deal of misunderstanding and some bad feeling because Caribair permits only a coach-class baggage allowance of forty-four pounds—with one exception. If you have made connections at San Juan after a first-class flight from the continent, they honor the 66-pound allowance previously allotted. Protests have been made to the Civil Aeronautics Board over what appears to be a show of favoritism, but evidently the practice is legally correct. Although Caribair has but one class of flight, they can call it first or coach as they will. But the baggage allowance is particularly important to the tourist in view of the heavy weight of the liquor quota which nearly everyone picks up to carry home.

Once you realize that St. Croix is not properly one of the Virgin Islands, you are less surprised to discover that physically it appears so totally different from St. Thomas. It does not look like a mountain violently propelled out of the sea. Instead, there is flat, rolling land (in one area peaks rise to 1,000 feet or so), a great deal of which is still given over to agriculture.

The towns themselves are curiously unlike Charlotte-Amalie. Christiansted, the capital, is a gorgeous perfection of Danish architecture—you recognize it immediately even if previously unacquainted with this Old Country charm—but, oddly, it is architecture of a different school. Frederiksted, on the other hand, was almost destroyed in what is known as "The Fire Burn" and rebuilt in an unusually light, delicate, and airy Victorian pattern.

St. Croix is larger than St. Thomas by about four miles in length and a mile or two in width, yet despite two towns, there are about a thousand fewer permanent residents and they are not so concentrated in urban areas. Christiansted, on the north shore, has about 5,500 inhabitants; Frederiksted, on the west coast, at most has 2,500.

Christiansted is decidedly the livelier center, but little Frederiksted boasts a good roadstead and it is here that the tramp and small ocean-going ships anchor. Occasionally a cruise ship puts into the harbor, but Alcoa makes a regular run every two or three weeks, carrying twelve passengers, and connections on other passenger-carrying cargo vessels can be secured in Miami and San Juan.

The airport is located almost in the middle of the island. From it to Frederiksted or Christiansted is a matter of a five- to seven-mile drive, the taxi fare ranging from $1.00 to $1.25.

There are only two hotels in Christiansted proper, the Club Comanche and the six-room Mahogany Inn, although good accommodations are available in a number of private homes, and quite a choice of restaurants is to be found. There is no hotel in Frederiksted, only a couple of guest houses. Most of

St. Croix's hotels are either beautifully renovated, great houses on old sugar estates or structures newly built to take advantage of the seaside.

Both rivalry and jealousy play a role in the relations between the St. Thomians and the Cruzans, as the inhabitants of the two islands identify themselves. Linked together politically as the Virgin Islands, they enjoy a joint legislature and good outward relations, yet both residents and visitors have a decided preference for one over the other. In terms of mode of living, the pace is quicker on St. Thomas and the tourist who wants constant gaiety prefers that island.

But St. Croix is by no means dull. For those who seek it, there is considerable entertainment. There are places to dance and there are steel bands to listen to, but the way of life in general is slower and more relaxed. The inhabitants prefer it that way, and they have no desire to see the tourist trade expand too greatly or too rapidly. St. Croix's tourist capacity is little more than half that of St. Thomas. Grapetree Bay, for instance, the newest and largest resort center, has ninety-six

Looking across the inlet at Christiansted, "a perfection of Danish architecture."

*Beach at Cane Bay,
where cottage colonies
are located.*

Estate Good Hope, a miniature Caneel Bay Plantation, has only twenty-two.

Costs are approximately the same as on St. Thomas, and there is just as wide a spread in hotel rates. One or two top hotels are as high as $50.00 double MAP, but the average is $35.00 and $40.00, reduced about a third in the off-season. Only a few places serve all three meals.

Because of the different type of life which St. Croix offers, many vacationers prefer housekeeping cottages, which rent on a weekly basis. Sometimes these are isolated, but generally they average about three cottages to a group. The largest concentration, at Cane Bay, is made up of two colonies—Cane Bay Cottages (six) and Village at Cane Bay (five) which also offers daily transportation for guests to Christiansted. Prices run anywhere from $75.00 to $150 a week, with an average of $60.00 in the off-season. Often there is a special rate for monthly rental. A full listing of cottages as well as of apartments and rooms can be obtained from the Virgin Islands Department of Tourism in New York or the Department of Tourism at Christiansted. The Chamber of Commerce, with an office facing the Christiansted wharf, is also very informative.

Apartments in both Frederiksted and Christiansted rent for

about the same amount as cottages. For those on a stringent budget, the two towns also have a wide listing of rooms for as little as $3.00 without bath and $5.00 with bath.

St. Croix has no such water shortage as St. Thomas. The rainfall is described as "sufficient," but the vacationer is fairly certain of a sunshiny holiday. The island does receive some welcome tropical showers, as is plainly evidenced by the green countryside.

As elsewhere, here too it is a great advantage to have your own car. Rental agencies are to be found in both towns, or rentals can be arranged through Caribair at the airport. In theory there is a bus service connecting Christiansted and Frederiksted, but its schedule is so uncertain that it cannot be recommended to the visitor. The only alternative to a drive-yourself, therefore, is to hire a taxi, for which your hotel will make arrangements. On an hourly basis, taxis charge $4.00 for up to four passengers, with an additional charge of $1.00 for the fifth passenger. For recognized runs, such as from an outlying hotel to the center of town, the charge is on a zonal basis as in St. Thomas.

Enjoyable and entertaining too are visits to different hotels. Calypso singers, steel bands, and dancing are featured at one or another on various evenings of the week. The Plantation Club in Frederiksted and the King Christian in Christiansted have dancing nightly, both equally appealing in a setting under the trees. Outside of Christiansted is Morningstar Club, its lovely outdoor bar and restaurant decorated by the clever use of curious patterns in driftwood. This is an enticing spot at any time, but on Saturdays they have an orchestra. It is the oldest, and still a favorite, gathering place for many Cruzans.

St. Croix This Week, counterpart of *St. Thomas This Week*, is an excellent source of information for the tourist. There are also three local newspapers, but they are not especially helpful to visitors.

The St. Croix Hotel Association has inaugurated a delightful scheme whereby after a week's stay, one night a week of your own choosing you may enjoy an exchange dinner at any other member hotel. You simply make a reservation by noon of the day you choose, through your own hotel, and they will issue you an exchange coupon. Thereby you can enjoy dancing on a particular night at St. Croix-by-the-Sea, informal dining by the pool at Clovercrest or Grapetree Bay, the Sunday special of Cruzan dishes and folk singing at Hotel-on-the-Cay, West Indian dance lessons at the Buccaneer, and so on. There are attractions to choose from every night in the week.

The hotels of St. Croix also provide a wide choice of luncheon restaurants. Many of them you will want to see anyhow in the line of sight-seeing. Sprat Hall, a beautiful ancient French manor house exquisitely furnished in antiques, is also a headquarters for fishermen and surf-riding enthusiasts. La Grange, another estate house near Frederiksted, has magnificent Danish furniture, silver, china, and glass. You feel as if you had been transported to the Old World. The owner, Mrs. Asta Fleming, *is* from Denmark rather than a native Cruzan, but she has been here long enough to have acquired a well-deserved reputation for her excellent cuisine. More about these estate hotels will be found in a later chapter.

In Christiansted itself are a half dozen restaurants, the two most outstanding of them being La Piazza and Café de Paris. La Piazza is named for the charming old Danish brick patio in which it is situated and, contrary to expectation, perhaps, does not serve Italian food. The owner-chef is Swiss and his wife, French, and, though the menu is somewhat international, the accent is on fine Swiss and French dishes. Café de Paris, an awning-covered outdoor restaurant, is French-Haitian; it, too, is excellent.

Besides these there are The Cellar and Hamilton House, both old favorites, and also Mahogany Inn, a delightfully transformed old warehouse stable on Company Street, where you can eat either in the converted carriage stalls or in the courtyard. King Christian, on the wharf, has a wonderful location and a garden restaurant.

Hotel-on-the-Cay, on a four-acre tree-shaded island which includes a beach, is a mere 150 yards across the water. The trip is made in a hotel rowboat—one is nearly always to be found against the pier. The row across takes about ten pleasant minutes, and waiting for the boat is no hardship on this lively water-front. Several inter-island sloops are usually tied up there unloading fruit and vegetables as colorful as the schooners themselves. On the flat just beyond the landing pier of the cay, beneath a mixture of such tropical trees as tamarinds, mahoganies, and coconut palms, is an outdoor bar with a smiling, friendly barman, and laid out on a trestle table near by is a hot and cold buffet lunch which costs $2.50. This lovely spot has a dreamlike quality with its offshore view of the fort in the foreground and the Danish town behind it. Like the majority of St. Croix's hotels, the Hotel-on-the-Cay—and, indeed, the islet itself—retains unspoiled the aura of an earlier epoch.

Reef and Sand is Frederiksted's most elegant establishment. Located in an early eighteenth-century town house, it combines a lovely tropical garden, a restaurant, a bar, and a shop. It also has four beautifully decorated guest rooms. Its luncheons feature French omelettes, and on Wednesday evenings there are round-the-world buffets, devoted to a different nation each week. The Seven Flags on the waterfront is a welcome newcomer, and Barbara McConnell's, next to the post office, is a long-established favorite. She is the daughter of Rea Irvin of *New Yorker* fame and a long-time Cruzan-by-adoption; her restaurant is the general meeting place for residents of the West End.

The clothes requirements here vary little from those of Puerto Rico and St. Thomas. It is summer the year around, but St. Croix, a trifle more directly in the path of the warm trade wind breezes, is a degree or two cooler than St. Thomas.

Men here do not seem quite so attached to shorts as a mode of attire. However, a warning appeared in *This Week in St. Croix*: "The Anti-Short Shorts Society composed of reasonably respectable members of the Island are deeply concerned that either women or men are appearing on the streets of Christiansted or Frederiksted in short shorts, or bathing suits..." Shorts, not too short, are suitable only in certain locales and in certain circumstances. Otherwise, there is an even greater informality in dress than on St. Thomas. This is part of the island's more leisurely way of life, and even during the Season a cocktail gown constitutes formal evening wear.

The remarks on shopping in St. Thomas apply, in general, to St. Croix. Christiansted is the larger shopping center. Although there are fewer shops in Frederiksted, Cavanagh's has opened a branch there which is considered equal to its main store in San Juan, and Christiansted's Danish House also has an offshoot there. Such popular shops as Compass Rose, Little Switzerland, and Continental have branches in Christiansted as well as in Charlotte-Amalie. There are others, too. You can go just as happily overboard buying dynasty silks, Danish silver, china, liquor, perfume, and cigarettes as on St. Thomas. Prices are the same, and the customs form no different.

In St. Croix also there is a slight accent on "home products"—meaning articles of straw and Virgin Islands rum, which is primarily "Cruzan Rum." A few other true souvenirs of the Virgin Islander are available, such as a record (or maybe several by now) of folk melodies by Marie Richards, a half-blind, native Cruzan who entertains at evening gatherings.

Cruzans unashamedly offer Cruzan food too, and a card I received at Christmas showed a fat old-timer over a miniscule charcoal stove, with an announcement in attractive red lettering: "Virgin Islands Recipes." Cruzan dishes are no different from those elsewhere in the Virgin Islands, but here they have discovered that some tourists are interested in them. The inner

Busy Saturday market at Christiansted.

fold of my card told of five unusual-sounding dishes quite difficult to execute elsewhere. "Kallaloo" was the first, for it is a mainstay dish of the natives. It demands, among other things, "one dozen eddo or dasheen leaves," which are best described as somewhat spinachy. They are combined with land crabs or other seasonings. According to my recipe, kallaloo should be "served with Foo-foo," that West Indian paste made of pounded plantains, which also can be mixed with other things,—combined in fish balls, for instance. "Fungi," a corn batter, occasionally replaces it. Two desserts, Mamey Apple Snow (that fruit was mentioned in the St. John chapter) and Mawby, whose basic ingredient is "1 heaping tbsp. of mawby bark," were included on my card.

At any rate, one can find entertaining and original cards in addition to the usual picture postals. And a number of hotels and restaurants feature "Cruzan" dishes from time to time, so that here Virgin Islands food is easy to investigate and assay. Some continentals like it very much.

Not all of St. Croix offers good sea bathing. In certain sections the coastline is too craggy, and in others the beaches run a poor second to those of St. Thomas. The very finest are south of Christiansted and a little east of Limetree Bay, just waiting to be discovered. As this region is still practically deserted, only a secondary road will lead you there, but a car can negotiate it quite handily.

There is one grave warning for all such explorers. A tree called manchineel has a fruit which has the tempting appearance of a crab apple—but *don't touch it*. It is deadly poison, so much so that it is believed the Indians prepared poison for their arrows from its juices. The juice and sap are a cyanide. A bite of the fruit will, at the least, cause blisters in the throat, and if the tree is used as a shelter in a storm, a drop of sap will do the same to the exposed flesh. The manchineel belongs to the entire Caribbean, and is not the exclusive property of St. Croix. But the tree is destroyed in all populous areas.

I should also add, as a cheering note, that the mongoose inhabits the Virgin Islands as well as Puerto Rico, and snakes, therefore, do not.

The excellent western beaches, less deserted, are one of the several charms of the Frederiksted area, but much of this stretch is private property. Nevertheless, Estate Good Hope has *two* nice beaches; Sprat Hall and Clover Crest are by the sea, and La Grange within easy access of its own sandy strip. Estate Carlton, a little inland, also has its own beach.

There are numerous coves to be explored and enjoyed at your leisure, but you can easily make arrangements for a swim at one or another of the hotels. In addition to those mentioned, St.-Croix-by-the-Sea has a good beach, and naturally the Buccaneer has one. Almost in sight of the Christiansted wharf is the beach of the Hotel-on-the-Cay, and in the town proper is the easily accessible salt-water pool of the Club Comanche, which also owns a beach outside the city limits.

The Club Comanche has a yawl—the *Comanche*—for rent, a favorite choice for picnic parties to Buck Island, which is about an hour's sail away. For individuals and small groups,

Merrymakers at Christiansted
Christmas Festival.

Queen of the Christiansted Christmas Festival and her consort.

Bill Miller, by the wharf, has daily excursions. Buck Island's gorgeous white sandy beach manages to delight even St. Croix's beach-blasé residents.

A couple of public beaches, with facilities, are in the planning stage, but the only existing one at present, Cramer Park, is ten miles east of Christiansted. If you rent a car, it is a pleasant spot for a day's outing. There are bath houses, a restaurant, and picnic tables for those who prefer to bring their own lunches.

St. Croix does not have a carnival, as such, but at Christiansted there is a genuine Christmas festival. In Frederiksted there is celebration, too, but the greatest activity is in the old capital. The festival runs for two weeks, from December 23 to Twelfth Night, and some of its charm is due to the Puerto Rican members of the community. A highlight is the singing of *aguinaldos*, or perhaps *villancicos* is even more exact, for the meaning is the miserable gifts which the poor make an effort to offer. It is this specific type of *aguinaldo* which represents the profferings of the biblical shepherds when they brought cake and honey to the newborn Christ Child. As the Spanish-speaking people have done for centuries, the guitarists walk through the streets to the wharves singing heavenly music.

There are also less solemn moments during the Christiansted festival. Until recently the main square of the town was the focal point of the festivities, but now they have been moved to the ball park on the nearby outskirts. The area has a maypole of lights over it like a tent and is referred to as "the village" because of the many thatched-roof stands which serve native food and soft drinks and shelter the standard games found at a fair. A queen is crowned, and there is a coronation ball; there are steel band contests, calypso singers and limbo dancers and fireworks. There are also street parades with floats, and a general carnival spirit prevails.

Another lesser but highly entertaining celebration is the Donkey Races held each year on February 22, alternating annually between the ball park at Frederiksted and the ball park at Christiansted. There are both cart and bare-back riding competitions, and if you have ever tried to ride or drive a donkey, you can appreciate what amusing confusion this pro-

The Winner: St. Croix Donkey Races.

Lining up for the start of the Donkey Races.

duces, as suggested by a tally card of races containing such titles as "Virgin Islands Futility," "Surrey Shambles," and "Cruzan Confusion." They are as unpredictable as the St. Thomas turtle races.

222

CHAPTER 9

The Second Discovery of America

(History of St. Croix)

THE "Orientals," at least those in the outlying islands, seemed a singularly hostile race to Columbus and his crew. A number of erudite men had concurred with him that the earth was round, but to secure incontrovertible proof he would have to find the passage to China somewhere among these snippets of land. He made the first landfall of his second voyage of search on Dominica, today a British Leeward Island, and felt he had gone too far south. Turning north, the ships stopped in the estuary of the Salt River on what the natives called "Ay-Ay" but which Columbus christened "Santa Cruz."

Instead of three, there were seventeen ships on this second voyage. As the Spaniards anchored in the bay, they beheld a few semi-attired reddish-skinned men on the cliff. Before them, a very short distance up the river, was a village. Some military members of the expedition disembarked, and captured and brought aboard a half-dozen of the natives, but they fought so incredibly fiercely that it was impossible to subdue them—at least, without killing them and thereby losing the evidence they were anxious to secure for Ferdinand and Isabella. So the Spaniards lifted anchor and moved on.

The Caribs had been in full control of Ay-Ay for some hundred years, and except for captured females, little evidence remained of the earlier Arawak tribes. These women, however, once members of a less warlike and more artistic clan of Indians, contributed their knowledge of pottery and fine carving. Even today, as in the farmlands of America, an occasional arrowhead is unearthed, but remnants of ornamented pottery and amulets

223

also come to the surface. The amulets frequently were semi-precious stones on which the frog motif, a symbol of fertility among most of these Indian tribes, was often carved.

The active resistance with which the Spanish fleet was greeted made it impossible to take on even a supply of greatly needed water. It was apparently in this quickly emptied village (with the inhabitants known to be waiting in ambush) that the hammock was first noted.

No European dared come near the island for almost a century and a half. Around 1625, the English and Dutch simultaneously decided to investigate its possibilities. The Dutch temporarily gained the ascendancy, but twenty years later were dispossessed by the still aggressive English. Five years later they themselves were driven out by a Spanish expedition from Puerto Rico. In the very next year a French force ousted the Spanish.

During those early days of colonization, title to land was considered valid purely by force of occupation. St. Croix was a fertile island and recognized as a valuable national asset. In all, seven flags flew over it. The French soon sold the island—but not before translating its Spanish name into their own tongue—to the Knights of Malta, who resold it to the French West India Company. On the revocation of that company's charter, it reverted to a Crown Colony.

Louis XIV badly needed money for the wars in which he was engrossed. The French had not expanded their colony, and they were glad to make a deal with the Danish West India Company, which netted the king some easy money to carry on his campaign against Poland. The Danish West India Company purchased both St. John and St. Croix. They surveyed the land and divided it into plantations of 150 acres, but after twenty years of monopolistic rule the dissatisfied planters petitioned the Danish king for the homeland government to take over control.

It was the eighteenth century which proved the golden era of prosperity. Some cotton was grown on the eastern, drier end of St. Croix, but the land was mainly planted in sugar. Sugar was considered so valuable a product by the Europeans that, during negotiations at the conclusion of the Seven Years' War, the English seriously debated the comparative worth of

Canada and Guadaloupe, wondering whether it might not be preferable to hold onto the latter!

At the time St. Croix was taken over by the Danes, it had a population of 10,200—but close to 9,000 of them were slaves and within the next one hundred years the slave population increased to over 27,000.

It is strange to discover how few of the old estates had Danish names. As a matter of fact, the majority of the settlers were either indentured servants or members of the landless lower classes—English and French, mainly—who moved in from the nearby islands. Some of the estate names are delightfully whimsical, as Upper Love, Lower Love, Anna's Hope, Eliza's Retreat, and Sally's Fancy. Of course many of these may, in the course of time, have been anglicized, but such names as La Princesse, Bonne Esperance, and Mon Bijou remain unchanged. On St. Thomas the plantations appear to have been largely of Dutch ownership; on St. John, a mixture —but on none of the three islands are Danish names in evidence.

This circumstance would seem to account for the lack of animosity—there is every evidence of sentimental attachment—

Ruins of old sugar mill on St. Croix.

Cosy harbor of Christiansted.

in the remarks of the not always expressive natives. The Danes were chiefly present in administrative capacities—both in private concerns and in governmental and military posts.

But on St. Croix, as on St. Thomas and St. John, English was the common language. Christiansted, if not an international harbor of the rank of Charlotte-Amalie, was nevertheless filled then, as today, with schooners from the Leeward Islands, the greatest number of which were British possessions.

For ten months between 1801 and 1802, the British were in actual occupation of the Danish West Indies, and again from Christmas, 1807, until the spring of 1815. Shortly after their departure the decline in prosperity set in, not attributable to the English withdrawal but to the increasing competition in sugar production throughout this region of the Western Hemisphere.

The condition of the slaves, although bettered, was still bad, and it was here on St. Croix that they forced the issue of emancipation in 1848, which was simultaneously enacted into law throughout the Danish West Indies. This surely would not have come about so abruptly and conclusively—although in the evolution of human events it would certainly have taken place soon—had it not been for the great Danish Governor Peter von Scholten, their first open champion and benefactor. So important was he that he deserves a separate chapter.

CHAPTER 10

"Massa Peter"

PETER VON SCHOLTEN was a man with an astonishingly advanced social conscience for his period, but his highly intelligent father had early imbued him with liberal beliefs. He first came to the Danish West Indies as an ensign at the time his father was appointed Commandant of St. Thomas. Twenty-three years later he was named Governor of all the islands, with headquarters at Christiansted, whence he was forced to leave in disgrace twenty-one years afterward.

With the British occupation of the islands, the father and son were shipped to England as prisoners of war, but they were released the following year and returned to Denmark. When Peter von Scholten next came to the West Indies, he occupied the position previously held by his father. In due course he was elevated to Governor-General of the Danish West Indies, the over-all capital of which was Christiansted on St. Croix.

Von Scholten arrived with a wife, who shortly deserted him and returned to Denmark. The causes of the marital rift are shrouded, but it is speculated that she might have been in disagreement with his advanced ideas. The break might, possibly, have been due to a more personal matter, for not many years after he settled in the West Indies, Von Scholten took a free-colored woman as his mistress, although apparently this was after the disappearance of his wife. In any case, his deep attachment to his mistress is unquestionable. They remained together until his forced return to Denmark at the end of his career, and even then hoped their separation would be temporary.

In all but a legal sense she was his wife. She acted as his official hostess and was accepted in government circles. Her father was a Dane, which accounts for her free-colored status. (About a fifth of the population was free-colored.) Since St. Croix was now his permanent home, Von Scholten built a country mansion, the estate called Bulow's Minde outside Christiansted, and the deed of ownership was made out jointly in her name.

From the beginning Von Scholten had been openly and violently opposed to slavery, an attitude which did not endear him to the plantation owners and managers. Of course the slave trade had been stopped and this limitation on replacements had led to a lessening of abuses, but slavery in itself was still a terrible thing, he thought.

Von Scholten's tenure as Governor-General was immediately marked by the mingling of blacks and whites at Palace social functions. He made constant appeals to the King for an improvement in the slaves' situation, and by 1834 had persuaded His Majesty to permit them to buy their freedom. Working hours were shortened, and the slave was allowed to choose whether or not to work on Sundays, but if he did work, he received payment for his labor. Many slaves also received money as gifts from humane white men.

These changes represented an enormous advance, but other improvements were also made. Pregnant women were prohibited from heavy labor. A more revolutionary development was opening certain military positions to blacks. Choosing the most intelligent, Von Scholten installed them in the lower ranks of the militia, in positions hitherto held exclusively by white men.

The Governor-General, or "Massa Peter" as he was fondly called, was naturally the Negro's hero. He continued to petition the King for further improvements, the most crying need being the opportunity for education. Five years after the first momentous changes this, too, was achieved—free instruction under the auspices of the churches, the Moravian Brethren in particular. Church funds being insufficient, the schooling did not really begin for another half-dozen years. At the time of the decree Princess Caroline-Amalie, a staunch supporter of Von Scholten's efforts and like most Danes a devout Lutheran, wrote him: "I was particularly glad to notice how you stress the religious instruction and the liberality with which you recommend the Moravian Brethren as the mission that has this instruction at heart."

All these ameliorations in the harsh treatment, especially the granting of educational rights, were simply preliminary steps toward eventual emancipation. In 1847 the proclamation finally came, but it did not signal immediate freedom. Children of slaves were now decreed born free, but for the adults there was to be a twelve-year transition period, the King perceiving a need to prepare them for that unknown responsibility of freedom, for which education was the most urgent requirement.

Von Scholten apparently agreed with the King. At any rate, believing the news of future emancipation to be joyful enough, he announced it on the King's birthday—September 18, 1847. But he had miscalculated. Instead of showing pleasure, the slaves grumbled loudly with disappointment and even demonstrated, bearing slogans, "Our children free, but we slaves." They learned of slave revolts on the French islands of Martinique and Guadaloupe and began making their own plans.

They were amazingly well organized. Their leader was an alert, thoughtful young man known as "General Buddo," who

Ruins of Bulow's Minde, von Scholten's country home.

Inviting beach near Frederiksted.

was a friend of the Governor's. The suspicion remains that Von Scholten was not unaware of the proceedings.

He had been over to St. Thomas on official business, and returned to St. Croix on July 2. Shortly after midnight he was awakened by the delivery of a note saying that the Negroes in Frederiksted were in a state of insurrection. The Governor ordered his carriage and prepared to go to the West End, but in view of the need for him, many in Frederiksted considered that he was unduly slow in arriving.

A group of slaves had gone to the chief of police demanding immediate emancipation. The police chief equivocated, awaiting the Governor. By the time Von Scholten made his appearance, a mob of 6,000 to 8,000 slaves stood before the fort, machetes in their hands. Within were just forty-eight men with sixteen guns amongst them. It was quite evident that the slaves had been instructed to wait calmly and not start trouble.

The Governor looked at them—their faces all turned trustingly to him—and said simply, "You are free now, you are hereby emancipated," and the crowd broke up peaceably. It was July 3 (how coincidentally close to our own Independence Day!) in the year 1848.

Unfortunately, back in Christiansted, against Von Scholten's explicit instructions, a shot had been fired from the fort. The slaves gathered there were already in an ugly mood, but now some had been killed, others wounded. The shot fired in Christiansted unleashed the pent-up hatreds. It was the cause of the burning and pillaging of estates throughout the island. On St. Thomas and St. John, in contrast, the Proclamation of Emancipation was received quietly. Only on St. Croix was there trouble.

But there was one very curious thing—*not one white person was killed!* This, it was admitted, was entirely due to the Negroes' great respect and affection for Massa Peter.

Von Scholten, however, was having great difficulty with the planters, who not only accused him of giving insufficient protection, but foolhardily refused to accept the Proclamation and threatened to resort to the language of the gun. Von Scholten was forced to act swiftly. He proclaimed martial law and ordered that everyone be searched for firearms, which were to be confiscated on the spot. Any opposition would mean immediate execution.

This stern handling of the situation sufficed to restore order, but not tempers. Complaints had already been forwarded to Copenhagen. Governor Von Scholten suffered a nervous breakdown under the great stress and, upon the advice of his physician, returned to Denmark.

His was a personal tragedy of the first magnitude. Not only was he forced to part from the woman who had been his close companion for over twenty years, but he left considering his career a failure. He resigned his post, but he was still forced to face court proceedings. Condemned, he appealed and was finally acquitted, but this was twelve years later when he was close to seventy years of age. At one time during his long trial—in fact, quite early—he was cheered by the receipt of a scroll of signatures from the colored people of St. Thomas. At about the same time, three hundred inhabitants of Christiansted, those of position, petitioned the King to give them back Peter von Scholten as Governor-General.

But he died not long after his acquittal. "Massa Peter is dead!" exclaimed the islanders in genuine sorrow.

CHAPTER 11

Christiansted—Capital of the Danish West Indies

(Fort Christiansvaern—Steeple Building—Something About Alexander Hamilton—Government House—Churches—Jewish Community)

CHRISTIANSTED is an absolutely fascinating Danish colonial city. So, too, is Charlotte-Amalie on St. Thomas. There are not many Danish colonial cities; in this part of the world there are only these two—why are they so different?

Charlotte-Amalie was an extraordinarily bustling, thriving, commercial city in its early days, but Christiansted was more staid, the capital city of the Danish Western Hemispheric colonies. It saw a good deal of commerce too, but this was—as it is today—interisland commerce. The slave trade and pirates' barter were concentrated in Charlotte-Amalie. But His Majesty's representative, the Governor-General, had his palace in Christiansted, its very size dominating the city.

Somehow these distinctions also affected the architecture. In the seventeenth and eighteenth centuries, Charlotte-Amalie's warehouses were strictly utilitarian and less attractive than nowadays. There were also a few warehouses in the main section of Christiansted, but they were used purely for local produce, and they blended into the permanent architectural scheme. One of the first contrasts you notice is Christiansted's colonnaded sidewalks—never quite even, with a step up here and another down there. In Charlotte-Amalie there are often balconies over the warehouses, certainly over most of the buildings.

Christiansted is built on flatlands, and so it is easier to walk about there. Everywhere you see lovely red-roofed stone buildings, washed in blue and yellow and rose, and houses with wrought-iron gates enclosing flower gardens of such quaintly named blossoms as "man's change of heart"—these are red at night and white in the morning.

The history of Christiansted is diversified, for it grew up under many flags. In contrast to Frederiksted, the town does not have a deep bay. It was never able to accommodate the larger trans-Atlantic ships as Charlotte-Amalie could, and was less propitiously situated for receiving and discharging long-distance transports. One wonders why the town did not grow up on the bay, which is the mouth of the Salt River where Columbus first landed. This is said to be a deeper anchorage, but a look at the map indicates it would also have been more vulnerable to attack. During the French occupation there was a fort on the bluff there, no doubt for that very reason.

In any case, the harbor of Christiansted today is delightfully cozy and picturesque. Alongside the wharf there are always sloops bearing foreign flags coming from Dutch Sint Maarten, British Antigua, French Guadaloupe, and smaller nearby islands. These are usually piled high with fine fruits and vegetables, for as a center of exchange—you might even say barter—Christiansted is still a vigorous port.

Colonnaded sidewalk in Christiansted.

Dominating and half-circling the bay is Fort Christiansvaern. Basically it is the oldest structure on the island, for its foundations date from the days of the Dutch occupation, when they were being harried by the English. The stalwart walls, however, were constructed in 1733 by the Danes, immediately after they purchased St. Croix. Additions were made throughout the next century, so that the date 1836 appears on the entrance gate and 1839 on the main building.

There is less of the air of industrious upkeep in St. Croix than in St. Thomas, and this insouciance helps preserve its look of authentic origin. The fort is a trifle shabby, but it is impressive, particularly when you walk out onto the ramparts where the promenade of old brick has won out against the cement overlay. Here you get a gorgeous harbor view, too, with Protestant Cay—better known today as Hotel-on-the-Cay—in the foreground. (This island, already mentioned, belonged to the harbormaster; his charming house—now the hotel—later served as the governor's summer residence.) Yachts, a schooner or two, perhaps a small steamer, are tied up in the nearby basin; the commons with bandstand is on the left, and in the background the green mountains hover protectively over the town.

The courtyard of the fort, dominated by an incredible flamboyant tree (tiny pyramids of cannon balls mark the corners of the green), is unadulterated loveliness, especially during the summer when the tree flaunts its red blossoms. The police station and local prison—a collection of miserable, tiny, lightless cells, each with a door facing onto the courtyard—were located here, but the prison has been transferred elsewhere. However, as all the cell doors were wide open at the time of my first visit, I decided that crime was even less a problem here than on St. Thomas.

Down in the square, standing alone, is the original old Danish Customs House. On the left, as you leave the fort via the alley of trees with the park on the far side, is a soft yellow building which served in colonial days as the post office, but now houses the library. Today's post office, rose with green shutters, takes up a full block. It was the old West India and Guinea Company warehouse. (The Guinea Company was the slave-trading organization; it soon merged with the Danish West India group.)

Across the street from the post office is what is referred to as the Steeple Building, now undergoing repairs, which has the classic lines of a church. There is much misinformation about it, one pamphlet stating it was built by the French prior to 1695. The design seemed curiously out of keeping with that date, and after some research I was able to find authentication of its construction in 1753, twenty years after the Danes took over St. Croix. Early prints, however, do show a church—though not the identical one—on the site; it may have been French Huguenot. The building was unused for so many years that its original purpose became obscured. It seems to me most probable that it was a Huguenot church until such time as the congregation was absorbed by the Danish Lutheran or some other Protestant sect.

The Steeple Building is being made ready to house the museum, which at present is confined to cramped quarters in the little library. The new location should afford the museum space for an excellent presentation indeed, but even the two small rooms presently allotted to it make an extraordinarily good, clear display. The history of the area is chronologically illustrated, with interesting details and examples from the Virgin Islands in general and St. Croix in particular. It is fascinating and extremely easy to grasp.

The old Danish street designations are being restored, so that for King Street the sign now reads "Kongensgade." Even in English, however, the retention of such names as "King Street," "Queen Street," and "Company Street" give flavor and atmosphere. Going down either King or the neighboring streets, under the stone arcades you find, as formerly, shops and offices. In colonial days a few served as small warehouses, others as stables, blacksmith shops, or, as in the case of the Little Guard House (a lovely antique shop now, by the way, where you are invited to browse), a military bootery.

At 76 King Street is a hardware store where (as indicated on the façade) Alexander Hamilton worked as a boy for a firm of New York merchants named Beckman & Cruger. Nicolas Cruger ran the Christiansted headquarters of the firm, and in 1766 eleven-year-old, precociously intelligent, young Alexander Hamilton was apprenticed to him. Rachel, Alexander's mother, was supporting herself by a small but prosperous store carrying plantation necessities such as meat, rice, flour, and apples. Cruger's business was on a much larger scale, and 76 King Street was the office and counting-house. Six years later Cruger, very ill, had a long enforced absence from his business, but his young clerk, then a mere seventeen, succeeded in running it superbly. The boy had such an obviously brilliant mind that Cruger, who had a fondness as well as admiration for him, helped him reach the mainland of America, where there was opportunity for further education and advancement. Young Alexander set off that very year for St. Thomas, where he took a boat for New York.

Until very recently, much has remained obscure about Hamilton's background, but it is known that he was orphaned. His father, James Hamilton, deserted his family the year Alexander went to work; his mother died a few years afterward, and if her relatives on the island were well-intentioned, they admittedly had few resources. (Further details about Hamilton and his family will be found later in the chapter.)

Only a short distance up King Street is the most imposing monument in all Christiansted—Government House. Approaching it from this direction, you see first of all the magnificent formal entrance up a flight of stone steps. Above the wide doors are REX 1830 and a crown. Government House has the authoritative grandeur due the official residence of the King's representative. It is a spacious building extending the length of two streets; actually, it is composed of two separate entities.

The farther two-story wing, or older part, originally the home of a Danish merchant, was purchased by the Crown and remodeled during the reign of King Christian in 1774. The later enlargement was so skillfully done that you must study it carefully to find the divisive elements. In its entirety it is a lovely building of soft yellow with white trim and green shutters. It surrounds a garden with a pond of water lilies in the center. The garden has not been given the formal care it needs, but it is still a lovely, tranquil spot, with balconies overlooking part of it and a gallery leading to today's downstairs government offices.

In the interior two quite distinct rooms stand out. The first

236

is the beautiful ballroom, also used for receptions, with long gold-framed mirrors filling the walls between the windows and doors, graceful candlesticks, and small settees—really little more than leather-covered stools. The furnishings are replicas, for the Danes removed the originals at the time of sale, as they did in Charlotte-Amalie.

Across the garden, on the side of the building with the balcony, is the famous kitchen; this whole section was obviously the servant or slave quarters. The kitchen is kept in its original appearance. The walls are painted a light ocher and the trim is black iron. Extending across one wall are the original charcoal burners—nine of them—flanked by bake ovens, with a flue in front of each to draw the smoke out of the room. On top of the stove are two graceful iron pots, with ring handles on either side as on Grecian urns. This kitchen, to me, is the most outstanding of all the attractions.

Government House is the termination of the guided tour, the official tour which begins at the fort. Tours are morning or

Entrance to Government House, Christiansted.

Formal ballroom at Government House, with its distinctive long mirrors, settees, and candlelight.

afternoon, Monday through Friday, at ten-thirty and three o'clock respectively.

Farther into town are some interesting old churches. The Evangelical Lutheran, housing the first congregation of that sect on the island, was built twenty years after St. Croix's purchase by the Danes. Its interior is finished in gleaming mahogany—from the rounded ceiling to the pews, the gallery, the choir stall on the left with its little roof, and the low circular rail around the altar. Marble slabs near the pulpit cover graves dated as early as 1755, two years after the church was built. Some are worn so smooth that they cannot be read. One, inscribed in Danish, does state clearly: "Maria Clausen, who was born in St. Thomas, wife of Peter Clausen, Governor General of the Danish American Islands in 1780 under his Royal Majesty of Denmark and Norway." It ends with the notation that her death came at "48 years, 10 months, and 7 days old."

These gravestones are often reminders of the turnover in national as well as personal fortune. In St. John's Anglican

Episcopal Church, for example, lies Sarah, wife of Turner Roope, who died the first of June, 1801, during the British occupation—it being proudly recorded in the carved lettering that he was the Assistant Commissary-General of His Britannic Majesty's forces.

St. John's, which was built within a few years of the Lutheran church, is a weathered pile of brick and stone from the outside, but the interior is unexpectedly beautiful. Tiles in solid colors of blue, green, and ocher, with a fleur-de-lis centerpiece, are used around and on the altar steps. This motif, though an early Christian sign of the trinity, is also carved on the posts of the pews, and is more likely an influence from the preceding French epoch. But considering the names of some of the plantations, you realize that many of those earlier settlers remained influential in the life of St. Croix. The knotted wood planks of the flooring of St. John's—except for the aisle filled with gravestones—are another unusual touch. The lacy wooden supports, not to mention the carved base of the gallery, are delicate and exceptionally lovely.

From St. John's, on February 19, 1768, was buried one Rachel Faucett Lavien, the mother of Alexander Hamilton. She was described then—even death bowed to the feminine vanity of

The old Danish kitchen at Government House, with the original charcoal burners and bake ovens.

falsifying age—as being thirty-two years old, but if that had been true she was only ten years of age when her eldest son was born. Gertrude Atherton, who wrote a very readable book of fiction, *The Conqueror*, about Hamilton's mother, erected a monument to her on Estate Grange outside Christiansted. Harold Larson, an Army historian who was not long ago Special Assistant to the Governor of the Virgin Islands, in erudite articles in 1945 and 1952, recorded his research into the facts and fiction of Hamilton's origins. He states that Gertrude Atherton declared she was glad she had not known the truth until after her novel was written. In Victorian parlance, Hamilton's mother was "not as good as she should be."

It is curious that although many Jews are known to have come to St. Croix as well as St. Thomas, there remains no synagogue to mark this fact. One was listed among the church buildings in the eighteenth century, and a Jewish cemetery still exists—just below the old hospital—now neglected and almost forgotten. The St. Croix Jewish community appears to have been less closely knit, and it is conjectured that the influx included more *marraños* (at the risk of repetition, those who during the Inquisition gave at least lip-service to the Catholic Church). One native-born Cruzan of Jewish descent was outstanding in the annals of the Confederacy—Judah Benjamin, who became Attorney-General, then Secretary of War, and finally Secretary of State in Jefferson Davis' cabinet.

In later years St. Croix has received another group of immigrants—Puerto Ricans, seeking employment. They have, on the whole, been absorbed in, as well as added their contribution to, the life of the community. In the restful blue-gray confines of the Roman Catholic Church, with its shuttered, vaulted windows, two out of three confessionals have "English-Spanish" written over them.

Deeper within the town there are also other relics of a bygone era. Queen Street is mostly a poor-to-slum area, but old houses with galleries still remain. Off Queen Street is the public market. And on the side streets all the way to the circle, where the modern attraction of a movie house is found, are delightful discoveries, not to mention some very excellent and attractive shops.

240

CHAPTER 12

Frederiksted and the Estates

(The Countryside—Estates Open to the Public—the Great Fire
of Frederiksted—More About Hamilton)

FIFTEEN miles separate Frederiksted from Christiansted, and in
the stretch between them there is a decided change of scenery.
Naturally, some prefer the western portion of St. Croix. As I
have said, the West End—its semi-official title—unquestionably
has the finer beaches. It also has a number of other charms.

You normally take Centerline Road to Frederiksted, but in
all likelihood you will want to make a number of detours to
see the old estates or plantations. You will certainly want to go
to the mouth of the Salt River just to see where Columbus
actually did stop. A fine stretch of green bluff, which has been
given to the government for future development as a public
park, makes an ideal vantage point from which to survey the
whole scene. But you need imagination to visualize that day
in 1493 when the Spanish fleet anchored off shore.

A map will be helpful in your peregrinations, and on St.
Croix they fortunately are easy to come by. The very lively
Chamber of Commerce, with an office facing the wharf, will
give you one, as will the car rental agencies and filling stations.

Many of the famous estates are private property and not
open to the public at all times, but during February there is
one guided tour a week which takes in a number of them, the
list varying somewhat each year. However, many have been
converted into hotels and other commercial enterprises, which
can easily be viewed at any time. At least one, Estate Whim,
is open as a public monument.

Of those regrettably not usually accessible to the public,

241

Bulow's Minde is of the greatest interest, for it was Governor von Scholten's private home. It was a superb, although not extraordinarily large, mansion of stone. Except for the wing which once constituted the ballroom and is now converted into most charming living quarters, it is a complete ruin, so crumbled as to be difficult to envision in its entirety. The chapel walls at the far end of this L-shaped house are fairly intact, although about seventy-five years ago it was used as a hotel. You see the shambles of an oven where the chapel was turned into a kitchen. Von Scholten's home, strangely, contained but one bedroom, a quite large one of the same size as the dining room beneath it. Except for the ballroom and chapel, these constituted the entire house. But a tiny outside staircase led directly to the Governor's personal quarters, with a short connecting path to the incredibly small stone cottage where his mistress fictitiously lived. Slabs of broken marble bear testimony of the onetime splendor of Bulow's Minde, for its sills and steps were overlaid by this fine quarried stone.

Estate Annaly is another private property, but public vehicles are permitted to pass through it. It is, in fact, included in one or two proposed tours which can be arranged with any taxi service. The listing of these tours, which may serve as a guide even if you drive yourself, can be secured through the taxi service or the Department of Tourism in Government House. As previously stated, taxi rates are $4.00 per hour for up to four people.

The chief reason for detouring via Annaly is the magnificent scenic drives. True, Mahogany Road is a main thoroughfare over which you should travel in any case. Here is suddenly a gorgeous tropical scene, an avenue of enormous old trees, mangoes as well as mahoganies, with vines like ropes—lianas—hanging from them. These, like orchids, it seems, are harmless air plants. Along this road especially—although they are used throughout the island—you are likely to encounter a donkey, or possibly a horse-drawn, two-wheeled cart.

Annaly has a vast acreage, and the road leading to it winds upward through beautiful countryside. Here are the highlands of St. Croix. The descent to the sea via the Scenic Drive one Cruzan, at least, deems the most spectacular trip of all—first an

Carts from the country, on scenic Mahogany Road, St. Croix.

air view of the entire island, then a drive through the tropical forest. Unfortunately there had been a bad downpour just prior to my visit, and we were advised against taking the drive, as it is a dirt road. It connects, however, with the paved coastal road which leads north from Frederiksted to Ham Bluff. Although a number of roads are not paved, most are moderately good and wide, flatter and much less winding than on St. Thomas, and the northwest coastline is a recommended trip.

There are no Great House ruins at Annaly, simply a sugar mill renovated into a home and generally rented, hence not open for public inspection. It is primarily for the scenic enjoyment that you drive through Estate Annaly.

Of the estates perennially open to visitors, the Great House at Whim comes first. These semi-ruins are being restored with private funds. The building is curiously interesting, encircled by a small moat designed for light, with semicircular end walls in an otherwise neo-classic design. Whim, it seems, was a nickname, the estate having been called John's Rest after an early owner, John Delaney. The present name dates from 1804, although the place has occasionally been erroneously referred to as the Old Dutch Church—for reasons that are definitely obscure. There is more reason to believe that it was built by Moravian missionaries, but to my mind it is far too grandiose for either sect. At any rate, there is a clear record proving that

243

a private family was living there in 1759, shortly after the advent of the Moravians. Possibly, true to their humble belief and calling, the Moravians were the masons.

Quite a different type of sight-seeing is provided by the sugar factory at Bethlehem or the Cruzan Rum Distillery at Big Diamond, both once big estates. The lower stories of the Big Diamond Great House are the original, as is the small mill, but that was used for water storage. (The smaller mills always were, the larger ones for grinding sugar being placed higher on the hill not only to catch the wind but to take advantage of gravity, allowing the juices to descend.)

Both these industrial properties welcome visitors. Robert Skeoch, a native Cruzan who runs the distillery, says that his grandfather, a Scotsman who reached the island back in 1850, was once the owner of Estate Carlton. This was after slave days. However, the Cruzan accent—distinct from that of St. Thomas—is a holdover from the days when Scots overseers were in the majority.

Many Great Houses either no longer exist or have since been so thoroughly transformed that no impression of earlier days remains. Estate Carlton is one of the latter, although a very fine hostelry with the special appeal of a nine-hole golf course. Of

The inner part of Frederiksted's old fort dates from the middle of the eighteenth century (1760). Its guns were the first to salute the American flag.

La Grange, restored Great House near Frederiksted, which has many other examples of unusually pleasing Victorian style.

interest, nevertheless, is the old mill, turned into a shop; the club house, a conversion of the original factory or boiling house; and the old slave quarters, separated from the main building, restored as guest cottages.

Sprat Hall, close to Frederiksted, is a hotel which has retained a great deal of the charm of an old mansion. It dates back to the seventeenth century and French colonial days, and its stately rooms are graciously furnished in antique mahogany.

Not far distant is La Grange, which stands out as an example of Victorian architecture, since it was reconstructed after the "Fire Burn."

Much of the damage to and destruction of the island's plantations, as well as of the town of Frederiksted, dates from October 10, 1878, when rioting laborers ran amuck with the rallying cry, "Burn down the West End!" The basic cause was the economic decline which set in after the freeing of the slaves and the stubbornness and embitterment of the former masters over demands for higher wages. That the former slave-owners were now feeling the pinch of poverty was neither overly evident to the ex-slaves nor, in any case, likely to arouse sympathy. The greatest wealth and the finest plantations had been concentrated at this end of the island, and Frederiksted was the headquarters of the owners. The terrible fire swept through both the town and the countryside.

Except for the fort, today's library and the customs house

are all that remain intact after the Fire Burn. On the foundations of the ruined buildings, the then popular Victorian style was superimposed. Its unusual gossamer charm here has been described as like "lace-paper valentines," and the description is indeed apt. Frederiksted and its environs have the most pleasing examples of Victorian style that I have ever seen.

The old fort, of course, was impossible to demolish. As in the case of its Christiansted counterpart, additions were made over the years, but here the basic structure dates from the middle of the eighteenth century and is therefore later than Christiansted's fortress. The main purpose of this stronghold was to curb the illicit trade in rum and sugar.

The fort also has a rather unique claim to fame—its guns were the first to fire a salute of recognition to the American flag!

Neither a listing nor a description of all the estates is possible. A great number are guest houses, often with accommodations for no more than a dozen visitors at the most. But they welcome the transient pausing for a drink or meal and a bit of painless sight-seeing. The Cruzana, which was the Great House of Estate Orange, is one of these, as is Good Hope, like Caneel Bay Plantation, a Rockefeller investment, but both have undergone much modernization and it is difficult to distinguish the original structure.

The Buccaneer, oldest of the fine hotels and still the second

Beach at the Buccaneer, the oldest hotel on St. Croix.

largest on St. Croix, claims the most ancient history. According to the owners, one wing was built upon foundations laid down by a Knight of Malta in 1653. Another wing is declared to have been the house where Alexander Hamilton passed some time as a child; this is possible but not probable.

Hamilton is known, of course, to have been born out of wedlock. A sound explanation for this circumstance is the fact that his mother, Rachel Faucett, was already married to another man. In due course she was divorced by John Lavien (the name sometimes shows up as Lavine and has even been corrupted to Levine; Faucett appears also as Fawcett, but these variations are attributable to the tendency toward phonetic spelling in that period) and, as the guilty party, was forbidden to remarry. In his complaint Lavien stated that she had "absented herself from him for nine years and gone elsewhere, where she had begotten several illegitimate children." Alexander Hamilton was among these offspring.

He was the second son of James Hamilton, born either on Nevis or St. Kitts, and in the summer of 1765 the father, mother, and two boys came to Christiansted. But the next year the father abandoned the family.

Rachel came from a so-called respectable family, but her mother before her had also been divorced—a rarity in those days. Afterward she had moved with her daughter from the British island of Nevis to St. Croix, where Rachel's older sister, already married to a planter, was living. A year or so later Rachel married Lavien, who had recently purchased the sugar plantation of Ruby.

The Buccaneer was known in those days as Estate Shoys, and Lavien did not live there then, at any rate. Whether Hamilton's father lived there during his somewhat brief connubial life is not recorded, but certain it is that the walls do not echo with happy memories of Alexander's youth. The misconception arose from an earlier supposition that Rachel married Lavien *after* being cruelly deserted by James Hamilton. Gertrude Atherton's novel added its weight to that fiction.

Even though it lacks particular historical significance, the Buccaneer can claim to be a fine old manor house. And as a hotel it has much to offer—superb setting, beach, attractive cottages, and other comforts and pleasures.

247

CHAPTER 13

Virgin Islands Sports

THE term sports in the Virgin Islands means sea-activities. For those who prefer other diversions, there is a nine-hole public golf course near the airport on St. Thomas and another nine-hole course at Estate Carlton on St. Croix, with exchange privileges for guests of other hotels. The top hotels on both islands provide tennis courts. Saddle horses are not numerous but a few can be rented. St. Croix, being less precipitous terrain than St. Thomas, is more suitable for riding, and Sprat Hall on the west end will take care of any equine needs.

St. Thomas claims to be unsurpassed for its underwater delights (although St. Croix, too, has a fine glass-bottomed boat trip), and proves it by the ease of finding equipment and instruction. The Virgin Islands Spearfishing School, a subsidiary of the Virgin Islands Pleasure Boats, advertises that they "teach beginners from 7 to 70" both skin-diving and water-skiing. The average beginning course for the former takes two or three hours; the graduation test is around the sunken Portuguese trawler mentioned in Chapter 6. Naturally this is rudimentary training but sufficient for enjoyment. Success in aqualunging, on the other hand, is equivalent to a college degree.

There is also Kriss (telephone: 552-J2), who offers three-hour boat trips for snorkelers, beginners included. The cost is $5.00, including picking you up and returning you to your hotel. A shop in Charlotte-Amalie carries every conceivable item a skin-diver might use. It is run by Claude Caron, father of the movie star Leslie Caron, and his prices are untouchable Stateside.

On St. Croix, too, there are skin-diving and aqualunging, but it is easier there to make arrangements through your hotel. Hotels with beaches usually provide for the needs of the snorkeler. Sprat Hall, outside Frederiksted, particularly specializes in everything to do with the sea—water-skiing, skin-diving, boats, and fishing gear. In fact, it calls itself the Fishermen's Resort.

Bill Miller, situated on the wharf in Christiansted, specializes in daily sails to Buck Island for a combined treat of swimming, snorkeling, and spearfishing, and provides the necessary equipment.

But the outstanding store for the purchase of equipment is Sailors' Center, near the Christiansted post office. It is also an information bureau on deep-sea and bonefishing, and rents sloops, yawls, schooners, and so on, with and without engines, by the hour, day, or week. Just about every type of boat, excluding an ocean liner, can be secured either here (officially called Sailors' Center Charter Service) or through the St. Croix Yacht Club. If you write in advance, the address in both cases is simply "Christiansted, V.I."

Charlotte-Amalie on St. Thomas, having the larger harbor, still remains a bustling port insofar as sailing craft are concerned. The number of ships available, from motorboats to

Guests at Sprat Hall, outside Frederiksted, have a wide choice of water sports: skiing, skin-diving, boating, and fishing.

Water-skiing, one of the delights of a stay on St. Thomas.

auxiliary schooners, is greater—and so is the demand—than on St. Croix. In the small sail class you can do no better than address yourself to Virgin Islands Pleasure Boats. They have "drive-yourself" sailboats for as low as $6.00 an hour, and larger ones for charter parties for around $50.00 a day.

The St. Thomas Charter Boat Association, Box 748, St. Thomas, V.I., can give you all the information you need for the more substantial trips. Should you have an itch to buy a yacht, Caribbean Charter and Sales, Inc., is an offshoot of the above. Then there is Colonel Henry Frew, owner of Blue Water Cruises, who not only rents boats and supplies the crew, but is unusually wise in the ways of fishing. He, too, can be reached through Box 748. (Yacht Haven is the actual headquarters for both groups.)

Game fishing in the Virgin Islands, incidentally, is not as good as in Puerto Rico, but there is still a fair deep-sea catch ranging from kingfish and pompano to small tuna and occasional sail and tarpon.

There is plenty of enjoyment for everyone in these Caribbean waters—fishing, swimming, snorkeling, or just sunning on the deck of a yacht. Or, for that matter, just *looking* at the water. It's pretty hard to beat.

250

Index

251

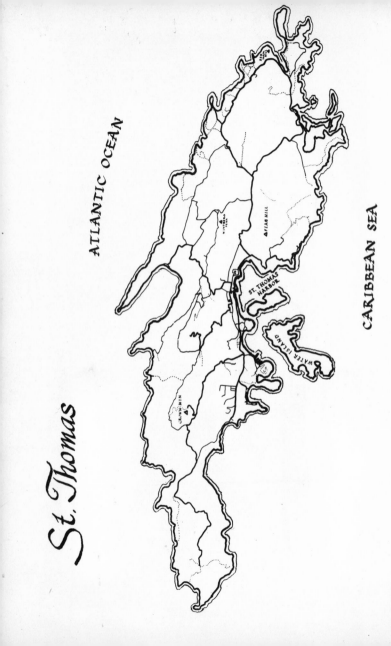

St. Thomas

ATLANTIC OCEAN

CARIBBEAN SEA